THE ROOTS OF AMERICAN LOYALTY

THE ROOTS

OF AMERICAN

LOYALTY

By MERLE CURTI

NEW YORK   ATHENEUM   1968

PUBLISHED BY ATHENEUM

REPRINTED BY ARRANGEMENT WITH COLUMBIA UNIVERSITY PRESS

COPYRIGHT © 1946 BY COLUMBIA UNIVERSITY PRESS

PREFACE COPYRIGHT © 1968 BY MERLE CURTI

ALL RIGHTS RESERVED

LIBRARY OF CONGRESS CATALOG CARD NUMBER 68-16409

PRINTED IN THE UNITED STATES OF AMERICA BY

THE MURRAY PRINTING COMPANY, FORGE VILLAGE, MASSACHUSETTS

BOUND BY THE COLONIAL PRESS, INC., CLINTON, MASSACHUSETTS

PUBLISHED IN CANADA BY MC CLELLAND & STEWART LTD.

FIRST ATHENEUM EDITION

To NANCY ALICE CURTI *and*

MARTHA MARGARET CURTI

PREFACE TO THE ATHENEUM EDITION

THE RELATED IDEAS of "Americanism," patriotism and loyalty have held a large and important place in our public thought and discussion. When this book was published in 1946 no systematic study had been made of either the roots or the growth of American patriotism and loyalty. Indeed, except for Thorstein Veblen, whose stimulating and contentious essay truly broke new ground, only two or three scholars seem to have given the subject even casual attention. Perhaps the academic world felt that the whole matter of patriotism belonged to the twilight zone of the intellect.

As the title of my book indicated, I was mainly concerned with the early or formative career of the ideas of national loyalty and patriotism: only about a third of the pages was devoted to the last hundred years. On the basis of a wide-ranging examination of both obviously "central" and out-of-the-way primary materials *The Roots of American Loyalty* presented in a chronological and topical organization an analysis of the forces, personalities, symbols and events that shaped the many and varied historic expressions of American patriotism and loyalty. The scope included political, constitutional, economic, social, religious and cultural facets of the theme.

On re-reading *The Roots of American Loyalty* the essential soundness of the analysis seems clear. Despite divisive influences (loyalty to state, section, class and group) patriotism, defined as love of country, pride in it, and readiness to make sacrifices for what was considered its best interest, developed gradually to the point at which it seemed capable of resisting centrifugal tendencies. To be sure, as the later chapters indicated, the identification of the national interest with one or another kind of group or self-interest deeply disturbed thoughtful and sincerely loyal Americans. In addition to the tensions between centripetal and centrifugal forces, the growth of patriotism and loyalty was related not only to "instinctive" or non-rational factors in

the nature of man and culture, as was true in other countries, but, in
addition, to the deep roots of a characteristically American ideology.
Although Americans did not achieve complete agreement as to the
meaning and operational implications of patriotism or the precise
nature of national welfare as the focus of loyalty, the discussion was
marked by a characteristically moral rationale. Challenged at times
by the exponents of a chauvinistic patriotism associated with an organic or integrated type of nationalism familiar to Europeans, the
major expression of patriotism and loyalty was twofold: discrimina-
tion between loyalty to officials and to "the general good" and an
emphasis on individualistic, libertarian and humanitarian values.
Such an ideology was functionally useful in enlisting the support of
nationalism and in providing a common ground for agreement at a
time and in a culture marked by ethnic diversity and an individualism
ranging from variety of expression to expatriation, war profiteering
and treason.

At the time of writing *The Roots of American Loyalty*, it was hard
if not impossible to foresee how this ideology might operate and even
change in the rapidly shifting character of America both at home
and in a new world role. That conflict between loyalty to America, in
traditional understandings, and to an emerging international community was certain to present great tension was, however, clear. But
any estimate of just how great this tension might become rested
necessarily on both an evaluation of the flexibility of American patriotism and loyalty in meeting new situations and on personal hopes
and faith. Nor was it possible to predict the intensity of the conflict
between traditional issues associated with the integration of various
ethnic groups and the militancy of the exponents of Black Nationalism—a movement stemming in part from the hardly anticipated vigor
of the civil rights movement and in part from the gulf between the
status and role of the great majority of Negroes in an era of affluence
and rising expectations of shared values and advantages making up
"the good life."

In the last two decades several studies in history and in the behavioral sciences have supplemented the record and analysis presented in *The Roots of American Loyalty*. Dr. Ruth Miller Elson's

Guardians of Tradition: American Schoolbooks in the Nineteenth Century (1964), begun many years ago in my seminar at Columbia, is an impressive addition to my own necessarily fragmentary treatment of the subject. Professor Harold Hyman's monograph, *The Era of the Oath: Northern Loyalty Tests during Civil War and Reconstruction* (1954), and his comprehensive study, *To Try Men's Souls: Loyalty Tests in American History* (1959), are the first thorough and wide-ranging examinations of an obviously significant theme. And I should mention Hans Kohn's *American Nationalism: An Interpretive Essay* (1957), which reflected its author's rich understanding of nationalism in many countries.

It was to be expected that in the era of the Cold War both public and scholarly interest in the problems of loyalty would reach major proportions. Not only was the sense of danger, urgency and crisis in the confrontation with international communism a heightened one. Social changes in mounting tempo at home also stimulated confusion, fear, uprootedness and malaise that provided a favorable atmosphere for suspicion, charges and countercharges, and demagoguery. New phrases and terms became household words: loyalty investigations, security risks, FBI personnel files, black lists, the invasion of privacy, rights of defendants, the plea of the Fifth Amendment, guilt by association, witch-hunt and McCarthy. While almost every sector of American life was affected, loyalty investigations in government, industry and colleges attracted special interest and attention.

Apart from the magnitude of the concern over loyalty and the role of the mass media in publicizing it, much of what was said, thought and done resembled what had happened before. Crusades for "Americanism" had enlisted the support of men of great wealth and of corporations and the approval of many men and women from the less advantaged ranks. All these had denounced anyone who favored social change in the direction of the "welfare state" as socialists, communists, as subversive, disloyal Americans. Political demagogues, at least on a local scale, had found it profitable to exploit alleged or actual radical and liberal protest and advocacy as "un-American." Nor were loyalty investigations on the governmental level unknown. Yet in some ways the situation was more than quantitatively different. A shift in emphasis from the positive aspects of patriotism and loyalty was reflected in the paramount and enduring concern over disloyalty. This was evident in the treatment of Japanese-Americans in the Second World War. It was evident in the vulnerability of atomic scientists and other government employees and advisors in sensitive areas. The alliance between genuinely concerned Americans for national security and of well-meaning but fanatical professional patriots on the one hand and anti-intellectualism on the other reinforced the non-rational components of loyalty. It seemed as if, to a greater extent and in more inelastic ways than in former crises, the traditionally important association of patriotism with individualism, nonconformity and humanitarianism was unable to meet the influence and power of those who regarded America, not as an unfinished process, but as a perfected achievement. Courageous Americans, many from what might be regarded as the conservative elite, did indeed speak out against identifying loyalty and conformity; did indeed insist on constitutional procedures, often denied; did indeed challenge the doctrine that obedience to the interpretations of loyalty made by the government in power were exclusive and imperative.

In the context of such major conflicts a number of writings appeared that will be indispensable to the future historian of loyalty during these years. Generally speaking, one group of these writings, while not lacking in factual accuracy or informative reliability, was marked by moral indignation and a call for the vigorous defense of the civil liberties and the right of protest as a valid, in fact, a necessary component of American loyalty and patriotism. Richard Hofstadter's *Anti-Intellectualism in American Life* (1963) did not explicitly relate the controversies about loyalty and disloyalty to the conspiratorial, demagogic attacks on non-conformity in political thought and action; but his broad treatment of anti-rational forces explored the role of democratic and "populistic" prejudices and convictions in the "paranoid" concern with political orthodoxy and conformity. Among the memorable discussions in this category were Carey McWilliams' *Witch Hunt: The Revival of Heresy* (1950), Alan Barth's *The Loyalty of Free Men* (1951), Francis Biddle's *The Fear of Freedom* (1951), Maurice Goldbloom's *American Security and Freedom* (1954) and

Henry Steele Commager's *Freedom, Loyalty and Dissent* (1956).

A second group of writings, while also *ad hoc* in origin, seems in terms of careful and precise documentation and of control of the technicalities of constitutional law to represent a somewhat different approach to the problem. Special mention must be made of the Cornell Studies in Civil Liberty, which, under the editorship of Professor Robert Cushman, examined the impact on civil liberties of current government programs designed to protect internal security. The volumes, combining high standards of scholarship with, in many cases, policy recommendations, include Robert K. Carr's *Federal Protection of Civil Rights* (1947) and *The House Committee on Un-American Activities* (1955), Walter Gellhorn's *Security, Loyalty and Science* (1950), Lawrence H. Chamberlain's *Loyalty and Legislative Action* (1951), Eleanor Bontecou's *The Federal Loyalty Program* (1953) and Professor Cushman's *Civil Liberties in the United States* (1956). To these should be added the contributions of David A. Fellman, especially *The Defendant's Rights* (1958), Ralph S. Brown's *Loyalty and Security Employment Tests in the United States* (1956) and Harold Guetzkow, *Multiple Loyalties: Theoretical Approach to a Problem in International Organization* (1955).

A third category of studies, reflecting the vogue for "analysis in depth," comparative approaches and the concepts of the behavioral sciences, probed into the social and psychological underpinnings and contexts of loyalty and disloyalty. The role of loyalties in the structuring of an individual life; the inability of many personalities to balance conflicts of loyalties; the bearing of family background on loyal and disloyal behavior; motivation and the implications of frustration and alienation—these and other factors gave new dimensions to an understanding of loyalty, disloyalty and patriotism. The encroachments of relatively new factors in the culture on the rights and values of privacy and of monolithic demands on a traditionally pluralistic society informed other studies. Those of special note include Edward A. Shils, *The Torment of Secrecy: The Background and Consequences of American Security Problems* (1956); Morton Grodzins, *The Loyal and the Disloyal: Social Boundaries of Patriotism and Treason*; and John H. Schaar, *Loyalty in America* (1957).

Whatever the limitations of these studies, one can hope, if not assume, that in new and difficult situations in which loyalty is again an uppermost issue these writings will provide factual and directional guide-lines for policy and action. But, as *The Roots of American Loyalty* showed, more is involved than scholarly understanding. It remains to be seen what the future history of American loyalty is to be. Whatever may come, the past, as revealed in the literature of which *The Roots of American Loyalty* was a pioneer, will in some degree affect the shape of the future.

MERLE CURTI

Lyme Center, New Hampshire
September 1, 1967

FOREWORD

THE PATRIOTISM which we tend to take for granted has a history and a future. But its history has not been written, and its future may be quite different from its past. Our scattered states, united and grown strong, have been a hope for those in all lands who longed for freedom and a democratic world. Whether America will provide an even larger freedom at home, an even stronger hope for the world, depends upon what citizens make of our country—depends not only upon the strength of our devotion to it, but also upon the character of that devotion. In a democracy blind, unthinking love of country must presumably give way more and more to intelligent and understanding patriotism, if that democracy as such is to survive. That being so, an examination of the sources and nature of American patriotism may be more than an academic exercise; and he who reads it thoughtfully may be helped toward more enlightened citizenship.

What is patriotism? Can one determine even approximately what it has meant at various times, in prosperity and depression, in war and peace, to the same individual in varying situations, to our leading thinkers, to Negroes, to farmers, to the women over the washtub and to the men on the assembly line? Did patriotic propaganda figure in the growth of American unity? How can patriotism be understood in terms of our federal system, with its peculiar set of double loyalties throughout much of our history? How may it be described in relation to the proximate assimilation of newcomers with their strange habits and alien ideas? Will antitheses or alleged antitheses of love of country such as lawbreaking, expatriation, war profiteering, treason itself, illuminate our understanding? This study will be concerned with these and similar questions.

Patriotism, though it has meant many things and been put to

various, even contradictory uses, may nevertheless be defined as love of country, pride in it, and readiness to make sacrifices for what is considered its best interest. What one man deems the best interests of the country, however, another declares to be mere class or sectional, rather than national, interest. What, if anything, constitutes a criterion for determining genuinely national interest? Man has a peculiar way of making himself—and others—believe that what is really in his own interest, is actually unselfish devotion to his fellows, and to his country. In view, then, of the tendency to rationalize one's conduct, to make the worse appear the better, what are the criteria for self-sacrifice? Obviously it is necessary to take into account not only words but actions as well.

Patriotism, so defined, is related to nationalism. A more inclusive and complex pattern of ideas and interests, nationalism has developed in the modern world as the philosophy of the national state. It has rested on the assumption that, by and large, the unified nation is the highest value in civilization. American nationalism is like the nationalisms to be found elsewhere in that it has expressed a faith in the superiority of a particular landscape, a special complex of traditions and institutions, a special mission. The story of American patriotism cannot be told without some recognition of its relationships to the patterns of national thought and feeling in the western world.

The term "Americanism," while closely related to patriotism and especially to nationalism, has been employed in a variety of ways by different people at different times. Jefferson used it as referring to an individualistic democracy, an experiment designed to realize at home the natural rights of all men to life, liberty, and the pursuit of happiness, and to point the way by example to the achievement of these values all over the world. Somewhat later the term was used to describe the Protestant tradition in America, especially the separation of church and state, lay control of ecclesiastical organizations, and the public school system. Militant Protestants denounced Catholicism as un-American and Catholics in their turn insisted that their faith in no way conflicts with patriotism. This controversy was a living issue as recently as the presi-

dential campaign of 1928. The term Americanism has been associated with still other values. At least since the First World War the
word has been used as necessarily implying *laissez-faire* capitalism,
private initiative and enterprise—the maintenance, in short, of the
general social and economic status quo.

The emphasis in this investigation of the materials relating to
American patriotism has been placed on what may be called the
formative period. By the centennial of the Declaration of Independence the main outlines of patriotic thought and feeling were
clear. The story of American patriotism from that time to our own
is included in this study, but it has been told with less detail. The
justification of this lies only partly in the fact that the foundation
period is the most important. More research is necessary for the
telling of the full story of patriotism within the period spanned
by the memory of living men—more research and more perspective,
which, of course, only the passing of time can give.

The study aims primarily to be a contribution to our knowledge
of a pattern of emotions and ideas. It is based on an extensive
investigation of materials, published and unpublished, letters, files
of newspapers and periodicals, government documents, Fourth of
July orations, and fugitive pieces, on *belles lettres*, on works of art,
and on the few secondary reports on American patriotism. The
story is not without its picturesqueness and humor. But chiefly
it is a story of human aspirations for prestige and for security and
for freedom. It is a story reflecting both the selfishness and limitations of Americans, and their altruistic idealism.

This book was begun in 1936 while I was a Visiting Scholar at
the Huntington Library, and I wish to thank the Trustees and staff
for making possible a year of research under virtually ideal conditions. I am especially grateful to Mr. David Stevens of the Rocke-
feller Foundation and to the Trustees of the Foundation for providing me with a semester's leave of absence in order to complete
the writing of the book. I wish also to thank Professor Paul Knap-
lund and the Research Committee of the University of Wisconsin
for a part-time research assistant during an academic year.

To former colleagues with whom I discussed the problems of

research in this field and who commented on my plans for the organization of material, I am grateful, especially to Carlton J. H. Hayes, Hans Kohn, J. Montgomery Gambrill, Erling M. Hunt, and Curtis P. Nettels. Thanks are due to Anna Lou Riesch who, as a research assistant, 1943–1944, collected material on relevant topics. I am also grateful to the students in my seminar at Columbia University who for five years studied with me problems in the history of American nationalism.

The staffs of several libraries, in addition to that of the Huntington, put me under obligation by reason of unusual courtesies. I wish especially to mention the Columbia University Library, the New York Historical Society, the New York Public Library, the Dartmouth College Library, the Charleston Library Society, the University of Wisconsin Library, and the Wisconsin Historical Society.

The manuscript was read by Bessie L. Pierce, Charles A. Barker, LaWanda Fenlason Cox, Howard K. Beale, and my wife, Margaret Wooster Curti. I am much indebted to them, and especially to Professor Beale for his honest and penetrating criticisms. I also wish to thank William Bridgwater of the Columbia University Press for his painstaking and intelligent help in preparing the manuscript for the printer, and Dr. Leslie Dunlap of the Library of Congress for his careful reading of the first proofs.

MERLE CURTI

University of Wisconsin
September, 1945

CONTENTS

THE ROOTS OF AMERICAN LOYALTY

Our country! In her intercourse with foreign nations may she always be in the right, but our country, right or wrong.

STEPHEN DECATUR, 1816

Our country, right or wrong! When right, to be kept right; when wrong, to be put right!

CARL SCHURZ, 1872

I: THE BIRTH OF LOYALTY

It is through this only [the Union] that we are, or can be nationally known in the world; it is the flag of the United States which renders our ships and commerce safe on the seas, or in a foreign port . . . In short, we have no other national sovereignty than as the United States. It would be fatal for us if we had—too expensive to be maintained, and impossible to be supported.

THOMAS PAINE, 1783

WHOEVER SEEKS THE BEGINNINGS of American patriotism might logically search for them in that Europe which men and women left in search of adventure, riches, freedom, and a new home more to their liking. In spite of all the ills and shortcomings of life in war-ridden and impoverished Europe, people cherished a feeling of kinship for the land of their birth. Its familiar associations, both sad and merry, were part and parcel of their make-up. Thus patriotism was one of the sundry values that Europeans brought along with their household treasures, their habits of speech, their religious views. Moreover, men and women in boldly leaving the old home carried in their hearts, dimly or vividly, dreams of a new country where life promised some day to be better. Such hopes, and such ardent faith, generated in the old countries, were the seeds of American patriotism.

Yet the beginnings of patriotism that is really American must be sought in America itself. The growth of loyalty was slow and unconscious. In the colonial period one can discern the same broad patterns in the growth of loyalty that appear in later stages of our history—such as the widening of attachment to a smaller area to include larger and larger units; the pride in natural beauty; the belief in a unique destiny; and the idea of a divinely chosen people.

Provincial self-consciousness was at first confined to a particular colony. Pride in a given province grew with concrete awareness that life there was not only different but also in some part fuller, richer, better, than the round still pursued by kinfolk and neighbors in the Old World, that in the new land dreams had come true (or were on the point of becoming true). Provincial pride sometimes took the form of local promotional activity. On other occasions it reflected mere boastful exuberance. The very first settlers were quick to see the generous hand of nature in the creation of the American terrain. "Of all the many places I have seen in the world," wrote William Penn of the pleasant Delaware River banks, "I remember not one better seated." [1] Decades later Benjamin Franklin was still rejoicing at the "salubrity of the Air, the healthfulness of the Climate, the plenty of good Provisions, the certainty of subsistence" [2] of his adopted Pennsylvania. The very vastness and scale of American physical environment evoked proud comparisons with England's miniature stage. In the mind of William Eddis the Thames by contrast with American rivers was "reduced to a diminutive stream." [3] The lusty joy of Captain John Smith in discovering the rich resources and unique features of Virginia was re-echoed a hundred years later by William Byrd.

Sensitiveness to the unique and superior features of the land kindled esthetic as well as utilitarian pleasure. To the versatile William Byrd even the Dismal Swamp in its never-dying verdure presented a delight for the eye. The Pennsylvania Quaker-naturalist, William Bartram, reveled in Florida's dark groves of cedars, myrtles, live-oaks, towering magnolias, meandering streams, fleecy clouds, green meadows, turbulent waters, and mysterious lagoons.

New England had no such lushness of course, but William Bradford not only could refer in plain and sinewy words to "the hideous & desolate Wilderness" but also could survey with satisfaction

[1] *Narrative of Early Pennsylvania, West New Jersey, and Delaware, 1630–1707,* ed. by Albert C. Myers in *Original Narratives of Early American History* (New York, 1912), p. 239.
[2] Benjamin Franklin, *Writings,* ed. by Albert H. Smyth (New York, 1906), VIII, 606.
[3] William Eddis, *Letters from America* (London, 1792), p. 6.

streams, and coves, and hills, together with "the fruits of the land." [4]
Ten years after landing at Plymouth the Reverend Francis Higginson wrote that "a sup of New England air is better than a whole
flagon of old English ale." [5] Morton of Merrymount, on exploring
Cape Ann, reported, "the more I looked, the more I liked it. And
when I had more seriously considered of the bewty of the place,
with all her faire indowments, I did not thinke that in all the
knowne world it could be paralel'd, for so many goodly groves of
trees, dainty fine round rising hillocks, delicate faire large plaines,
sweete cristall fountaines, meads . . . which made the Lande to
mee seeme paradice: for in Mine eie 'twas Nature's Master-
peace." [6] In conquering their own stern coasts and sterile lands
New Englanders came to love the rocks and rills, the woods and
templed hills. Indeed, as Timothy Dwight, president of Yale, wrote
toward the end of the eighteenth century, "the variety which Mil-
ton informs us Earth has derived from Heaven, 'of pleasure situate
in hill and dale,' is nowhere more extensively found" than in New
England itself. [7]

The growing pride in America was now and then expressed in
historical writings. Ministers frequently compressed into election-
day sermons accounts of the colonial past. A famous but by no
means unique example is that of William Stoughton in 1668. "God
sifted a whole nation that He might send Choice Grain over into
this Wilderness," he declared. [8] The identification of New Englanders in particular as God's chosen people became habitual.
More formal celebrations of the distinctive colonial past were Cotton Mather's *Magnalia Christi Americana* (1702), the Reverend
Thomas Prince's *Chronological History of New England* (1736–
1755), John Lawson's *History of Carolina* (1709), the histories of

[4] William Bradford, *History of Plimoth Plantation* (Boston, 1898), pp. 95,
106.
[5] Francis Higginson, *New-England's Plantation* (London, 1630), p. 11.
[6] Thomas Morton of Merrymount, *New English Canaan*, in Peter Force, ed.,
Tracts and Other Papers (Washington, 1838), II, 41–42.
[7] Timothy Dwight, *Travels in New-England and New-York* (London, 1823),
I, 83.
[8] William Stoughton, *New-England's True Interest* (Cambridge, 1670), p. 19.

Virginia by Robert Beverley and William Stith, and those of Pennsylvania, New Jersey, and New York by Robert Proud, William Smith, and Samuel Smith. In this mounting literature pride in American forefathers and their achievements and pride of place found frequent expression.

More indicative of the rise of an American self-consciousness during the colonial era were predictions of future greatness. In some instances these were confined to a particular colony or city. Thus in 1730, when Philadelphia was only a small town, a local enthusiast in the spirit of Bishop Berkeley's famous "westward the course of empire takes its way" predicted that

> *Europe shall mourn her ancient fame declined*
> *And Philadelphia be the Athens of mankind.*[9]

But frequently the predictions of future eminence were expressed in terms of the American seaboard rather than of a single province. Ecclesiastical brethren thus shared the conviction of Jonathan Edwards that Providence had singled America out as "the glorious renovator of the world." The prophecies of a magnificent American future were also often coupled with predictions of Europe's decline.

By the middle of the eighteenth century the belief in the degradation of the Old World and the mounting fame of America had become widespread. No one gave more reasoned expression to this than the loyal subject of the crown and warm admirer of England, Benjamin Franklin. "I have long been of the opinion," he wrote in 1760, "that *the foundations of the future grandeur and stability of the British empire lie in America.*" Again and again, while still an advocate of union with Great Britain, Franklin declared that "America, an immense territory . . . with all advantages of climate, soil, great navigable rivers, and lakes, etc. must become a great country, populous and mighty; and will, in less time than is generally conceived, be able to shake off any shackles that may be imposed on her." [10]

[9] Moses Coit Tyler, *A History of American Literature* (New York, 1878), II, 239.
[10] Franklin, *Writings*, IV, 4; V, 20–22.

Colonial Americans differed from stay-at-homes not only in their more generally optimistic faith in the future, and especially in the destiny of America, but in other respects as well. The story of the modification of British institutions and points of view has been told often and well. Remoteness from England and the peculiarities of American environment figured prominently. So did the fact that more and more non-British stock settled in the colonies: Dutch, Irish, and Germans, Walloons and French. The presence of these non-British stocks, making up on the eve of the Revolution perhaps a fourth of the population, weakened the ties with the motherland, facilitated the growth of American self-consciousness, and contributed to the modification of British-inherited institutions and ideas. Thomas Paine's remark that "Europe, and not England, is the parent country of America" was not without point.

It must suffice here to mention only a few examples of colonial alterations of institutions and ideas which figured in an important way in the growth of American self-consciousness. One was the weakening of devotion to royalty as an institution and a faith. Royal governors, to be sure, kept up a certain pomp and circumstance, and maintained in some degree in the royal provinces ceremonials that reminded colonial Americans of the crown and the king. But inevitably such rituals were less impressive and less frequent than in England, and more and more the monarch became a somewhat shadowy figure. This was especially true for the non-British immigrants who came in impressive numbers in the eighteenth century.

Other institutions were definitely modified in the course of colonial experience. Laws of land inheritance and land tenure became more flexible. The idea developed that all communities must be represented in legislative assemblies, a concept that was not common in Great Britain. Gradually the authority of state-established churches over dissenters weakened.

Another condition making for increasing divergence of American from English and European life was the greater class mobility in the new country. The relatively easy access to land provided greater opportunities for humble folk to get ahead than in the Old World. All these actualities meant that the plain people came to have, despite class distinctions, limited suffrage, and a dominant aristocracy, a far greater stake in America than ordinary men in Europe had in their countries. America, in other words, was coming, even in the colonial era, to be associated with human rights. This association was a backlog of loyalty.

The point may be concretely illustrated in the views which John Adams at varying times expressed on the subject. Writing in 1765 the Massachusetts leader expressed a fairly common faith, a faith almost certainly held by innumerable indentured servants, mechanics, shopkeepers, and farmers. "I always consider," he wrote, "the settlement of America with reverence and wonder, as the opening of a grand scheme and design in Providence for the illumination and emancipation of the slavish part of mankind all over the earth." [11]

It became natural to think of a country offering special opportunities to plain people as one destined to be independent of autocratic Europe. Adams, however, was almost certainly reading into the past a purposeful intention on the part of allegedly independence-minded colonists when, in writing to Dr. Benjamin Rush in 1807, he declared that the idea of independence, far from being a "late invention," had been familiar to Americans "from the first settlement of the country." In this letter to Dr. Rush, John Adams went on to say that the concept of independence was "as well understood by Governor Winthrop in 1675, as by Governor Samuel Adams, when he told you that independence had been the first wish of his heart for seven years." [12] Nevertheless the shift from Anglo-American patriotism in the few months before the Declaration of Independence to a paramount loyalty to independence was amazingly sudden and can be understood only by taking into account another statement of John Adams. The real American Revolution, he insisted in 1816, was the radical change in the principles, opinions, sentiments, and affections of the people. The Revolution, continued Adams, "was complete in the minds of the people, and the union of the colonies, before the war commenced in the skirmishes of Concord and Lexington." [13]

[11] John Adams, Works, ed. by Charles Francis Adams (Boston, 1854), III, 452n.
[12] Ibid., IX, 596.   [13] Ibid., X, 197.

The growth of American self-consciousness was reinforced in still other ways. The Atlantic Ocean and swift-flowing navigable rivers often helped to break down the isolation of any one colony from its neighbors. The growing means of communication slowly softened the fierce rivalries and jealousies that had existed when the colonies were in closer touch with the mother country than with each other. The improvement of roads and postal facilities, the circulation of newspapers beyond the confines of the province in which they were issued, the wanderings up and down the seaboard of printers, artists, and itinerant evangelists, the more frequent contacts of fellow-Masons, students, lawyers, and physicians, aided the faltering but none the less genuine advance of an intercolonial culture and the development of intercolonial points of view.

In the hinterland the rise of an inchoate new section, stretching westward from the falls in the navigable rivers and cutting across provincial boundaries, also stimulated colonial like-mindedness. For in the backcountry life differed from that in England far more than did life in the tidewater area. The backwoodsmen of New Hampshire, western New York and Pennsylvania, Virginia, and the Carolinas had more in common than they did with the seaboard inhabitants of their own colony: they were all on the make, they resented with heat and fury and even violent protest the greater privileges which men on the seaboard enjoyed in economic, social, and political affairs. Used to doing things for themselves in their own way, they tended to regard England with more independence and indifference than did the colonists at, or within easy reach of, seaport towns. In the new western section, moreover, fear of French aggression had been most acute, and there the menace of the Indian was most serious. In view of the role which fear and the threat of an enemy play in the growth of social coherence, it is easy to see how the frontiersmen of every colony came to feel ties with those of their rank and place in almost every other province.

The awareness that provincial and British interests differed at many points only gradually crystallized. It found sporadic expression in the colonial tendency to magnify provincial privileges and to defy the authority of British officers. This was the case when they interfered with encroachments of colonists on the king's naval reserves and with colonial desires to increase the supply of circulating money by printing paper currency. It was illustrated in the resentment of land speculators and backwoodsmen and would-be backwoodsmen at the restrictions placed on westward migration by the Proclamation of 1763. Most important of all, the awakening consciousness of a conflict between colonial and British interests was sharpened by the efforts of the king's ministry, after the French and Indian War, to enforce and strengthen the acts of trade and navigation. When the shoe began to pinch, the conviction that British and American interests differed became an important factor in the growth of American self-consciousness.

It took the Stamp Act to bring colonial leaders together in common council. Plan after plan for some sort of union had been proposed ever since the end of the seventeenth century when William Penn outlined his project of colonial cooperation for defense. Indifference and jealousy had thrown all these blueprints to the winds. Now in the heat and tumult of a widely resented grievance colonial boundary disputes were overlooked, quarrels over the due proportion of troops from one colony or the other for defense against the Indians and the French in the late wars were forgotten, irritability aroused by the issues of trade and currency were pushed into the background.

The agitation evoked by the Stamp Act, and the growing colonial self-consciousness it brought to a focus, were expressed again and again in the tense year of 1765. In a notable pamphlet Richard Bland insisted that America, though a part of the British empire, was "no part of the kingdom of England" and was under no obligation to obey the laws issued by England's parliament.[14] John Adams put into words a sentiment that must have been in many minds when he declared there was "something exceedingly fallacious in the commonplace images of mother country and children colonies. . . . Are we not brethren and fellow subjects with those in Britain, only under a somewhat different method of legislation, and a totally different method of taxation?"[15] In Boston the Rev-

[14] Richard Bland, *An Inquiry into the Rights of the British Colonies* (Williamsburg, 1766), p. 20.
[15] Adams, *Works*, III, 461–462.

erend Jonathan Mayhew, whose centenary sermon in 1749 on the execution of King Charles I had renounced the doctrine of passive obedience and asserted the right of tyrannicide, now sanctioned the right of citizens, under certain "extraordinary conjunctures," to take the administration of government into their own hands.[16]

In the contentious pamphlet literature of the Stamp Act agitation, resistance to the British crown was definitely associated with the idea of union. One ballad, typical of others, was popular in every colony:

> Come join hand in hand, brave Americans all,
> And rouse your bold hearts to fair Liberty's call!
>
> Then join hand in hand, brave Americans all
> By uniting we stand, by dividing we fall.[17]

Patriotic newspapers, remembering Franklin's cartoon at the time of the ill-fated Albany Congress of 1754, now placed above a design of a snake broken up into thirteen fragments the boldly printed letters UNITE OR DIE. Yet after the Stamp Act was repealed and the crisis passed, it was difficult for the merchants in the several colonies to unite effectively in defense of their economic interests when these were menaced by new parliamentary legislation. The promising movement for intercolonial cooperation encountered a new obstacle a few years later when a period of relative prosperity set in.[18]

Although the agitation for colonial rights and for colonial self-determination within the British empire weakened in some measure loyalty to England and to the king, that loyalty was still deep. In spite of colonial indifference to calls for the support of the French and Indian War, in spite even of the weakening of British traditions and institutions and the gradual rise of a provincial self-consciousness, colonists still in general loved and revered England, felt

[16] Jonathan Mayhew, A *Discourse concerning Unlimited Submission and Non-Resistance to the Higher Powers* (Boston, 1750), especially pp. 29, 36–37; *The Snare Broken* (Boston, 1766), p. 42.

[17] Frank Moore, *Songs and Ballads of the American Revolution* (New York, 1856), pp. 37, 39.

[18] Arthur M. Schlesinger's *The Colonial Merchants and the American Revolution, 1763–1776* (New York, 1918), illustrates this point in detail.

loyalty to the English king, and took pride in the British empire. This duality of loyalties to America and to England was well expressed by Franklin when he took heart at the fall of French Canada before British might in 1760: he did so as an American fully aware that provincial interests were at stake, and, at the same time, as a proud and loyal Briton. Thus there was an Anglo-American patriotism—loyalty to a particular province along with an inchoate American self-consciousness and, at the same time, devotion to the British connection. Anglo-American loyalty meant—and the point is important—devotion both to America and to England, and thus differed from the loyalty cherished by Britishers in England. Until almost the eve of the Declaration of Independence there seems to have been for the most part a feeling that any conflicts between loyalty to the king and the mother country and loyalty to colonial rights and interests could somehow be resolved.

The Anglo-American patriotism that had long found outlet in words and deeds was not, then, destroyed by the mounting passion and tumult in the decade which ended in the bloodshed at Lexington and Concord. In that decade more than one provincial who later took up the American cause with enthusiasm expressed himself on visits to England in terms of warm admiration for the mother country. Dr. Benjamin Rush, returning to Philadelphia from study in Edinburgh, sailed past the white cliffs of Dover contemplating "in silence this pensive retrospect of the finest country in the world." [19] Another future leader of the revolt against England, Arthur Lee, saluted his motherland as "the Eden of the world." The ardent admiration and affection for England may have been less marked in the minds of the great rank and file who could not afford to cross the seas, but even many of these shared the sentiment in some degree.

In the hearts of many who spoke explicitly for colonial interests and rights, devotion to England was no less genuine than it was for Rush and Lee. Ten years before signing the Declaration of Independence dapper young Francis Hopkinson set forth a common

[19] Benjamin Rush, *A Memorial Containing Travels through Life, or Sundry Incidents* (Philadelphia, 1905), pp. 49–50.

sentiment. "Are we not one nation and one people?" he asked. "We in America are in all respects Englishmen, notwithstanding that the Atlantic rolls her waves between us and the throne to which we all owe our allegiance." [20] That spirited foe of parliamentary taxation, Oxenbridge Thacher, could in the same breath denounce the acts of the British ministry, "avow love to the country" that gave him birth, "exult in the name of Briton," and hope that "the whole English empire, united by the strongest bonds of love and interest," might "happily possess immortality." [21] In the pre-Revolutionary agitation for colonial interests the very frequency of the appeal to "the rights of Englishmen" makes it clear that even the more outspoken provincial champions were loyal both to the British traditions of liberty and to British authority. In his intemperate, vivid, and piercing *Rights of the British Colonies*, James Otis spoke for countless fellow provincials when he wrote, "We all think ourselves happy under Great Britain. We love, esteem, and reverence our mother country, and adore our king. And could the choice of independency be offered the colonies, or subjection to Great Britain upon any terms above absolute slavery, I am convinced they would accept the latter." [22]

Until within a few months before the Declaration of Independence was adopted Revolutionary leaders vouchsafed attachment and loyalty to the king and mother country and hope for reconciliation. The Continental Congress that had appointed Washington as the leader of the patriots' armies against the king's troops assured the world that it did not mean "to dissolve that union which has so long and so happily subsisted between us," and which it wished sincerely to see restored. Two months after the Battle of Bunker Hill, Jefferson wrote a member of his family that he was "looking with fondness towards a reconciliation with Great Britain." [23] All

[20] Cited in Evarts B. Greene, *The Revolutionary Generation* (Vol. IV of *A History of American Life*, New York, 1943), p. 182.

[21] Moses Coit Tyler, *The Literary History of the American Revolution 1673–1783* (2d ed., New York, 1898–1900), I, 55–56.

[22] James Otis, *Rights of the British Colonies Asserted and Proved* (Boston, 1764), p. 51.

[23] Thomas Jefferson, *Writings*, ed. by Paul Leicester Ford (New York, 1892–1899), I, 482.

this and much more evidence supports Thomas Paine's remark in *Common Sense* that on the eve of the appearance of his pamphlet in January, 1776, Americans esteemed the British nation, however much they disliked its ministry; that their attachment to the mother country was obstinate, however much they suspected its government; that they regarded as treasonable any talk against the connection with the empire; and that their single object was reconciliation.[24] This is true if the published writings of almost all the leaders of the Revolution express their sincere sentiments and the feelings of their less-articulate fellow provincials. The abiding depth of Anglo-American patriotism is further suggested by the fact that, in spite of all the bitterness the war bred, many a good patriot could, like President Ezra Stiles of Yale in 1783, recall "the antient national affection, which we once had for the parent state, while we gloried in being a part of the British empire," and could in the same breath hope that men might come to glory in the name Columbian or American, as they once had in the name British.[25]

Nevertheless, the renewal of strife in the early 1770's, occasioned by economic depression and a bungling English government, had led many colonial Americans to wonder whether the equilibrium of loyalties to king and empire on the one hand and to colonial interests on the other was less stable in fact than almost everyone had assumed and hoped. The British rejection of colonial plans for a virtual British commonwealth of nations confirmed American doubts and fears. The agitation for colonial rights and for self-determination within the British empire did not break the bond of loyalty to the king and to England. But it is plain that all this agitation did greatly weaken the tie and did bring the colonists into closer association the better to promote a common cause.

The subtle process by which the cords were at length broken and allegiance transferred from the crown to the somewhat vaguely defined republic cannot be understood without taking into account the feelings of the more radical leaders of tradesmen, mechanics,

---

[24] Thomas Paine, *Writings*, ed. by Moncure D. Conway (New York, 1894), I, 69 ff.
[25] Ezra Stiles, *The United States Elevated to Glory and Honour: A Sermon . . . May 8, 1783* (New Haven, 1783), p. 31.

and farmers. The hearts of these men were set on securing the gains they had made in suffrage and influence in local affairs and on extending these gains still further. The radicals were quick to build up a strong central organization of committees, well knit in an intercolonial chain, and to identify with the agitation against Great Britain their own aspirations for rule at home and their own antipathies toward the influential and well-to-do gentry and merchant class. But they held that the best way of retaining what they had won and of winning new victories over the colonial aristocracy was to support only a loose union of the newly declared states. In concentration of authority and power, whether in London or in Philadelphia, they sensed danger to their own aspirations. Thus it was largely a burst of rhetoric when the radical leader, Patrick Henry, exclaimed in 1775, "the distinctions between Virginians, Pennsylvanians, New Yorkers and New Englanders are no more! I am not a Virginian, but an American." [26]

The more cautious and well-to-do merchants, planters, and lawyers favored a union of conservative forces in the colonies only partly as a safeguard against British encroachments on their economic interests and their liberties. They also saw in a union an instrument for checking the power of turbulent mechanics, tradesmen, farmers, and frontiersmen to regulate commerce and monetary exchange in accord with their own democratic lights and interests. Many substantial citizens wanted to postpone independence—if independence were to come—until a strong union could be built for insuring victory over Britain and over the radicals, whose strength lay in their control of particular provinces.

Still others who had cooperated in the movement of protest against British authority and who were genuinely devoted to America now parted company with their associates and took their stand with the British. Their ultimate loyalty was to the crown, to the traditions and the authority of the motherland, to the concept of the empire. This loyalty was strengthened in many instances by their fear of radicalism within the colonies themselves.

[26] William Wirt Henry, *Patrick Henry; Life, Correspondence, and Speeches* (New York, 1891), I, 222.

The transfer of loyalties in the mind of any one man cannot, of course, truly represent that of others in whom different temperaments, different motives, and different backgrounds operated. Nevertheless, it is illuminating to consider the steps Washington took in this process of transferring his loyalty to the cause of American rights and an American nation.

The autumn of 1774 found the Virginia leader somewhat suspicious of the radical Massachusetts men. Perhaps, after all, the frequent accusations both in England and in America that what they were really up to was independence might be true. Washington himself at this time had no conscious leaning in that direction. Before deciding to go along further with Samuel Adams and his crowd, Washington satisfied himself that they merely wanted to maintain the rights of life, liberty, and property, that they could not be diverted from the defense of those rights into a drive for independence. Apparently he was still of this mind throughout the next spring. Jonathan Boucher, an Anglican clergyman and a friend of Washington, is authority for a story which, if true, indicates the Virginia planter's attitude toward independence in May, 1775, after blood had been shed at Concord and Lexington. Meeting Washington on his way to take command of the Continental army, Boucher warned his friend that his errand would lead to civil war and to a movement for independence. Vigorously scouting any such idea Washington remarked, according to Boucher, that if he ever joined in any such measure, the clergyman might set him down for "everything wicked." [27]

Yet, according to his own testimony, Washington suddenly abandoned all idea of an accommodation to England on hearing of the measures the king and ministry adopted after the battle of Bunker Hill. "I would tell them," he wrote to his military secretary, Joseph Reed, on February 10, 1776, "that if nothing else could satisfy a tyrant and his diabolical ministry, we are determined to shake off all connections with a state so unjust and unnatural. This I would tell them, not under covert, but in words as clear as the sun in its

[27] Jonathan Boucher, *Reminiscences of an American Loyalist* (Boston and New York, 1925), p. 109.

meridian brightness." [28] At this point the conservatives in Congress suffered a notable defeat when James Wilson's resolution denying the purpose of independence was rejected.

No one can weigh the various factors that entered into Washington's relatively early willingness to shift loyalty from king and empire to American self-determination. We may be sure that, like many others, he was affected by colonial self-consciousness, even though he did not feel so keenly as did Franklin that England denied humble folk the chance to get ahead and that Britain shared in the decadence of the Old World. There were, however, other reasons for disliking the English connection. Some have assumed that Washington cherished from young manhood a grudge against the British because of cavalier treatment by redcoat officers during the French and Indian War. Certainly as a speculator in western lands he resented the barriers imposed by the British government to the rapid development of the trans-Allegheny region. Nor is it unreasonable to suppose that he shared the irritation of so many Virginia planters who, year after year as they cast accounts, chafed at their indebtedness to Scottish and British merchants.

As an aristocrat of Virginia, a province entirely rural, Washington was less prone to sense danger from democratic forces in the towns than men like John Dickinson, Gouverneur Morris, Robert Morris, and Robert Livingston, all of whom chose reluctantly and almost at the last moment to cast their lot with the movement for independence. Again, as the leader of the military opposition to Great Britain Washington must have sensed the frustration and opprobrium he would feel if the colonial cause collapsed or even if some sort of a compromise were made.

Nor can one be certain that Thomas Paine's *Common Sense* played no part in Washington's decision. If his memory served him correctly when he said that he had given up all hope of reconciliation shortly after Bunker Hill, then, obviously, his resolution could merely have been confirmed when he read *Common Sense* within two weeks after its appearance in January, 1776. "My countrymen,

[28] George Washington, *Writings* (Bicentennial ed., Washington, 1931–1936), IV, 321. The later quotation about Paine's *Common Sense* is from *ibid.*, p. 455.

I know, from their form of government, and steady attachment to royalty, will come reluctantly to the idea of independence," he wrote on April 1, 1776; "but time and persecution bring many wonderful things to pass; and by private letters, which I have lately received from Virginia, I find 'Common Sense' is working a powerful change there in the minds of many men." The knowledge that numberless men, including such leaders as General Charles Lee, to whom *Common Sense* was a "masterly, irresistible performance," were moved by Paine's arguments to accept independence as inevitable and desirable must at least have fortified Washington's own intellectual and emotional shift of loyalties.

What *Common Sense* did was to brush aside as irrelevant all the cloudy issues of constitutionalism that had confused men's minds. It built the case for independence on common-sense analogies and arguments. Undermining reverence for the British monarchy, Paine argued that kingcraft was an intolerable way of governing mankind; that if England was in reality the mother of America, then her treatment had been more shameful than that of brutes, who do not devour their young; that even if it be conceded that America had flourished in the empire, one could no more conclude that separation should be avoided than assert that a child who had thrived on milk should never eat meat.

The tie with England, Paine further argued with epigrammatic asperity, involved America in the wars of Continental Europe and set Americans at odds with nations seeking their friendship. It rested in the last analysis on the preposterous idea that a great nation on one side of the Atlantic should remain in a state of permanent pupilage to a nation across the sea. "In no instance," Paine urged, "hath nature made the satellite larger than its primary planet; and as England and America, with respect to each other, reverse the common order of nature, it is evident that they belong to different systems. England to Europe: America to itself!" [29] Only in America could freedom find a true asylum, and then only if America were free from oppression. Such, in brief, were the pungent

[29] Paine, *Writings*, I, 92.

arguments popularized by Thomas Paine and so welcome, apparently, to Washington.

In many hearts the old ties of loyalty were broken with great difficulty and in many more—a majority, no doubt—there was no enthusiasm and much downright opposition to what Paine called "the new method of thinking that hath arisen." Families, friends, and neighbors divided; some among the least-privileged classes took the Tory side, and many among the most aristocratic ranks threw themselves into the patriot cause. But by and large, with many qualifications, to be sure, the transition from loyalty to crown and empire to loyalty to American rights, to a vague but emerging idea of an American nation, owed much to the conviction of innumerable plain people that the British connection strengthened privilege and caste, fettered opportunity for the common man, and threatened future liberties and well-being.

The struggle for freedom from Great Britain drew together those who, for reasons widely divergent and in some cases even contradictory, had taken their stand for separation. This sense of unity was enhanced, of course, by the presence of the foe, both the British redcoats and the large number of Loyalists and their sympathizers. It was on some occasions intensified and on others diluted by the existence of a large number of men more or less indifferent to the struggle. From the ranks of those who took the Revolutionary side some actually went over to the British when their troops occupied New York, or Philadelphia, or great stretches of the Carolinas. Yet in spite of such exceptions it was clear that the decision to strike for independence had welded the provinces into a sort of fighting unity.

It was the morale rather than the loyalty of civilians and soldiers among the patriots that failed often to meet the test of sacrifice and endurance. Washington labored against the countless local attachments and distinctions among those who supported the cause. "But I have found it impossible to overcome prejudices," he wrote sadly to the president of the Congress on December 20, 1776. How often Washington deprecated jealousies among the troops from the different provinces! How often he pleaded for unity in "the noble Cause in which we are engaged, and which we ought to support with one hand and one heart." [30] In his General Orders of August 1, 1776, the great American earnestly begged officers and men "to consider the consequences; that they can in no way assist our cruel enemies more effectively than making division among ourselves; that the Honor and success of the army, and the safety of our bleeding Country, depends upon harmony and good agreement with each other; that the Provinces are all United to oppose the common enemy, and all distinctions sink in the name of an American." [31] When men deserted; when officers carried over provincial rivalries into personal antagonisms; when the Congress and the states were unable or unwilling to supply the armies with a bare minimum of essentials; when provisions were refused the Continental armies only to be sold at a fat profit to the enemy for good British gold; when military disasters piled up one on another; when in the dark days at Valley Forge there was a growing fear that the people might become completely disunited and supine, or even yield to the enemy's peace offer: facing all these dangers, Washington was as a rock of adamant. His courage inspired officers and men, his loyalty to the embryonic nation inspired Americans of that day and of the future.

Sorely tried, the "father of his country" was too wise to rely merely on patriotism to effect the purpose to which he and those who stood with him were committed. "Men may speculate all they will," he wrote from Valley Forge in April, 1778; "they may talk of patriotism; they may draw a few examples from ancient story, of great achievements performed by its influence; but whosoever builds upon it, as a sufficient Basis for conducting this Bloody war, will find themselves deceived in the end. We must take the passions of Men as Nature has given them; and those principles as a guide which are generally the rule of Action. I do not mean to exclude altogether the Idea of Patriotism. I know it exists, and I know it has done much in the present Contest. But I venture to assert, that a

[30] George Washington, *Writings*, ed. by Worthington C. Ford (New York, 1890), V, 117.   [31] *Ibid.*, pp. 361–362.

great and lasting War can never be supported on this principle alone. It must be aided by a prospect of Interest or some reward." [32] And so Washington struggled to put the army on a "respectable footing," to convince soldiers and civilians that the cost of defeat would be immeasurable, the rewards of freedom sweet and lasting.

If the letters of soldiers are sufficient evidence of their sentiments, fighting men in all wars are preoccupied most of the time with thoughts of food, drink, mud, lice, and sex rather than with patriotic sentiment and sustained, conscious devotion to country. This was true of Revolutionary soldiers. It was true in spite of the fact that for Mrs. John Adams—and no doubt for many other ladies—the lowest subaltern with a cockade appeared "of double the importance he used to be." [33] The plain fact was that notwithstanding the sacrifices, the fervor, and the nobility within the ranks, the soldiers only now and then expressed in the letters that are available to us the deepest patriotic sentiments.[34] Nor is this cause for wonder, since the Revolutionary soldier knew nothing of a national government and was not even too clear about just what his country was. His loyalty and patriotism were in one sense negative: he was against what seemed to him wrong and oppressive. Only falteringly did he come in a positive way to associate American rights with an American nation, and when he did so, that American nation was an abstraction. For an American nation might exist as an idea, as an aspiration, as it did in Dr. Benjamin Rush's mind when he exclaimed in 1776, "We are now a nation!" It hardly existed as an actuality.

All this becomes clearer when one examines the uses which colonists made of the terms "country," "America," and "American" in the decade prior to the famous resolution by Congress on September 9, 1776. On that day it declared that thenceforth the term "the United States" would replace "United Colonies" on all commissions and other official documents issued under the author-

[32] Washington, *Writings* (Bicentennial ed.), XI, 286–287.
[33] Charles Francis Adams, ed., *The Letters of Mrs. John Adams* (Boston, 1848), p. 38.
[34] William Matthews and Dixon Wecter, *Our Soldiers Speak*, 1775–1918 (Boston, 1943), Chapter 1.

ity of the Congress.[35] It is not certain at just what point colonists generally began to refer to their own province or to the seaboard provinces collectively as "my country."

What Franklin did in this connection may or may not have been representative, but it in any case illustrates the pattern of his own thought and feeling. On preparing in 1764 to leave Pennsylvania for England he wrote to a friend, "I am now to take leave (perhaps a last leave) of the country I love, and in which I have spent the greatest part of my life." [36] He could have referred to Pennsylvania alone or to the American colonies in general. That it was in the latter sense is suggested by the fact that throughout the 1760's he used the term "America" not only in the sense of the thirteen colonies, but of the whole continent, the "New World." In 1768 he wrote to an unknown correspondent that the English thought him "too much of an American." It is significant that he did not use the expression, "too much of a Pennsylvanian," inasmuch as he was the official agent of that province. Early in 1774 he was commonly speaking of his "sincere affection to my native Country," of "my countrymen." And on July 5 of the following year, twelve months before the Declaration of Independence, he wrote to an acquaintance, "You are a member of Parliament, and one of that Majority which has doomed my Country to Destruction." [37] That it was fairly common to refer to the thirteen colonies at this time as "America" is suggested by the fact that Burke used that expression rather than "colonies" in his famous speech on reconciliation.

The fighting unity into which at least that portion of the population which took the American side was welded found a verbal expression in the Declaration of Independence itself.[38] Yet the meaning of many terms in the document was none too clear. Jeffer-

[35] *Journals of the Continental Congress 1774–1779* (Washington, 1906), V, 747, XV, 1310, XXVI, 169; Edmund C. Burnett, ed., *Letters of Members of the Continental Congress* (Washington, 1934), VII, 265.
[36] Franklin, *Writings*, IV, 285.
[37] *Ibid.*, VI, 407.
[38] For an illuminating discussion on this point, see Charles A. Beard, "Nationalism in American History," in Waldo Leland, ed., *Nationalism: Papers Presented at the Fourth Chicago Meeting of the American Association for the Advancement of Science* (Bloomington, Indiana, 1934), pp. 39 ff.

son spoke of "one people," but the term "them" rather than the collective expression "it" was used in the same context. There could be no doubt that the Declaration was a declaration of the newly created states speaking with one voice; but there could be no doubt that thirteen different states were speaking. Throughout the Revolution and long afterward John Adams called both Massachusetts and the United States "my country." James Madison likewise spoke of both Virginia and the United States as "my country." So did Jefferson, to the very end of his life. As Irving Brant has noted, so common was this duality of meaning that both during and after the war men spoke of state and nation as "our country" even in the same sentence! [39] This confusion of loyalties is demonstrated by a vast mass of evidence.

As the war approached its end even the fighting unity seemed to be vanishing into state separatism. On May 31, 1780, Washington wrote that he could "see one head gradually turning into thirteen. . . . I see the powers of Congress declining too fast for the consequence and respect which is due to them as the grand representative body of America." [40] The commander in chief again and again deplored the weakness of national sentiment and of genuine national interest.

That weakness again and again revealed itself, notwithstanding one notable achievement—notable at least for its potentialities. The Confederation acquired a domain to administer, thanks to the refusal of Maryland to ratify the Articles until the states with claims to western lands ceded these to the general government. This in itself was of great importance in giving substance to the new Confederation. No less significant was the famous decision by Congress to admit in due time new western states to the union, on terms of equal partnership with the original thirteen. This meant that the feeble union could develop from a mere Atlantic coast strip into a vast country bounded only by the Mississippi; and that the western states, admitted as equals, were likely to be loyal to the union. Had

[39] Irving Brant, *James Madison, the Virginia Revolutionist* (Indianapolis, 1941), Chapter 18.
[40] Washington, *Writings* (Bicentennial ed.), XVIII, 453.

the colonies in ample time been given equal partnership with the mother country, it is probable that their loyalty to Britain would have been able to cope with whatever tensions developed. In any case, the lesson was not lost. The twofold decision to endow the new Confederation with lands for temporary administration as territories and ultimate admission as equal states was a foundation stone for the growth of loyalty to the inchoate nation. Washington, discouraged though he was at the lack of true zeal for the American cause, took heart.

In his Circular Letter to the states, issued at Newburgh on June 8, 1783, the commander in chief had reminded his countrymen of the blessings America possessed in its variety of soils and climates, its vast theater of operations, and "the fairer opportunity for political happiness" it enjoyed than "any other Nation has been favored with." Most important of all, it was embarking on its future career, not in an age of ignorance, but at an epoch in which the rights of man were better understood and more clearly defined than ever before. All this assumed that America was a country, a nation. Yet if the United States was to survive as an independent power, Washington laid down four essentials: an indissoluble Union of the States, under one federal head; a sacred regard to public justice; the adoption of a proper peace Establishment; and the prevalence of "that pacific and friendly Disposition, among the People of the United States, which will induce them to forget their local prejudices and policies, to make those natural concessions which are requisite to the general prosperity, and in some instances, to sacrifice their individual advantages to the interest of the Community." [41]

Washington continued to be troubled by the weakness of national sentiment and national interest. The outward and formal process of making a nation had achieved a victory in 1781 when the Confederation was at length ratified; that outward and formal process was to be completed when the Constitution was adopted in 1787. The inward process of fusing discordant communities into one people had made only slight headway, had only barely begun the long course which is even today unfinished. Washington was

[41] Washington, *Writings*, XXVI, 483 *ff.*

therefore sensitive to anything that threatened to upset the delicate equilibrium. Thus he advised Bushrod Washington on November 15, 1786, of the dangers in "patriotic societies" designed to instruct the delegations of states in the general congress. "In speaking of national matters I look to the federal Government, which in my opinion it is the interest of every State to support; and to do this, as there are a variety of interests in the Union, there must be a yielding of the parts to coalesce the whole." Any county, district, or even state, Washington went on, might decide on a measure, "which, tho' apparently for the benefit of it in its unconnected state, may be repugnant to the interests of the nation, and eventually to the State itself as a part of the Confederation." [42]

Others who shared Washington's hopes for a genuinely united nation sensed danger in anything that suggested an *imperium in imperio*. John Jay, writing to John Adams in May, 1786, declared that it was one of the first wishes of his heart "to see the people of America become one nation in every respect," to have them look on their state legislatures as standing to the Confederation, "in the same light in which counties stand to the State of which they are parts, *viz.*, merely as districts to facilitate the purposes of domestic order and good government." [43] Somewhat later James Wilson, a conservative Pennsylvania lawyer, in speaking to the newly assembled Constitutional Convention, reviewed the tendency in the first Continental Congress to bury local interests and distinctions. But, he lamented, the tables turned once the state governments were formed, and jealousy and ambition began to display themselves until "at length the confederation . . . became frittered down to the impotent condition in which it now stands." [44]

"The interests of the States," wrote Jefferson to Monroe from Paris in 1785, "ought to be made joint in every possible instance, in order to cultivate the idea of our being one nation, and to multiply instances in which the people should look up to Congress as their

[42] Washington, *Writings*, XXIX, 67–68.
[43] William Jay, *The Life of John Jay, with Selections from His Correspondence* (New York, 1833), I, 249–250.
[44] Max Farrand, ed., *The Records of the Federal Convention* (New Haven, 1911), I, 166.

head." [45] Twelve years later, in May, 1797, Jefferson expressed himself as happy in believing "that, whatever follies we may be led into as to foreign nations, we shall never give up our Union, the last anchor of our hope, and that alone which is to prevent this heavenly country from becoming an arena of gladiators." [46]

Thomas Paine was no less outspoken. In *The American Crisis* (1783) he insisted that "our great national character depends on Union of the States. . . . It is through this only that we are, or can be, nationally known in the world; it is the flag of the United States which renders our ships and commerce safe on the seas, or in a foreign port." [47] The division into states was, Paine maintained, a mere matter of local convenience. Such a distinction ceased the moment an American went abroad. "In short, we have no other national sovereignty than the United States. It would be fatal for us if we had, for it would be too expensive to be maintained, and impossible to be supported. . . . Our great title is AMERICANS—our inferior one varies with the place." [48] The fact that Jefferson and Paine so vehemently contended for loyalty to the collective whole shows that at the end of the Revolutionary War even these stout champions of the more democratic values saw nothing incompatible between them and national loyalty and power.

It is a difficult task to weigh the motives of the men who took the initiative in framing the Constitution and in fighting for its ratification. We may be sure that these motives were complex and that the men themselves were only partly aware of them. We may be sure that some men were moved by their fear that if the central government were not made sufficiently strong to protect property rights everywhere and to put down insurrections, anarchy lay ahead. We may be sure that others felt hope for their fortunes only in a national government sufficiently strong to assume the debts contracted by the old Confederation and the states during the War for Independence, a government able to protect the frontier against the Indian and to promote white settlements across the Alleghenies, where land speculators had already staked out claims in anticipation

---

[45] Jefferson, *Writings* (Ford ed.), IV, 52. [46] *Ibid.*, VII, 122.
[47] Paine, *Writings*, I, 374.   [48] *Ibid.*, p. 375.

of future profit. That others saw in a truly national government more satisfactory measures for the regulation of trade and currency is also evident. But in the minds of these same men, an emotionally patriotic devotion to America and a conviction that only a strong central government could maintain the republic also played a large role—how large, who can say?

The Constitution did not proclaim the existence of a nation: the word national does not appear in the document. Yet on May 30, 1787, the Convention adopted, by a narrow margin, a resolution declaring that "a national government ought to be established." Luther Martin, one of the minority, withdrew because he believed the convention intended to set up a national, rather than a federal, government. The debates indicate that a substantial majority of the framers favored a strong central government. Gouverneur Morris probably spoke for the majority who wanted a national government when he defined a confederacy as "a mere compact resting on the good faith of the parties" and a national government as one with supreme, complete, and compulsive operation.

But this was skating on thin ice. Charles A. Beard has imagined cautious statesmen expressing concern lest such frankness disrupt the convention by encouraging others to follow the example of Luther Martin in quitting it. He has pictured wise heads drawing back from the use of the word national on the score that such a document would almost certainly be rejected by voters in view of the intensity of local and state interests. The suspicion of some that a strong national government might become an instrument for the destruction of popular rights and interests is well known. Thus it was that a substitute resolution was adopted, a resolution declaring that "the government of the United States ought to consist of a supreme Legislative, Judiciary, and Executive."

In later years champions of the idea that the Constitution had established a nation in which the states had only limited powers cited the preamble of the document as proof of their contention. But it is clear from the records of the Convention that the phrase, "We, the people of the United States," was not meant in any collective sense, was not intended to convey the idea that the Constitution was establishing a consolidated nation. The original draft of the preamble began by listing the several states: "We, the people of New Hampshire, Massachusetts, Rhode Island," and so on. Since no one could anticipate just which states would first ratify the Constitution and just which would not, it was deemed wise to shift the phraseology to some more general term. After due search that was found in the famous introduction, "We, the people of the United States."

On other issues, too, the specific intentions of the framers on the whole question of the national character of the new government were vague. In the matter of citizenship, a crucial test of nationality, the Constitution speaks of citizens of the states and citizens of the United States. When references were made in the debates to the question whether the colonies, in throwing off the authority of Great Britain, achieved their independence individually or unitedly, members of the Convention failed to see eye to eye. Some took their stand with Luther Martin, who contended that when the colonies became independent of Great Britain they had also become—and had remained—independent of each other. Even men who, like James Wilson, took the opposite view and maintained that an American nation actually existed during the Revolution, spoke on occasion as if the Constitution itself had established the nation. This assumption seems, at any rate, to have been in Wilson's mind when, on the Fourth of July, 1788, he triumphantly declared in an oration in Philadelphia, " 'Tis done! We have become a nation!" [49]

In the heated debates between those who championed the adoption of the Constitution and those who opposed it, occasional remarks of framers suggested that in their minds a nation did actually exist. Writing in The Federalist John Jay declared "this country and this people seem to have been made for each other. . . . As a nation we have made peace and war: as a nation we have vanquished our common enemies: as a nation we have formed alliances and made treaties." [50] To Jay, at least, the American people, united as they were in religion, language, and principles of government, con-

[49] James Wilson, Works (Philadelphia, 1804), III, 299 ff.
[50] The Federalist, ed. by Paul Leicester Ford (New York, 1898), p. 9.

stituted "one united people," one nation, to which supreme loyalty is due. Other champions of the Constitution probably saw the people as already a nation in the essentials of culture and purpose, or else they believed that a nation was rapidly appearing and that the Constitution was a necessary instrument in the process.

Many, to be sure, sharply dissented from such a view. In their minds a national government seemed likely to bring the dominance of aristocracy and even tyranny. "If the United States are to be melted down into one empire," exclaimed the antifederalist Samuel Bryan, in a broadside designed to defeat the ratification of the Constitution in Pennsylvania, "it would not be difficult to prove, that anything short of despotism, could not bind so great a country under one government; and that whatever plan you might, at the first setting out, establish, it would issue in a despotism." [51] This was so, he felt, because in so large a country no supreme national government could properly regard the needs and wants of local areas.

Such fears proved groundless. The Constitution was a necessary instrument in the process by which the Americans did become a nation which they could love and to which they could be loyal. The wisdom of the framers in outlining a structure of government and in broadly sketching the outline of federal relations was to be demonstrated over and over again. Interpreted as a national document by the Supreme Court, especially by Chief Justice Marshall, the Constitution greatly promoted the development of the powers of the federal government. Eulogized by patriotic orators like Daniel Webster, it became in due time an emotionally charged symbol of national unity and loyalty.

The Constitution could hardly have been written, let alone adopted, if a variety of ideas and interests that may be called national had not already been forming. Nor could it have served in the further growth of national unity and loyalty if these ideas and interests had not continued to operate. What these ideas and interests were, and how they were consciously nurtured, constitute memorable chapters in the history of loyalty to the American nation.

[51] Samuel Bryan, *Centinel: To the People of Philadelphia* (Philadelphia, ca. 1787).

II: THE LOYALTY OF TIME AND PLACE

Look round on your country, Columbians, undaunted,
From Georgia to Maine—from the Lakes to the Sea!
Is one human blessing or luxury wanted
That flows not amongst us unmeasur'd and free?
Our harvests sustain half the wide eastern world,
Our mines and our forests exhaustless remain;
What sails on our great Fishing-Banks are unfurled!
What shoals fill our streams from the depths of the main!
The fruits of our country, our flocks and our fleeces,
The treasures immers'd in our mountains that lie,
While discord is tearing old Europe to pieces,
Shall amply the wants of our people supply.

THE AMERICAN PATRIOTIC SONG-BOOK, 1813

Geography was chiefly American, and the United States was larger
than all the universe beside. . . . In the same way our history was
American history, brief but glorious. We despised monarchical
countries and governments too thoroughly to care much about their
histories and if we studied them, it was that we might contrast their
despotisms with our own free happy institutions. We were taught
every day and in every way that ours was the freest, the happiest, and
soon to be the greatest and most powerful country in the world.

T. L. NICHOLS, 1864

IN SOME SHADOWY PAST when nomads settled down into pastoral culture the sentiment of loyalty to homeland was born. In every Old World country devotion to the land itself played a telling role in the growth of national loyalty. Over a long period of time men and women came to associate the sentiment they felt for their own locality with a larger area or a whole country. During the slow growth of civilization, people had been profoundly influenced by soil and climate, by local attachments and innumerable associations which had, bit by bit and unconsciously, come to be identified with this larger region, or, when nations had come into being, with a nation.

In America the situation was different. Francis Grund, an Austrian visitor, pointed out in 1837 that Americans had entered their homes, not as children nurtured in the bosom of the land, but as masters determined to subdue it. They could not love what was not their own, and when the land became theirs, "they had already changed its face." [1] This interpretation was supported by comments of other visiting foreigners. Charles Mackay, also writing in 1837, said of the American that "his affections have more to do with the social and political system with which he is connected, than with the soil which he inhabits. The man whose attachments converge upon a particular spot of earth, is miserable if removed from it; but give the American his institutions, and he cares little where you place him." [2] Moreover a great many Americans did not spend their lives in the neighborhood of their birthplace, and thus failed to develop, in the same degree as Europeans, deep and abiding attachments to particular localities. This migratory portion of the American people did not for any great length of time submit to what Constance Rourke has called "the discipline of place." They were far too mobile for that. This mobility was one factor in the bustle and activity which came to be regarded as a national characteristic.

Although devotion to a native soil was a less important factor in

[1] Francis J. Grund, *The Americans in Their Moral, Social, and Political Relations* (London, 1837), I, 266.
[2] Charles Mackay, *Life and Liberty in America* (New York, 1837), I, 174 ff.

the growth of national loyalty in America than in Europe, it was nevertheless a powerful force in the New World. In a suggestive essay Arthur M. Schlesinger has shown how the very abundance of land made the Americans not only a rural people, but a rural people unlike any in the Old World.[3] Nature was indeed generous in her lavish setting for the American stage. This generosity eased the transfer of loyalty from the old home, whether in Europe or in the older American settlements, to the new area. Americans grew more and more conscious that their land was wide and held a wealth of distant fertile fields to which any man might move if he chose. The very spaciousness of territory, along with the mobility of the people, fostered loyalty to localities and pride in the land as a whole.

It is true that in some instances the immensity of America and the gigantic scale on which nature had worked hampered the development of love of the land in its entirety. In commenting on the intense patriotism of the English, Hawthorne ascribed it to the size of the island, which was "not too big to be taken bodily into each of their hearts." Admitting with regret that he himself was not particularly patriotic, Hawthorne remarked that the limited sense of kinship he felt with the soil sprang from the circumstance that "we have so much country that we have really no country at all." [4] Hawthorne returned to this theme in *Dr. Grimshawe's Secret*, in which the Englishman remarked to his American friend that if an American's heart were very large he might take in, he might come to know intimately and love, at the most, the soil of New England. The American agreed, adding: "Our space is so vast that we shall never come to know and love it, inch by inch . . . for where land changes its ownership every few years, it does not become imbued with the personalities of the people who live on it. It is but so much grass; so much dirt, where a succession of people have dwelt too little to make it really their own." [5]

[3] Arthur M. Schlesinger, "What Then Is the American, This New Man?," *American Historical Review*, XLVIII (January, 1943), 225–244.
[4] Nathaniel Hawthorne to Henry Wadsworth Longfellow, October 24, 1854, cited in Lawrence S. Hall, *Hawthorne, Critic of Society* (New Haven, 1944), p. 71.
[5] Nathaniel Hawthorne, *Works* (Boston and New York, 1891), XI, 470.

Whatever truth there was in what Hawthorne wrote in his more nostalgic moods, his position was in no sense characteristic of the great majority of Americans who expressed themselves on the subject. As the vastness of America and the gargantuan features of its physiography were increasingly revealed to Americans, their pride and boastfulness knew no bounds. Jedidiah Morse's ubiquitous school textbooks underlined the superiority and the distinctiveness of American geography. The tendency to emphasize the vastness and the variety of the American scene, and to find it both superior and unique, was reflected in the remark of an observer that in American schools "geography was chiefly American, and the United States was larger than all the universe beside." [6] The pastime of comparing America's geographical features with those of Europe was popular. One rhymester, writing in the *New York Magazine* in 1795, told of a fictitious dinner party in Edinburgh, where at length the single American rose to defend his country against the charge of inferiority:

> *Why, Sir, we in America have Pools*
> *In which we might douse Britain's Island whole,*
> *And though your ablest navigating squires*
> *With steady diligence, and patience meek*
> *Might seek the wandering realm of their desires,*
> *They would not find them in a week!* [7]

In like vein Elkanah Watson, merchant, philanthropist, and traveler, rhetorically exclaimed, "What are called mountains in Europe, are hills in America; rivers are reduced to brooks; trees to bushes, and lakes to ponds!" [8]

The appreciation of the singular American landscape in the colonial era mounted during the first half century after independence, when the Romantic movement swept over the United States. Romanticism, with its worshipful attitude toward nature, provided in Europe a good deal of inspiration for the rising national spirit that

[6] Thomas L. Nichols, *Forty Years of American Life* (London, 1864), I, 62.
[7] *New York Magazine*, I (1795), 15.
[8] Elkanah Watson, *Men and Times of the Revolution* (New York, 1861), p. 77.

marked the first half of the nineteenth century. In America it fed even more the growth of patriotism. For Romanticism glorified the primitive wilderness and so deepened enthusiasm for the American landscape. Exuberant European Romanticists, however critical they might be of American institutions and customs, were eloquent in describing the lush picturesqueness of American scenery. Americans themselves were not slow to echo the refrain in still louder tones.[9]

Just as God's dumb creatures love their surroundings, so by a kind of instinct, argued a New England divine, "the mountains and the valleys, the brooks and the meadows, the hamlets and the cities, which delighted us when young, delight us when old."[10] Another parson some decades later confessed that the softest warblings of a nightingale were poorer melodies in his ears than the shriek of a nighthawk swooping through the New England sky. A Massachusetts clerical leader and historian, Jeremy Belknap, discovered for Americans the wild beauty of the White Mountains. Joel Barlow celebrated in his long epic, *The Columbiad*, the magnificent rivers, the stupendous mountains, the vast forests and plains of the republic. Nor was the romantic impulse in these matters by any means limited to New England, as Cooper, Irving, Paulding, Simms, and a host of lesser lights bore witness. In some degree the admiration of the landscape and scenery of each region was felt in every other.

The exaltation kindled in the first generations on the seaboard and reenforced by Romanticism was repeated as West after West was discovered, charted, and occupied. Guidebooks for settlers commented not only on the fertile soils, salt springs, navigable streams, and salubrious climates, but on picturesque landscapes. "Whoever undertakes a Description of the *Walnut* Hills," wrote one traveler, "must have a fertile Imagination, be happy at Landscape Painting, and use Something of Romance or he will fall infi-

[9] Mary E. Woolley, "The Development of the Love of Romantic Scenery in America," *American Historical Review*, III (October, 1897), 56 ff.
[10] John Lathrop, *Patriotism and Religion: A Sermon Preached on the Twenty-fifth of April*, 1799 (Boston, 1799), p. 6.

nitely short of that Eulogium which the Place so justly merits." [11]
William Cullen Bryant wrote of the "Encircling vastness of the
prairies" and had no doubt that

> The hand that built the firmament hath sheathed
> And smoothed these variant swells, and sown their slopes
> With herbiage, planted them with island groves,
> And hedged them round with forests.[12]

Mrs. R. J. Avery in her *Wood Notes Wild* (1843) sang of the ex-
quisite landscapes of France and Italy, of their flowers and parks
and formal beauty, but hastened to add

> Our bouquets simple tho' they be,
> In our own native woods they bloom,
> Uncultured,—in our Tennessee
> They yield perfume.
>
> Take them!—nor crush them in their bud!
> Rural wreathes of natural growth,—
> No foreign charms were ever wooed,
> To give them worth! [13]

The appreciation of American landscapes was both reflected in
and accented by pictorial representation. In the second quarter of
the nineteenth century the Hudson River School of painters,
Thomas Cole, Frederick Church, Asher B. Durand, and Thomas
Doughty, depicted the Catskills and the Adirondacks with a technical skill that employed, now lines of needlelike precision, now
poetical gray and silver tones with charming effects of light and
shadow. The consciousness of American natural beauty and the
pride in it, which these paintings furthered, fed the streams of
patriotism.

[11] John Pope, *Tour Through the Southern and Western Territories of the
United States of America* (Richmond, 1792), p. 28.
[12] William Cullen Bryant, *Prose Writings*, ed. by Parke Godwin (New York,
1883), I, 229.
[13] Mrs. R. J. Avery, *Wood Notes Wild* (Nashville, 1843), pp. 8–9.

A wider public was reached through elaborate gift-books, beautifully embellished with American views. *The Scenery of the United States* (1855) was typical of scores of such volumes. "The beauty of American scenery is proverbial throughout the civilized world," wrote its editor. "Nowhere else on the globe is Nature lovelier, grander, less austere, and more varied and picturesque, than upon this continent." [14] Vast canvas panoramas brought some part of the magnificence of the Father of Waters to countless Americans, and the Currier and Ives prints familiarized an even larger number with the majesty of the Niagara, the sweep of the prairies, the opulent vegetation of the Southland, the wooded roads and snowy hills of New England.

The diversified character of the land opened by the westward movement continued to evoke admiration. Even when this admiration was not explicitly identified with love of the country, it laid part of the foundation for loyalty. Readers of Francis Parkman's robust *Oregon Trail* must have taken satisfaction in identifying with their country "the faintly defined outline of the distant swell" of the prairies; they could hardly have resisted the suggestion of the strength and beauty in "the low, undulating line of sandhills" bounding the horizon. Subsequent explorers, reveling in the unexpected, shared their appreciation with an enchanted reading public. John Wesley Powell, the geologist who brought to light the esoteric beauties of the Colorado River in the 1870's, graphically pictured the wilderness of colored rocks, the weird canyons, the blunted mesas, the snow-clad peaks. Among the writers who familiarized Americans with the details of western beauty Raphael Pumpelly, Clarence King, and John Muir did yeoman service. Whatever informed critics might say of the lack of warmth and technical subtlety in the vast canvases on which Albert Bierstadt painted Laramie Peak and the Yosemite Valley, his work awakened awe and pride in many hearts. Frederic Remington's spectacular paintings of the dazzling Great Plains appealed, even more than did Bierstadt's majestic mountains, to men, women, and children in every part of the land.

[14] *The Scenery of the United States* (New York, 1855), Preface.

The curiosities of the new country, the variety and unfamiliarity of flora, fauna, and terrain, and the half-hidden potentialities in the acres stretching west to the sun naturally moved such professionals as explorers, artists, and writers to expression. Yet the wonder and delight were shared, too, by rank and file Americans little given to writing about their feelings. Letters of pioneers often spoke of the beauty as well as the fertility of their new homesteads, often found words for their loyalty to the new region. Love for the land moved a Michigan pioneer to write:

> Down the banks of Flint river,
>   This beautiful stream,
> Where my cottage remains,
>   I've returned home again,
> And who, in his senses,
>   Can help but believe
> That this was the garden
>   Of Adam and Eve? [15]

"Passed through the most beautiful country I ever saw," noted another Michigan settler, "the ground all along the road richly ornamented with wild flowers and dotted with crimson by the thousands of strawberries which cover it everywhere." [16] Still another believed that "for untold thousands of years, Nature had been at work, in the air, in the snow, in the water, in combining and secreting vivifying material in the soil for the coming men." [17]

Now and again the advantages as well as the beauties of the new land were explicitly associated with patriotism; for example, the Michigan pioneer who believed that a "sturdy race of honest and patriotic men grow up to counterbalance the effeminacy and wickedness of the old cities of the east. But for this, ruin and decay would have long since marked the gradual downfall of our great

[15] W. R. McCormick, "Sketch," *Pioneer Collections; Report of the Pioneer Society of the State of Michigan* (Lansing, 1906), IV, 364–373.
[16] L. R. Swan, *Journal of a Trip to Michigan in 1841* (Rochester, 1904), pp. 18–19.
[17] Charles W. Jay, *My New Home in Northern Michigan* (Trenton, 1874), p. 43.

republic. There is today more of the leaven of national salvation, right here by the lonely shores of the mighty waters of Lake Michigan, than in all the borders of all the cities of the corrupt civilization of the older east. The wide extent of our country is the conservative influence that will save it from the fate of the ruined dynasties of the old world for ages yet to come." [18]

When the frontier moved to the treeless prairies farther west, pioneers waxed equally enthusiastic, even though fortune did not always smile on them. The letters of newcomers ring with praise of the "beauty and loveliness of the rich and rolling prairies . . . the dry, pure air, the clear, blue skies, the winding stream skirted with timber along which the buffalo and antelope graze." [19] Although the first Nebraskans had their hardships and fears, although they contended with prairie fires, grasshopper plagues, and terrible blizzards, they quickly discovered that nature had made provision there for agricultural abundance. "Never on earth did nature present a fairer field for the use of man," declared a speaker at the Nebraska State Fair in 1878, "never one more beautiful for his eye to survey, or his heart to admire and love." [20]

Grim nature did much to discourage the weak-hearted, but once a given set of obstacles had been surmounted, it was argued, the salubrity of the climate and the thrill of life on the plains had a transforming effect on taciturn, resolute men who became, under the Nebraska sun, enterprising and venturesome.[21] Many a letter confessed a sinking disappointment at the first sight of the "Desolate, wind-swept prairie" stretching out uninvitingly, but in time the same person often might take pleasure in the cottonwoods along a winding stream, revel in the sight of a grove with a homelike look, or feel uplifted on beholding the tens of thousands of wild prairie

[18] Jay, My New Home, p. 48.

[19] Henry T. Davis, Solitary Places Made Glad; Being Observations and Experiences for 32 Years in Nebraska (Cincinnati, 1890), p. 24.

[20] A. S. Paddock, An Address delivered at Lincoln during the Nebraska State Fair (Lincoln, 1879), p. 2.

[21] L. L. Correll, "The Lure of the Prairies," Collection of Nebraska Pioneer Reminiscences (Nebraska Society of the Daughters of the American Revolution, Cedar Rapids, Iowa, 1916), p. 274.

flowers.[22] "Out of the elements at hand," wrote a Nebraska pioneer, "we made the rudiments of a home on land that was to become ours —our very own—forever." [23]

"It is impossible to imagine the beauty of a Texas prairie when in the vernal season its rich luxuriant herbage, adorned with many thousand flowers of every size and hue, seems to realize the vision of a terrestrial paradise," wrote a settler. "Methinks the veriest infidel would here be constrained to bow and worship." [24] An occasional witness, to be sure, looked in vain for beauty in the grandeur of Texas scenery, or was overpowered by dreary solitude and loneliness, but even some of these doubters often came to "be filled with the immensity of the picture." [25]

Pioneers of the mountain West set a new high in lyric appreciation of the country that spread out before them. They were impressed by the diversity of a country which presented every variety of scenery from the most grand and sublime to the most beautiful and picturesque.[26] "Such sunsets as we have!" exclaimed one. "Tongue cannot describe the beautiful scene that the God of nature has unfurled," declared another.[27] In speaking of Mount Hood and Mount St. Helens, of the beautiful valleys and rolling hills, one pioneer declared she had never been so much affected by any scenery in her life.[28] Many were convinced that such country stimulated the body to active industry, prompted the heart to noble deeds, and inspired the mind with elevated thoughts. Paeans of appreciation were chanted by men as well as by women over every

[22] E. G. Everett, "Experiences of a Pioneer Woman," *Collection of Nebraska Pioneer Reminiscences*, p. 32.

[23] G. L. Shumway, "Pioneering," *Collection of Nebraska Pioneer Reminiscences*, p. 265.

[24] D. W. C. Baker, *Texas Scrap-Book* (New York, 1875), p. 330.

[25] Abbé Domeneck, *Missionary Adventures in Texas and Mexico* (London, 1858), p. 27.

[26] This sentiment is expressed again and again in the writings of the early settlers. See the documents in Oregon Historical Society, *Collections*.

[27] Wallis Nash, *Two Years in Oregon* (New York, 1882), p. 27.

[28] Mrs. Marcus Whitman, "A Journey Across the Plains in 1838," *Nineteenth Annual Reunion of the Oregon Pioneer Association, Transactions* (Portland, 1893), pp. 55–56.

type of landscape. The fertile reaches of the Mississippi which Tocqueville declared to be "God's own country," the boundless prairies,
the wind-whittled mountains of New Mexico, even the alkali flats
of Wyoming and Nevada, called forth expressions of interest in, and
loyalty to, the land.

As men made the wild land their own through years of labor,
they learned to love it. As they came to love it, they developed that
sense of pride which made it at length easier to cherish a loyalty to
the nation which was springing to maturity on that land. Hungry
peasants from the Old World revered the stubborn and frequently
cruel prairies, even when their womenfolk resented the droughts
and the snows, the vastness and the loneliness of the semiarid
plains. In Rölvaag's *Giants in the Earth* the Dakota soil conquered
Beret, who despised it. But her husband, Per Hansa, adored it. In
Willa Cather's *O Pioneers!* Alexandra Bergen, like Per Hansa, first
conquered and then loved the prairies. Many a cowboy felt the thrill
of Andy Adams in "the stillness of those splendid July nights" of
the moonlight drives, felt a deep love for the "lone prairie" even if
he sang tenderly of the youth who did not want to be buried on it.
When Walt Whitman in his magnificent poems celebrated the
American land and sang of loyalty to it, he was only a more articulate one among countless Americans whose letters, diaries, and
songs bear testimony to their love of the soil.

Always this esthetic appreciation is closely related to a realization
of the usefulness, the abundance of the land. What pride the almost limitless natural resources stirred in the hearts of Americans!
"All that the wish of an epicure, the pride of a beauty, or the curious
mind of a naturalist can ask to variegate the table of luxury, increase the shine of splendor, or delight the endless thirst of knowledge, is showered in profusion on this, the favorite land of heaven,"
declared President Timothy Dwight of Yale in 1787.[29] That same
year an academic orator at the College of Philadelphia praised
the pure atmosphere and the moderate seasons of America, which
made it "the granary of the world." Thanksgiving sermons spared
no hyperbole in celebrating the richness of American resources.

[29] *American Magazine*, I (December, 1787), 43.

"We suck the abundance of the sea, and the treasures of the land,"
declared the Reverend David Osgood of Medford, Massachusetts,
in 1783. "We have many hundred leagues of sea coast for the advantages of trade. No longer confined to one market [England], our
commerce receives an unbounded extension." [30] And so it did, for
the very next year an American ship set sail for China, the first of
thousands of vessels to make that long journey.

Southerners as well as Northerners took pride in the natural en-
dowments of the whole American domain. "With what rapture
must the American patriot reflect on the brilliancy of our career, and
anticipate the future destinies of our country," declared John Jersey
Mawyer in a Fourth of July oration in Charleston in 1819. "Formed
by a beneficent Creator, to be the world's 'last treasure and best
hope,' He has extended it to every clime, and afforded it every
natural advantage for composing a great and mighty people. It
abounds with luxurious plains, filled with the spontaneous productions of the earth, groaning under the weight of majestic trees.
Broad, mighty, and navigable rivers intersect the country, on whose
placid bosoms the riches of the interior float to the seaboard. . . .
Yes, America shall reach a height beyond the ken of mortals." [31]

Appreciation of the rich beauty of the land thus went along with
belief in its superior destiny. Typical of scores of orations is that of a
New York patriot who in 1794 asked whether Americans did not
have ample resources within the bosom of the country "which require nothing but our united exertions to serve every useful purpose?
Invested by nature with strength, it belongs to us to avail ourselves
of it." [32] In 1841 the Phi Beta Kappa orator at Union College likewise voiced the thought of countless other orators in asking, "Who
can cast his eye over the broad map of our country, without an expansion of feeling, and a proud exultation, which doubt cannot

[30] David Osgood, *Reflection on the Goodness of God in Supporting the People
of the United States during the Late War* (Boston, 1784), p. 24.
[31] John Jersey Mawyer, *An Oration Delivered to French Calvinists, The Fifth of
July, 1819* (Charleston, 1819), pp. 16–17.
[32] John B. Johnson, *An Oration on Union, Delivered in the New Dutch Church
in the City of New York, on the Twelfth Day of May, 1794* (New York, 1794),
p. 6.

shake, nor ridicule suppress? If ever the hand of nature visibly pointed to the seat of empire, it will be on the Continent of North America." [33] In view of such widespread sentiments and convictions the nationalistic historian George Bancroft was at a loss to understand how Americans could coolly "calculate the value of the Union." Looking about them, they might observe "the air of cheerful industry and successful enterprise, the sobriety of order, the increasing wealth of our cities, the increasing productiveness of our land, our streams crowded with new establishments, and the appearance of entire success, stamped on every part of the country." [34]

After the civil war there was a growing tendency to associate the richness of the land with industrial wealth. In 1866 a Massachusetts patriot spoke in thanksgiving for the late triumph of the Union. "The American citizen may indeed look with delight upon broad rivers, as channels for communication with the open seas; upon smaller streams, as of great wealth in motive power; on vast forests, with treasures of timber; on almost numberless acres, matchless for wheat, cotton, and corn; on mines of coal, iron, lead, copper, silver and gold; on rocks which pour out rivers of oil . . . a continent which contains all that will delight the senses, all that will gratify the investigating philosopher—a variety of soil, differences of climate, more than two thousand miles of seacoast, large and navigable rivers, bearing on their bosom all that imagination can paint, all that our necessities require, into the very core and heart of our country." [35] It is safe to say that no school child failed to hear such sentiments on more than one occasion, that few men or women in the mainstream of American life were unfamiliar with such doctrine.

The foundations of loyalty to place included not only pride in the vastness, the distinctive landscape, and the resources of America but also the conviction that nature had intended a separate and a

[33] William Kent, *Address Pronounced before the Phi Beta Kappa Society at Union College, July 27, 1841* (New York, 1841), p. 4.
[34] George Bancroft, *Oration Delivered on the Fourth of July, 1826, at Northampton* (Northampton, 1826), p. 14.
[35] A. W. Ide, *A Sermon Preached at Stafford Springs, on Thanksgiving Day, November 29, 1866* (Holliston, Massachusetts, 1866), pp. 5, 13.

united nation to rise on the shores of the Atlantic. Just as nationalists in Germany, Italy, and other European countries found in geography a powerful argument for unification of the political state, so American patriots developed the theme of natural boundaries. Geography, declared John B. Johnson in an oration delivered in the Dutch Reformed Church in New York in 1794, clearly points to the fact that "Providence designed us to be a great and a *united* Nation. Our lines are marked by the very hand of nature. . . . Within these limits marked by invariable lines, and abundantly extensive for the purposes of one empire," man clearly must not defeat what nature had intended.[36]

The conviction that national unity was inherent in American geography also found its champions in the South. "Nature, as well as policy, cries aloud for union," exclaimed a Fourth of July orator in Charleston in 1820. "Do not our mountains, which run from North to South, bind us in indissoluble union, like the sacred chain in nature which links all her jarring elements in peace? Do not our rivers rise in one state and run into another, receiving the tributary streams of both, and fertilizing with their waters, as rich as those of the Nile, the meadows of all through which they hold their majestic course, without distinction or regard to local prejudices?"[37]

The New England Unitarian minister Thomas Starr King was a powerful force for national loyalty on the Pacific Coast, where he had settled. "God designs that each country should wear a peculiar physiognomy," he declared. "Every patriot must guard against every disease that would cripple the resources, degrade the face that God has shaped. . . . God grooved our noble rivers, and stretched our prairies on their level base, and unrolled our rich savannahs, and reared the prompt of our coasts with generous ocean waves, and wove all these diversities into one, to be the home of no mean people, and the theater of no paltry destiny."[38] Both before and during the Civil War this distinguished patriot again and again cited

[36] Johnson, *op. cit.*, p. 6.
[37] Francis D. Quask, *An Oration Delivered on the Fourth of July, 1820, before the Cincinnati and the Revolution Societies* (Charleston, 1820), p. 20.
[38] Thomas Starr King, *Patriotism and Other Essays* (Boston, 1864), pp. 36, 53.

the character of American geography as proof that God had intended it as the seat of one and only one nation. "God has moulded the North American continent on an opposite plan from Europe and Asia: He has made it one immense fertile basin, having mountain walls over a thousand miles apart, with easy slopes and plentiful passes from East to West, not hindering but inviting the march of immigration down into the plains, and still on and over, if they choose, to a powerful sea. Does this mean that God intended this land for hostile armies and separate states?" [39]

Thus the doctrine of divinely ordained boundaries which figured in the contentions of national expansionists in European countries continued to flourish in the United States, although the main boundaries were not actually determined even so recently as a hundred years ago. Nor was there any general agreement at any particular time regarding the true limits of the national domain. Just before each new accession of territory the argument was advanced that nature had marked the desired territory for our own.

Many speeches in Congress and editorials in the press illustrated this at the time of the taking-over of Louisiana in 1803, of Florida in 1819, of Texas in 1845, of Oregon in 1846, and of New Mexico, Arizona, California, Nevada, and Utah in 1848.[40] Thus in venting dissatisfaction with the Spanish occupation of the mouth of the Mississippi, Secretary of State Madison spoke of "the manifest indications of nature." In Congress an ardent expansionist similarly announced that "God and nature have destined New Orleans and the Floridas to belong to this great and rising empire." The renunciation of American rights to Texas in 1819 aroused the passionate indignation of another Congressman, who insisted that "the great Engineer of the Universe has fixed the natural limits of our country, and men cannot change them." Others declared that the Rio Grande was "the boundary prescribed by nature." Oregon enthusiasts, not to be outdone, quoted Vergil: "our empire is bounded by the ocean, our glory by the stars."

[39] Thomas Starr King, *American Nationality* (San Francisco, 1863), pp. 5–6.
[40] This thesis is abundantly documented in Albert K. Weinberg, *Manifest Destiny: A Study of Nationalist Expansionism* (Baltimore, 1935), from which these quotations are taken.

From the time of Jefferson on, another argument for expansion was employed, that is, the right of the Anglo-Americans to the coveted lands by virtue of their superior use of the soil and their superior institutions. The doctrines of natural growth and political gravitation were also used. These arguments were employed particularly by agriculturists. They were cited to justify the purchase of the Louisiana territory, and they were invoked at later times when agrarians desired the lands of Florida, New Mexico, California, and Oregon.

Just as the Jeffersonian-agrarian type of argument was invoked at different times in our history when fresh acquisitions were in the offing, so too was the opposing Federalist type of doctrine regarding such matters. The Federalists, representing mercantile and embryonic industrial interests, feared that the balance of power in the federal government would be upset by new agricultural domains. Thus they stood out against the annexation of Louisiana by Jefferson in 1803; they bitterly resented the agrarian effort to seize Canada and the Floridas in the War of 1812; they grudgingly accepted the admission of Louisiana to the Union—"the new state of Louisiana—though she is the illegitimate child of the Twelfth Congress," exclaimed a Federalist toastmaster in 1813, "yet the United States must acknowledge her as a sister-in-law." In like manner the successors of the Federalists, the Whigs, saw little merit in taking over from Mexico the arid Southwest and remote California.[41]

The geographical argument was made to work both ways. George Perkins Marsh of Vermont, who shared the eastern Whig fear of the potential dominance of the West, wanted to know in the fateful year 1848 just what common interests Boston had with the Bay of San Francisco, or New York with Monterey, or Charleston with Puget Sound. Even if Anglo-Americans took possession of the remote area beyond the great Rockies, Marsh insisted, it belonged nevertheless by geographical predestination to the Orient. "What, then, God hath joined together, let no man put asunder."[42]

[41] In addition to Weinberg, *op. cit.*, consult on this Charles A. Beard, *The Idea of National Interest* (New York, 1934), Chapters 3–5.
[42] George Perkins Marsh, *Remarks on Slavery in the Territories* (Burlington, Vermont, 1848), p. 12.

This impassioned appeal to a particularized version of the doctrine of natural boundaries was, of course, only an incident in the larger contest of rival interests in the whole business of expansion. Once the flag waved over all these lands they were accepted as part and parcel of the Union. With the acquisition of Texas, Oregon, and the far-stretching New Mexico–California country in the 1840's, the national boundaries were at last charted.

The rounding-out of the national domain and the acceptance of the newly won areas by even the stoutest antiannexationists did not mean, of course, that all Americans took to their bosoms all parts of the land with equal enthusiasm. The land was laced with more and more lines of communication and the people were increasingly mobile, but local pride and state loyalty did not wither. Indeed, in the older parts of the country, local pride continued to exert a mighty pull in thought and feeling. The mournful epitaph of John Randolph of Virginia was extreme, but it excited no great comment among ardent state-proud Virginians:

> Beyond Virginia's border line
> His patriotism perished.

Although enduring local pride was perhaps less evident in the West, where the state was the creature of the national government and where people from many states and lands mingled together, pride in state and region was by no means absent. In the 1830's and 1840's intellectuals in the Ohio valley began to preach the doctrine of western regionalism. In the pattern of thought thus woven the favored features of western physiography vied in emphasis with the concepts of a particularized destiny as a distinct region. This regionalism was to cast its spell over the literary endeavor of a western generation yet unborn.[43]

In the antebellum South growing political and economic antagonism to the North called forth declarations of Southern cultural independence. For this movement Southern geography and climate provided cornerstones. In an address at the Virginia Military In-

---

[43] For illustrations, see Merle Curti, *The Growth of American Thought* (New York, 1943), Chapter 11.

stitute in 1857 James W. Massie declared that "American civilization is properly divisible into two; in common parlance, Northern and Southern civilizations. . . . These two systems are in principle and in results widely different. We possess a common language, and in some part, a common ancestry; in these we resemble each other, and I might almost say, in nothing else." [44] The Southern nationalism of this speaker, and of many another, rested in part on the assumption of a unique Southern geography. When civil war itself convulsed the South, Confederate poets sang of the God-given beauties of Dixie Land. Even after the struggle had been fought to a finish the idea of a distinctive terrain and climate survived as a part of that lively loyalty to the South which the memories of the war and, especially, of Reconstruction did so much to invigorate.

Local and regional loyalties did not necessarily conflict with loyalty to the nation. Some patriots insisted, indeed, that love for the place one knew best in no way dampened, but in fact enhanced, devotion to country. Towns, counties, states, and their unnumbered institutions have each their own independent spheres of action, wrote Nahum Capen in 1848. "Their growing and diversified strength," he declared, "is a perpetual source of power to the Union." [45] The same point was made by Francis Lieber, a German political scientist who became a faithful adopted American. Attachment to the community, Lieber pointed out, was, after the family, the great focus of national loyalty. A man without love for his hamlet would seldom risk his life for his country, still less live and toil for the nation. [46]

Scientific analogies from the Newtonian system were on occasion made to buttress this point of view. Insisting that in the social as in the physical realm every atom of matter was bound by ties of eternal fealty to some spiritual lord, Thomas Starr King suggested, in a popular lyceum lecture of the 1850's, that "the oneness of the

[44] James W. Massie, *An Address Delivered before the Society of Alumni of the Virginia Military Institute, July 3, 1857* (Richmond, 1857), p. 22.
[45] Nahum Capen, *The Republic of the United States of America* (New York, 1848), p. 23.
[46] Francis Lieber, *Manual of Political Ethics* (Boston, 1838), p. 158.

nation is the unity of the galvanic current that is generated from the many layers of metal and acid." [47] Even the staunchest advocates of state loyalty, such as Lieutenant Matthew Fontaine Maury, the Virginian father of oceanography, maintained, in arguing for the economic resuscitation of his native commonwealth, that in view of Virginia's mediating role in the Union national interest would be served by the promotion of Virginia's strength and well-being.[48]

Nor was the argument that local and state loyalty fed the springs of national fealty lost sight of in the years that lay ahead. Thus in 1908 a Fourth of July orator declared that the "relations between local pride and national pride are everywhere close and certain; they are overlapping, and are intertwined with the most intimate association and development. . . . One may delude oneself with the notion that one is a true American because one cherishes the Declaration of Independence, while feeding his heart with the most dreadful dislike of his own place of residence, and all that is concerned with it." [49] Thus was reasserted in the midst of a highly integrated and interdependent national culture the ancient concept that man's love of and loyalty to the larger unit must rest on his firsthand experiences with the more immediate and the more local. Finally as the sense of place declined with new facilities for getting about, the significance of the cult of place as an element of cohesion has been asserted and implemented by such recent projects as the Williamsburg restoration.

Loyalty rested on more than esthetic impulses, utilitarian considerations, and the belief that God had designed America to be a single united nation. Throughout a good part of the nineteenth century the faith was widely held that America had been destined by heaven to remain aloof from Europe's age-old jealousies and

[47] Thomas Starr King, *Substance and Show, and Other Lectures* (Boston, 1877), pp. 13–14, 390.

[48] Matthew Fontaine Maury, *Address Delivered before the Literary Societies of the University of Virginia, on the 28th of June, 1855* (Richmond, 1855), p. 13.

[49] Barr Ferree, *Sentiment as a National Asset* (New York, 1908), p. 12.

bloody wars. Timothy Dwight gave words to a common sentiment when he wrote:

> See this glad world remote from every foe,
> From Europe's mischiefs, and from Europe's woe.[50]

Scores of sermons, Fourth of July addresses, and commencement orations popularized this view. "Nor is it the least of our advantages," declared a typical speaker, the Reverend Andrew Lee, in an election day sermon at Hartford in 1795, "that we are so far removed from those who could do us essential injury . . . God grant that the ocean may forever guard us against the violence, and separate us from the vices, follies, and politics of Europe." [51] The next year Washington crystallized this pattern of thought in the Farewell Address. In warning against the temptation to let sympathies with foreign nations divert the American ship of state from the course of its true interest, in calling attention to the risks of entering into permanent alliances with any country, Washington assumed that the physical separation from Europe made his advice practical.

Belief in the advantage of geographical independence was expressed again and again by American statesmen and intellectuals alike. "The European nations," Jefferson wrote to the Baron von Humboldt in 1813, in the midst of the second war with England, "constitute a separate division of the globe; their treaties make them a part of a distinct system; they have a set of interests of their own in which it is our business never to engage ourselves. America has a hemisphere to itself. . . . The insulated state in which nature has placed the American continent should so far avail it that no spark of war kindled in the other quarters of the globe should be wafted across the wide oceans which separate us from them." [52] Similar convictions lay back of the policies of John Quincy Adams.

[50] Timothy Dwight, *Greenfield Hill: A Poem* (New York, 1794), pp. 151–152.
[51] Andrew Lee, *The Origins and Ends of Civil Government* (Hartford, 1795), p. 33.
[52] Thomas Jefferson, *Writings*, ed. by Paul Leicester Ford (New York, 1892–1899), IX, 431.

The Monroe Doctrine was, of course, of the same pattern. Indeed, long after steam and steel had reduced the distance from Europe, long after physical isolation had gone, this conviction of geographical separateness haunted men's thoughts and dreams and buttressed one type of loyalty to the American nation.

Loyalty to place was closely related, as it was in the nationalist thought of Europe, to consciousness of the past. Enlightened Americans were aware that their own history was part and parcel of universal history. Rufus Choate, in his Fourth of July address on "American Nationality" in 1858, expressed what was in the mind of many of his fellow citizens in asking whether all history was not the recital of the achievements of nationality. In any case, from the very first years of the Republic, Americans felt that nothing short of a reinterpretation of man's total past sufficed if history were to be an effective instrument for inculcating national loyalty. A considerable body of opinion held that Americans must look at universal history, not through the eyes of Old World historians, prejudiced as they were by monarchical and aristocratic sympathies, but through republican and American perspectives. Judge Nathaniel Chipman of Vermont, writing in 1793, urged less emphasis on the dynastic intrigues and wars of Europe and more on the struggles of the people in the "upward march of civilization." [53] Another exponent of a new American type of historical writing, Alexander Kinmont of Cincinnati, admitted in 1836 that he felt ashamed "that all we know about our older sister republics of the earlier ages, should be through monarchical historians. I cannot bear that the whole history of the world's philosophy should not be read over again in the writings of its contemporary witnesses, with American eyes and American perceptions." [54]

No one developed this theme with more eloquence than George Perkins Marsh, who in an address at Union College in 1847 maintained that historians had scorned and neglected essential sources

[53] Nathaniel Chipman, *Sketches of the Principles of Government* (Rutland, Vermont, 1793), p. 32.
[54] Alexander Kinmont, *Discourse on the Ends and Uses of a Liberal Education* (Cincinnati, 1836), pp. 25–26.

of information. "It is only by a familiar knowledge of the every-day life of a people," declared Marsh, "that we can acquire that sympathy of feeling which is an indispensable condition for the profitable or intelligent study of the history of any nation. To this end, we must know what has been the fortunes of the mass, their opinions, their characters, their leading impulses, their ruling hopes and fears, their arts and industry and commerce." [55]

But the conviction that Americans ought to study their own history was uppermost. In all the discussions of this theme it was assumed that such a study would strengthen the loyalty of Americans to the nation. Thus Marsh, in addition to espousing the cause of what he described as popular history, declared that Americans should study their own past because in it they would find an epitome of all history. "Society has thus passed through all its phases of life-time of one of its members, and there is many a living American whose own experience will confirm the remark of Volney, that American society, in its range from the life of the backwoods to that of the city, presents a synopsis of the history of many ages of European progress. . . . In our brief annals, we have exemplified the distinctive virtues and vices, the predominance and succession of which characterize the epochs and progress of society." [56]

Marsh was not alone in expressing this idea. George Burnap, in a discourse at Baltimore in 1853, maintained that the birth of American nationality took place in the colonial period itself—that shortly after the founding a certain national feeling began to spring up on this side of the Atlantic. Upon the publication of the first genuine newspaper in Boston in 1704, "then and there," declared Burnap, "the great American soul, already incarnate, began to breathe forth its inspiration, and carry vitality to the remotest members. Then and there the American mind began to react upon itself, and fuse into one mass the various materials of which the colonies were composed." [57] If Americans properly

[55] George P. Marsh, *The American Historical School* (Troy, 1847), pp. 27–28.
[56] *Ibid.*, p. 24.
[57] George W. Burnap, *Origin and Causes of Democracy in America: A Discourse* (Baltimore, 1853), pp. 27–28.

understood these facts in their history, their loyalty to the Union, he concluded, would be more deeply rooted.

In the brief span and rapid tempo of our history others found specific incentives to loyalty. Thus Theron Metcalf in a Fourth of July oration at Dedham, Massachusetts, in 1810, said that "no nation can examine its early history with so little abatement of satisfaction and pride as our own. We are not obliged to resort to fable for our origin, nor to conjecture for our progress. The whole is spread before us in unfaded colours. Nor are we disgusted with a picture of our former barbarism and cruelty. Our ancestors were not outcasts from civilized society—they sought these shores, not as a refuge from punishment, but as an asylum for liberty." [58]

This was the note struck most frequently of all: the glorious deeds of the fathers, the inspiration of their record, the obligation to remain steadfast to their ideals, admiration of the achievements for which they suffered and sacrificed themselves. "We have learned to love our country, because we are near it, and in it . . . because the sweat of our fathers' brows has subdued its soil; their blood watered its fields, and their revered dust sleeps in its bosom; because it embraces our fathers and mothers . . ." said a Boston minister in 1798, denouncing the cosmopolitan loyalties of "certain metaphysical reformers and tyrants." [59] Important among the unifying forces in the country's past was, according to Judge Nathaniel Chipman in his *Principles of Government* (1793), the common pioneer struggle of the fathers in establishing themselves in a new land. "This was the germ of that general union of counsels and sentiments, which produced the American Revolution." [60]

Orators and writers seeking inspiration for loyalty to American institutions chose to emphasize the unique features of the American Revolution, and in so doing they contrasted that struggle with the upheaval in France. Men of a conservative temper especially

[58] Theron Metcalf, *Oration, Pronounced at Dedham, July 4, 1810* (Boston, 1810), pp. 3 ff.
[59] John Thornton Kirkland, *An Oration, Delivered at the Request of the Society of Phi Beta Kappa, July 19, 1798* (Boston, 1798), pp. 13 ff.
[60] Chipman, *op. cit.*, p. 241.

loved to dwell on the differences between the two revolutions: that in America undertaken reluctantly and only as a last resort, not for destructive ends, but to safeguard all that was most precious in the heritage of the past—the rights of life, liberty, and property; that in France, impetuously embarked on by desperate men with no respect for order, private possessions, the sanctity of the home, for God Himself. "Our hoary patriots would rise up, and disclaim their share of the disgrace," declared John Lowell, eminent Massachusetts Federalist, in 1799, the year of quasi war against Revolutionary France, if they could know that firebrands attributed to their holy experiment the shame and degradation of Old World Jacobins. "Our departed Heroes and Statesmen would burst their cold imprisonments, and vindicate their memories from the unmerited reproach." [61] From that time until our own, conservative patriots have consciously or unconsciously overlooked the violence meted out to Tories and ignored the social aspects of the American Revolution, lest, perhaps, the example of these give aid and comfort to latter-day radicals.

An important factor in American patriotism was the conviction that the hand of God had guided American experience from the very start. Colonial Puritans had held fast to this notion, and it came to find much support in every part of the country. In speaking of the late revolution a minister in 1784—and he was only one of a hundred—declared that "the divine hand hath been so signally displayed in the events and occurrences which hath led to it, that those who are not convinced of the government of Providence over the affairs of nations by what has passed before them in these late years, would not have been persuaded if they had been eye-witnesses of the mighty works which God hath wrought in the midst of His peculiar people." [62] Benjamin Trumbull in like vein began his *General History of the United States* (1810) with a sentiment which could be duplicated in hundreds of other quotations, "Very conspicuous have been the exertions of

[61] John Lowell, *An Oration, Pronounced July 4, 1799* (Boston, 1799), p. 10.
[62] Samuel McClintock, *Sermon Preached before the Senate and House of New Hampshire, June 3, 1784* (Portsmouth, 1784), p. 17.

Providence in the discovery of the new world, in the settlement, growth, and protection of the states and churches of North America." [63]

It remained for George Bancroft to do full justice to this theme and to give it the democratic turn. Believing as he did that history is the record of God's will, he saw the hand of God in the American past. The history of his own country, he thought, was in a peculiar sense a divine revelation inasmuch as, in the Land of the Free, God's purposes had been less fettered by outworn human customs and arbitrary authority than elsewhere. Furthermore, since all men are endowed with a direct intuition of "the world of intelligence and the decrees of God" and since "the best government rests on the people and not on the few, on the free development of public opinion and not on authority," the voice of the people is the voice of God. All the American past seemed to Bancroft to bear this out and to augur well for a future in which God's purposes would be even more fully realized. His flamboyant pages, which filled ten large volumes before he finished and which took the reading public by storm, amplified the theme expressed in his basic conviction that "in the fulness of time a republic arose in the wilderness of America. Thousands of years had passed away before this child of the ages could be born. From whatever there was of good in the systems of former centuries she drew her nourishment; the wrecks of the past were her warning. The fame of this only daughter of freedom went out into all the lands of the earth; from her the human race drew hope." [64] This was all as Providence designed. Bancroft's *History* gave the American people pride in its past and confidence in its future. By associating both of these with the will of Providence and the will of the people, the work provided a bulwark for national self-consciousness and patriotic sentiment.

It was usual to elaborate the general thesis of the hand of God in American history by explaining that America had not been

[63] Benjamin Trumbull, *A General History of the United States of America* (New York, 1810), p. 9.
[64] George Bancroft, *Memorial Address on the Life and Character of Abraham Lincoln* (Washington, 1866), pp. 4–6.

revealed by God to man until the stage was properly set. God did not intend to have America beclouded by ignorance, superstition, and feudalism, declared Charles Russell in a Fourth of July oration in Boston in 1851. He reserved the momentous discovery until the time was ripe, until feudalism had crumbled, until the human mind had begun to throw off its thralldom and conscience had asserted its high and holy prerogative.[65] Nor did the theme lose its appeal. In lectures delivered in 1856 in Washington, Professor Henry Reed of the University of Pennsylvania brought together all these and like arguments. Surveying the past, this scholar saw the hand of God in a very special sense at work in welding together the diverse materials of the colonies into a federal union.[66]

Even after the dawn of the twentieth century the theme of the hand of God in American history found its exponents. The plain implication in all this writing was that, if the Christian American were true to his God, then he could hardly be lukewarm to his country inasmuch as Providence had so clearly guided its course over the centuries.[67] Comparable, though obviously not identical, doctrines characterized, of course, much nationalistic thought in the Old World.

While historians interpreted the American past in terms of patriotic thought and feeling, artists were busy representing vividly the dramatic incidents of the heroic age. In spite of many artistic failures, including his work in the rotunda of the National Capitol, John Trumbull, himself a veteran of the Revolution, captured the imagination of innumerable Americans who saw the war through his eyes. His *Battle of Bunker Hill*, painted in the studio of Benjamin West in London, lacked something of the spirit of the battle, but it was excellent in coloring and grouping. His subsequent historical pieces, which included *The Declaration of Independence* and *The Surrender of Cornwallis*, are explicit in design, cool in

[65] Charles Russell, *Oration Delivered before the Municipal Authorities of Boston, July 4, 1851* (Boston, 1851), p. 11.

[66] Henry Reed, *Two Lectures on the History of the American Union* (Philadelphia, 1856), *passim*.

[67] Robert E. Thompson, *The Hand of God in American History* (New York, 1902), *passim*.

color, and for the most part historically accurate. Popularized through engravings and reproduced widely in schoolbooks, Trumbull's pictorial reports of the Revolution helped to keep alive memories of a valorous past.

To glorify the past and to hold it up as the criterion for judging a supposedly decadent present seemed to some patriots to encourage supineness rather than thoughtful loyalty to the nation. On the eve of the Civil War the Reverend Orville Dewey, a Unitarian minister in New York, belittled the current talk about the descent of the country from the dignity and virtue of olden times. Reminding his countrymen that the fathers who were now idealized had in their own time been denounced with acrimonious and violent words, Dewey argued that an honest historical evaluation of the country's record should not lead to defeatism, should not paralyze action by exaggerating the indifference of Americans toward their civic duties or by giving undue weight to the mob violence and the rancor of the day. In point of fact, Dewey urged, there was now less intolerance, less slander, and more justice, frankness, and fearlessness than in "the good old days." [68]

Yet the good old days provided a chart on which patriots relied when storms were threatening. Whatever the course the ship might take in the days ahead,

> We know what Master laid thy keel,
> What Workman wrought thy ribs of steel,
> Who made each mast, and sail, and rope,
> What anvil rang, what hammers beat,
> In what a forge and what a heat
> Were shaped the anchors of this hope! [69]

In 1876 and in succeeding years the centennials of the Declaration of Independence, the adoption of the Constitution, and the inauguration of Washington were celebrated with joyous enthusiasm. The Union had been saved from disruption, material progress was everywhere apparent, and the new school of critical historians

[68] Orville Dewey, On Patriotism: The Condition, Prospects, and Duties of the American People (Boston, 1859), pp. 5 ff.
[69] Henry Wadsworth Longfellow, Poetical Works (Boston, 1883), I, 517.

had not yet arisen to puncture fondly cherished legends of the nation's past.

Here is one example of the patriotic oratory of the centennials: "If ever there were a nation favored of Heaven, and under the special protection of Almighty God, that Nation is the United States of America." The speaker was the Reverend Cornelius Brett, and the solemn exaltation was characteristic of the centennial sermon: "The booming cannon which ushers in and salutes the last of the long line of centennial celebrations, the waving banners, the streaming decorations, the moving hosts, the blare of trumpets, the clash of cymbals, the roll of drums, the shouts of lusty patriots, and the softer voices of the singers, will fail to celebrate the completion of our first centenary, unless pious fervor shall swell a Te Deum, a grateful love-inspired Hallelujah." [70] Oratory setting forth the "providential view" of the nation's history and the patriotic implications of that version resounded far and wide over the land.

The half-legendary past was praised as an abstraction, but it was not an unpeopled ideal.[71] Heroes were another essential element in the growth of loyalty to the nation. Hero worship was, to be sure, both an expression of, and a stimulus to, national loyalty in every European land, but American hero cults had their own flavor. From the time that Cotton Mather looked back with nostalgia on the spiritual titans of early New England, it was customary to glorify the great men of the past and to find incentive in their lives. Local communities and regions cherished their own heroes, built monuments to them, celebrated their birthdays, and in public exercises commemorated their exploits. Sometimes these local giants were adopted as national heroes. As sectional rivalries became acute, orators magnified the contributions their own state or regional heroes had made to the struggle for freedom. "The history of our country is before us," exclaimed a fire-eater in Charleston during the secession crisis of 1850. "We know from which sec-

[70] Cornelius Brett, *The Centennial of the American Presidency: A Sermon Preached April 28, 1889* (n.p., n.d.), p. 2.
[71] Dixon Wecter, *The Hero in America: A Chronicle of Hero-Worship* (New York, 1941), is an excellent study.

tion sprang the great minds of the Revolution; we know whose blood was illustrated by the history of three great national wars." [72] In New England and in the Middle States orators similarly claimed for their particular sectional heroes the major share of glory in winning freedom from England.

Nevertheless the cult of heroes served on the whole to buttress a larger loyalty to the nation. This was true although many patriotic men decried the "proverbial indifference" of the Republic toward its heroes, an indifference evidenced, so the word went, by America's negligence in erecting monuments to her glorious dead. The countries of Europe, they said, had eternalized praise of their heroes in marble and metal, but the United States had few monuments of dignity and beauty. This lack was, thanks to a few hard-working enthusiasts, later filled.

Of the national heroes Washington, of course, led the host. Dixon Wecter has noted that, in contrast to so many of the most popular heroes, Washington was by most tests a conservative. Yet in the popular mind he was associated with innovation. In spite of his own conservatism and the support he had as President given to the Federalists—a support which led to bitter criticisms from liberals and radicals—Washington came to be pictured as a man above partisan strife. The picture of him that Freneau, the Jeffersonian democrat, drew on the occasion of Washington's entrance into Philadelphia, became a stereotype:

> O, Washington! thrice glorious name!
> What due regards can man decree—
> Empires are far below thy aim,
> And scepters have no charm for thee.
> Virtue, alone, has your regard,
> And she must be your great reward.

This was the figure widely popularized in the orations at the time of Washington's death, and the reverent portrait did much to make the father of his country the model of patriotism: the orators

[72] W. H. Trescot, *Oration Delivered before the Beaufort Volunteer Artillery, on July 4th, 1850* (Charleston, 1850), p. 13.

dwelt on his religious faith, his courage, his selfless service to the country. The appearance, a few years after his death, of John Marshall's *Life of George Washington* (1805-7) eloquently defended Washington against any and all criticisms, and, though disparaged by Jefferson and his disciples by reason of its Federalist bias, the book powerfully influenced the American mind.

As the years passed the figure of Washington more and more became fixed in the minds and hearts of Americans, old and young, as a symbol of disinterested patriotism. In the hands of some popularizers he was sentimentalized and overidealized. This was notably true, of course, of the widely read life of Washington which Parson Weems wrote early in the nineteenth century. It was only a little less true of the sketch in the highly popular *Lives of the Benefactors* which Samuel Goodrich ("Peter Parley") published in 1844. Goodrich did, in emphasizing the nobility of Washington's character, focus attention on a quality in his hero's life which somewhat more nearly corresponded to the truth than the extreme idealizations which were current. "Another reflection," wrote the famous author of moral stories for youth, "and a grateful one to the American bosom, is, that our country has furnished the finest character—that acknowledged by the civilized world to be the finest—in the annals of our race, at least in modern times. The value of Washington's example, aside from his great deeds in our behalf, is beyond calculation, if we use it aright." [73] Thomas Starr King declared in the crisis of 1850 that it was better for the country in such an ordeal of its history "to have lost its collected treasures, to have parted with half its territory and half its citizens, than to have been robbed of the heart of Washington." [74]

Sculptors and artists joined with writers in the cult of hero worship. No statue of the father of his country, it is true, achieved general popularity. The colossal marble of Horatio Greenough, the product of eight years of devoted and patriotic labor, met with indifference or disapproval; the public was shocked at the half-nude

[73] *Lives of Benefactors by the Author of Peter Parley's Tales* (Boston, 1844), p. iii.
[74] King, *Substance and Show*, p. 28.

seated figure in neoclassical style which was meant to suggest republican virtue and dignity. But if the sculptor failed to engrave a likeness of Washington to satisfy the minds of the people, the painter succeeded. The many portraits of Washington which Charles Willson Peale made were, if uninspired, more truthful than the better-known likenesses of Gilbert Stuart. These, particularly the famous "Athenaeum" portrait, with which almost every schoolchild came to be familiar, endowed the President with an aloof, patrician majesty. The same quality in a heightened form characterized Emanuel Leutze's stilted and tumid *Washington Crossing the Delaware*. This celebrated picture, with the theatrical pose of the hero and with inaccuracies in detail, presented a concrete and lasting image to countless Americans.

In the development of loyalty to the nation faith in the future of America outstripped even the pride taken in the memory of great deeds and great men. Every leading European nation had cherished a conception of its unique destiny or mission—a pattern of thought reinforced by Hegel's philosophy of history. The fundamental and widely held dogma that America was destined to become a nation of great wealth, power, and culture, the home and beacon light of liberty, the Elysium of the common man, prevailed over all competing conceptions of the future.[75] This tremendous confidence lay back of the vainglory that both baffled and irritated visiting foreigners in the first half of the nineteenth century. The almost ubiquitous boasting, as puerile as it was flamboyant, rested on the conviction that America was leaping ahead.

Both during the "critical period" of the 1780's and again after Jefferson took the reins in 1801, dour conservatives, citing the downfall of the classical republics, prophesied that America too might well be facing catastrophe. But more optimistic Americans replied that their fellow countrymen excelled the ancients in the science of government and in "true philosophy." Pessimists looked with grave concern on party strife and saw in it the seeds of the destruction of the Republic. But optimists answered that in a

[75] Arthur E. Ekirch, Jr., *The Idea of Progress in America, 1815–1860* (New York, 1944), is a useful and readable study.

democratic state differences of opinion were both inevitable and wholesome and insisted that a prudent and temperate course on the part of government would induce moderation and acquiescence on the part of the people. Hard times now and again followed hasty economic expansion, but the ailment always proved to be only temporary. More grave, to be sure, were the recurrent threats of disunion, most serious of all the fact that thoughtful men could not be certain of the permanence of the nation. But as the shadows cast by the Hartford Convention, the Missouri crisis, the nullification ordinance of South Carolina, and the threatened withdrawal of the Southern states in 1850 faded away, faith in inevitable progress, in a glorious future, was more than confirmed.

This faith in the future of America was confined to no one section. It was quite as common for Southern Fourth of July orators to wax eloquent over the national destiny as it was for those in the North. "Here shall be seen statesmen, and warriors, and patriots, surpassing the rest of the world in disinterestedness, courage, and virtue," declared a Charleston orator in 1819. "Here shall Poetry ascend to the sublimest, highest heaven of invention; and her sisters Painting and Sculpture equal, nay, surpass all that Greece, all that Rome e'er boasted. Here, will an admiring world exclaim, is the land of 'Freedom, Arts, and Arms.' " [76] *DeBow's Commercial Review*, a Southern organ devoted to the commercial and agricultural development of the South, printed article after article down to the very threshold of the Civil War in which the glorious destiny of the United States was proclaimed with high exuberance.

Thoughtful newcomers, ready to identify their adopted land with a glorious destiny, joined in the prophecies. Writing to a friend in Germany in 1854, Philip Schaff, an eminent theologian, confessed his belief that "the grandest destiny is probably reserved for the American people. . . . If anywhere in the wide world a new page of universal history is to be unfolded, it is in America. Either humanity has no earthly future, everything is tending to destruction, or this future lies—I say not exclusively but mainly—there, accord-

[76] Mawyer, *An Oration Delivered in the French Calvinist Church*, p. 17.

ing to the victorious march of history from east to west." [77] Such sentiments again and again found their way into the letters of the more articulate immigrants.

The democratic aspects of American destiny, the sharing of material, intellectual, and esthetic goods among all the people, tended to elicit loyalty in plain men and women. "While in the aristocratical and monarchical governments of the Old World," wrote a Wisconsin collegian in 1856, "not only wealth and fame, but knowledge is monopolized by the privileged classes, here a highway to honor, wealth, and renown is open to all—monopolized by no aristocracy but that of merit and genius. May we not, relying on the past as a pledge for the future, predict that this Republic has, under God, an exalted destiny to fulfill? May not here be realized the golden age of which poets have sung, when literature and science shall flourish upon the same soil, the foster-children of government? When the province of the scholar will be not only to think but to act, to blend theory and practice, beauty and utility, the ideal and the real?" [78]

The habit of linking national virtue with material progress as a necessary factor in the full realization of the national future was well illustrated in William H. Seward's lecture, "The Destiny of America" (1853). "No! No!" declared the New York political leader, "we cannot indeed penetrate the Eternal Counsels, but, reasoning from what is seen to what is unseen, deducing from the past probable conjectures of the future, we are authorized to conclude that if the national virtue shall prove sufficient the material progress of the United States, which equally excites our own pride and the admiration of mankind, is destined to indefinite continuance." [79] Even the dark shadow cast by slavery only served to make antislavery men like Seward reiterate all the more firmly the faith that America, like Israel, had been appointed by God the nation above all others to "promote justice, freedom, and the rights of

[77] David S. Schaff, *The Life of Philip Schaff* (New York, 1897), p. 145.
[78] *Beloit College Monthly*, IV (October, 1856), 28.
[79] William H. Seward, *Works*, ed. by George E. Baker (Boston and New York, 1886), IV, 125.

man," and that defection could only result in a "fearful over-throw."

No more characteristic expression of the idealistic view of American destiny could be found than the sermon which the Unitarian minister Edwin H. Chapin preached in Boston in 1841. Our mission, Chapin declared, is "to carry out the great ideas of a new dispensation, to elevate and improve the individual, to establish on the highest degree of the scale of human progress the standard of national greatness; to teach man to govern himself, to love his fellow, to love his God; to teach the nations that all are equal, that physical power is not the highest force; that extent of dominion is not the greatest conquest, that these old outbursts of passion and revenge and rapine and war, are not in accordance with the Christian law; to teach them to kindle on all their altars the light of religion, to reverence human rights and bestow human privileges, to raise up the downtrodden, to sheathe the sword and furl the banner and live in peace so that the links of human brotherhood will brighten round the earth and reach the skies, and man live for his duty and destiny; to teach all this chiefly by example, to teach that 'Wisdom is better than weapons of war.' " [80]

More worldly-minded men advanced other views of the nation's destiny, to be sure. Some of these have already been cited in connection with the movement for territorial expansion. The concept of Manifest Destiny, of inevitable physical growth, was made to rest on biological and other analogies. Stephen A. Douglas spoke for a whole company when he declared, "This is a young, vigorous, and growing nation, and must obey the law of increase, must multiply, and as fast as we multiply we must expand." [81] But closely associated with all this was the argument that, in expanding, America would spread liberty all over the continent. Those who called themselves in the 1850's Young Americans even visioned the future positive role of the United States in the Old World—a role as

[80] Edwin H. Chapin, *The Responsibilities of a Republican Government* (Boston, 1841), p. 18.
[81] Quoted by John Bach McMaster, *A History of the People of the United States* (New York, 1913), VIII, 339.

liberator of suppressed peoples, missionary of republican institutions, champion of free and untrammeled trade.

Idealism and materialism thus met on common ground. In a genuine sense that common ground was the universal identification of America and an open future, an association of the nation with eternal youth. When a French statesman politely asked an American, "If such is the youth of the republic, what will be its old age" he was startled to hear Senator Lewis Cass of Michigan reply, "Sir, it will have no old age." [82] America was to prove, in short, that no senescence would overtake her, that she had drunk at the fountain of perpetual youth.

When Union arms triumphed at Appomattox, the perpetuity of the nation seemed to be assured. Charles Sumner, idealistic humanitarian and nationalistic expansionist, collected an array of brilliant prophecies about America that had issued over the centuries from the pens of eminent Europeans. All these celebrated the faith in America already possessed by the common men and women who did not read such books.

It was not until well toward the end of the century that Brooks and Henry Adams ventured a pessimistic conception of American destiny. This failed to win any general support. Indeed, not until the verge of the Second World War did any considerable number of people question the quasi-axiom that America was to bring to the common man plenty, comfort, opportunity, adventure, and peace. Then the old near-Calvinistic conception of the fundamental evil in the universe, the basic weakness of man, the tragedy of his fate, brought forth foreboding words among a small circle of intellectuals.[83] A considerable number of the plain people still believed in America's destiny, though less exuberantly, to be sure, than in former times.

[82] *Congressional Globe*, 29th Congress, 2d session, Appendix, 1192.
[83] See, for example, Reinhold Niebuhr, *Beyond Tragedy* (New York, 1937) and *The Nature and Destiny of Man* (New York, 1941–43).

III: THE LOYALTY OF A NEW PEOPLE

I think there never was a period since the fall of man, nor a country to be found in the globe, where peace and plenty so generally abound as in the northern states of America.

FROM AN IMMIGRANT LETTER, 1828

IN AMERICA as in Europe the concept of a unique people has occupied a strategic place in the growth of national loyalty. The sense of unity and of likeness in relation to other peoples has, in fact, been one of the strongest forces in modern nationalism. In the colonial period the idea of a distinctive Anglo-American people began to emerge slowly and almost imperceptibly. It became somewhat better defined on the eve of the American Revolution, when James Wilson prophetically declared that the new American commonwealth was based, not on men's differences, but on their similarities. In the decades that followed the winning of independence the concept of a distinctive American people was more fully elaborated and more widely spread. At no point did all Americans agree on the unique characteristics of the American people. Yet these differences of opinion did not blot out the notion that there had come into existence a unique American people.

The vast, rich, and magnificent physical setting of the new land not unnaturally suggested that a people exposed to such bounty should develop superior characteristics. Especially at the end of the eighteenth century American sons of the Enlightenment—and many others—responded to the idea that natural environment molds the basic characteristics of a people.

Nothing did more to focus attention on the whole matter than a controversy over one of the most popular beliefs current among European naturalists. This was the theory that American physical environment, American climate particularly, bred specimens in the animal and vegetable kingdom inferior to their type in Europe. This was bad enough in American eyes, but indignation could hardly be held within bounds when Old World naturalists began to declare that the deleterious effect of American climate and soil could be noted in the human species as well. Jefferson wrote the *Notes on Virginia* in part at least to refute this mistaken and intolerable notion. Good scientist that he was, he presented European savants with actual specimens of American boars and other mammals, to show how ridiculous was the notion that American environment reduced the size of our native representatives of the species. Not to be outdone, the wily Franklin, seeking to dispel once and for all the European illusion on this point, asked all guests at a dinner party in Paris, Americans and Frenchmen alike, to stand up and note how much taller his countrymen were!

The argument, nevertheless, continued. In 1814 DeWitt Clinton examined the evidence concerning the supposed noxious effects of American climate upon the human body and concluded there was no adequate scientific support for the European thesis. He took pains to add that "the imputation of an unfriendly influence upon the mind is equally groundless." [1] Decades later, however, an Englishman, Robert Knox, announced the degradation of the American physical type and with equal dogmatism noted a corresponding lapse of mental power.[2] The ghost would not die until the United States surgeon general in the Civil War ordered measurements of foreign-born and native soldiers. The irony was that the evidence, such as it was, turned the tables by showing the superior physical caliber of native-born Americans! [3]

The idea of a unique American people did not rest merely on the conviction that the environment of the New World favored the development of a superior, not an inferior, human stock. It will

[1] DeWitt Clinton, *Introductory Discourse, Delivered on the 4th of May, 1814* (New York, 1815), pp. 43–44.
[2] Robert Knox, *The Races of Men* (London, 1862), p. 51.
[3] B. A. Gould, *Investigations in the Military and Anthropological Statistics of American Soldiers* (New York, 1869), and J. H. Baxter, *Statistics, Medical and Anthropological, of the Provost-Marshal General's Bureau during the Late War of the Rebellion* (Washington, 1875).

be recalled that another leading factor in the growth of the concept of a unique people was the notion, current among English Puritans and widely held in New England, that the Puritans were God's chosen people.[4] During and after the Revolution the popularity of certain Scriptural texts showed that the idea was still very much alive: [5] *Hitherto hath the Lord helped us. . . . He hath not dealt so with any nation: and as for His Judgments, they have not known them. . . . Happy art thou O Israel: who is like unto thee, O People Saved by the Lord.* Again and again preachers compared the early Jews and the Americans: He had led both out of bondage into freedom; He had shown special mercy and favor to the one as to the other. On some occasions men of the cloth dwelt on these parallels, "not to raise our national vanity, as if we had an indefeasible title to peculiar divine favor; but rather to excite our pious caution, that we may not forfeit it." [6] In any case this conviction must have given a sense of group solidarity as against the outside world.

The idea of a chosen people comparable to Israel was by no means confined to New England, nor was it enunciated merely on occasions of thanksgiving. In the midst of the yellow fever epidemic in Philadelphia in 1793 a New York minister insisted that "Jehovah has a controversy" with His chosen people, the Americans, whose "national sins are enormous; their cry ascendeth up to the very heavens: and we all have had our share in them." [7] Calvinist sermons in South Carolina struck the same note. "The citizens of the United States," declared Isaac Keith of Charleston, "are the object of divine providential care." [8]

---

[4] For examples see William Stoughton, *New-England's True Interest* (Cambridge, 1670), p. 19, and William Vinal, *A Sermon on the Accursed Thing That Hinders Success and Victory in War* (Newport, 1755), p. 5.

[5] A classic example is the election sermon of Ezra Stiles, *The United States Elevated to Glory and Honor* (New Haven, 1783).

[6] A characteristic example is Abiel Abbot, *Traits of Resemblance in the People of the United States of America to Ancient Israel* (Haverill, Mass., 1799).

[7] John M. Mason, *A Sermon, Preached September 20th, 1793* (New York, 1793), pp. 8, 47.

[8] Isaac Keith, *The Friendly Influence of Religion and Virtue upon the Prosperity of a People* (Charleston, 1789), p. 5.

In various situations the concept of a chosen people was subsequently evoked. Thus on the Fourth of July 1845, the editor of the Charleston *Courier* used the stereotype in support of a widely held version of Americanism. "We are the peculiar people, chosen of the Lord," the editorial ran, "to keep burning the vestal flame of Liberty, as a light unto the feet and a lamp unto the path of the benighted nations, who yet slumber or groan under the bondage of tyranny." [9] A Louisville minister about the same time pointed out the "remarkable coincidence between our people and the Jewish" and insisted that children be taught the dangers of the disunity that had wrought such havoc to Israel. Indeed, the history of the Hebrew commonwealth was cited as proof of the God-given nature of national loyalty. "We doubt not that a pure and ardent patriotism did glow upon the altars of Eden," exclaimed the Louisville preacher, "and mingle in the morning and evening worship of our first parents in their unfallen state." [10] And off in Wisconsin a contributor to the *Beloit College Monthly* in 1857 wrote that the founders of our nation lifted up their voice from the house of a spiritual Egyptian bondage, that God heard their cry, and that the people from the exodus who dotted the Atlantic shore from Plymouth to the Carolinas had risen as His chosen people into a mighty nation.[11]

On both sides of the Atlantic, America was looked on as an asylum for the oppressed. Thus it was natural for the belief to develop that the American people are unique in their love of freedom. The Puritan sermons of the late eighteenth century and hundreds of Fourth of July orations, in recounting the early history of America, idealized the forefathers for having fled from wicked oppression. There was seldom any hint that it might have been well had they stayed at home and fought for liberty in the land that gave them birth.

This belief that America was the asylum for the oppressed from all the world found considerable favor both in the Revolution and

[9] Charleston *Courier*, July 4, 1845.
[10] L. J. Halsey, *A Discourse Delivered in the Chestnut Street Presbyterian Church, Louisville, Kentucky, July 4, 1852* (Louisville, 1852), pp. 14, 17.
[11] *Beloit College Monthly*, IV (June, 1857), 177.

in the decades that followed. Thomas Paine maintained in *Common Sense* that "this new world hath been the asylum for the persecuted lovers of civil and religious liberty from *every part* of Europe." He saw in that fact one of the unique characteristics of the rising nation.[12] Freneau put into couplets the widely held belief:

> From Europe's Proud, despotic shores,
> Hither the stranger takes his way,
> And, in our new-found world, explores
> A happier soil—a milder sway.[13]

The Continental Congress lent support to this idea by assuring the Irish that in case the nonimportation policy brought distress to Ireland, "the fertile regions of America would afford you a safe asylum from poverty, and in time, from oppression also." [14]

Yet there were dissenters from this general view. Without explicitly rejecting it, Washington believed that in immigration, as in all other matters, American interests rather than universal philanthropy should guide American policy, and he urged that Europe be enlightened on this point. John Adams shared his opinion. Even Jefferson, favorable as he was to the advance of liberty and to all human progress, was no unqualified friend of the asylum idea. The great Virginian feared that immigrants might not easily surrender the habits and loyalties of their native monarchical lands, and that their languages, customs, and ideas might infuse into American society "their spirit, warp or bias its direction, and render it a heterogeneous, incoherent, distracted mass." [15]

Challenged as it was again and again by various competing ideas and interests, the belief that the American people was uniquely liberty-loving remained an important part of the American faith. The constant reinforcement of the American people by freedom-

---

[12] Thomas Paine, *Writings*, ed. by Moncure D. Conway (New York, 1894), I, 87.

[13] *American Museum*, I (February, 1787), 159.

[14] *Journals of the Continental Congress, 1774–1789*, ed. by Worthington C. Ford (Washington, 1905), II, 215.

[15] Thomas Jefferson, *Notes on Virginia*, in *Writings*, ed. by Paul Leicester Ford (New York, 1892–1899), III, 189.

bent newcomers would, it was argued, perpetuate the distinctive-ness, the superiority, of the population. When periods of reaction in Europe coincided, as they often did, with years of rapid eco-nomic growth in the United States, the idea of the American asylum loomed large in the discussions of the nature of the American peo-ple.[16] Nor was the idea invalidated by the fact that land specu-lators, railroad builders, and industrialists had reasons of their own for wanting the gates kept open. In immigration they saw a supply of cheap labor. When aspersions were cast on their motives for favoring immigration, they could honestly reply that the new-comers were discontented with their lot in Europe, ambitious, and anxious to seek a new home. Not until the end of the nine-teenth century did the idea of an asylum for anyone and everyone meet with legislative check, and not until the third decade of the present century did the quantitative and qualitative restriction of immigration seal its future.

The very presence of so many ethnic groups early inspired the conviction that the American people were becoming a blend, en-tirely unlike people in any one of the European lands that sent im-migrants to our shores. In all the colonies and especially in the mid-dle and southern provinces newcomers from the Continent found a generally cordial welcome. In spite of the fact that the English language, law, and political ideas predominated in every colony, it was ever more clear that non-English-speaking peoples had made and were making significant contributions to colonial life.

One of the most penetrating early analyses of this fusion of peo-ples was that of J. Hector St. John de Crevècoeur, a Franco-American farmer and essayist. In his famous *Letters from an Ameri-can Farmer* (1782) he called attention to the cosmopolitan character of the American people. "They are a mixture of English, Scotch, Irish, French, Dutch, Germans, and Swedes," he wrote. "From this promiscuous breed, the race now called Americans have arisen. . . . Here individuals of all nations are melted into a new race of men." Crevècoeur also added pointedly that every

---

[16] Robert Ernst's "The Asylum of the Oppressed," *South Atlantic Quarterly*, XL (January, 1941), 1–10, is a good, brief treatment of the subject.

intelligent immigrant from the Continent was a clear gain in the struggle for intellectual freedom which was in the offing, chiefly because this type of newcomer had no emotional ties with England, and few, indeed, with the land of his birth. Most of the downtrodden who left Europe, Crèvecoeur went on, were tied to the old land merely by knowledge of the language and by the love of a few kindred as poor as themselves. The country of such an immigrant was likely to be, not the land that gave him birth, but the "country which gives him land, bread, protection: *ubi panis ibi patria*." [17]

It is uncertain to what extent this idea found popular support, but it was frequently expressed by thoughtful Americans. "We can boast," declared DeWitt Clinton in 1814, "of our descent from a superior stock. I speak not of families or dynasties; I refer to our origin from those nations where civilization, knowledge, refinement have erected their empire; and where human nature has attained its greatest perfection . . . The extraordinary characters which the United States have produced may be, in some measure, ascribed to the mixed blood of so many nations flowing in our veins; and it may be confidently predicted that the operation of causes, acting with irresistible effect, will carry in this country all the improvable faculties of human nature to the highest state of perfection." [18] In Charleston some twenty years later a Fourth of July orator in speaking of the uniqueness of the American people declared that here in our country the old Milesian blood of Ireland, with its gallantry, genius, and humor, mingled with that of the realistic Frank, the ardently earnest Spaniard, the profound and sagacious German, the flexibly sensitive Italian.[19]

In 1858 David A. Wasson, a sensitive writer of Massachusetts, carried still further this general theme in a striking article in the *Atlantic Monthly*. Here he claimed that the American of his day was in truth a "new man." The offshoot of Protestant Northern

[17] J. Hector St. John de Crèvecoeur, *Letters from an American Farmer* (London, 1782), pp. 51–53.
[18] Clinton, *op. cit.*, p. 29.
[19] C. B. Northrop, *An Oration, Delivered in St. Mary's Church, before the Washington Society* (Charleston, 1843), pp. 10–11.

Europe, he came from no "scurvy nation," but from peoples of resourcefulness and talent. The American was, in brief, a new physical and moral type, lean, paler than the Englishman, with a sharper face and slighter build, and "more in conversation with the heart and pure spiritual fact of humanity than any other people of equal power and culture." Wasson insisted that nowhere in modern times had thought and action approached each other so nearly and so intimately as in the American people; "nowhere is speculative intellect so colored with the hues of practical interest without limiting its own flight; nowhere are labor's executive powers so receptive of pure intellectual suggestion." [20] All these traits Wasson attributed in part to the physical environment, in part to the blending of peoples.

The antebellum South, receiving as it did relatively few immigrants and resenting the more rapid growth of population in the North, did not in general tend to favor the melting-pot idea. Yet even Southerners on occasion expressed at least a qualified faith in the ultimate superiority of the American type. Thus, to cite a single example, on the very eve of the Civil War a writer in *De-Bow's Review*, after citing the fact that the best men of Europe and the United States had issued from the blood of many Caucasian tribes, hoped that the immigration to the United States from all quarters of the globe might culminate in "a race of men nobler than any which has hitherto worked to adorn God's beautiful earth." [21]

In the decades between the Civil War and the First World War the concept of an American people unique by reason of its cosmopolitan make-up won wide acceptance. President Woodrow Wilson was expressing a familiar idea when he declared "we are a composite and cosmopolitan people . . . of the blood of all the nations that are at war." It would be a mistake to assume that all Americans, or even, perhaps, a majority, accepted the idea that the mixture of nationalities had produced a superior people. Protests against the incoming of dissident groups and the growing movement to put up barriers suggest a strong undercurrent of opposition. Yet

[20] *Atlantic Monthly*, II (October, 1858), 527.
[21] *DeBow's Southern Commercial Review*, XXX (January, 1861), 25, 30.

many thoughtful, idealistic Americans, both from old American stock and from the newcomers, maintained that the American population was not only distinctive but better by reason of its eclectic composition.

Eager to recruit settlers, colonial authorities favored a liberal naturalization policy by which Continental immigrants easily won the boon of citizenship. Until 1740 each colony bestowed its own provincial citizenship on foreigners, but in that year Parliament took a step of consequence. Thereafter a foreigner who had lived in a colony for seven years, who had taken the oath of allegiance, and who had become a communicant of the Anglican Church, was entitled to civil rights in all the colonies; and the religious tests were modified in the law to permit the naturalization of Jews and Quakers and sometimes were broadened in practice to include other dissenters. Thus naturalization was made easier than in the Old World and a sort of colonial citizenship was recognized.

The liberal naturalization procedure of provincial America became the foundation of the national policy after independence was won. In 1790 Congress for the first time provided for uniformity of naturalization procedure in all the states. During the discussion of the bill, which granted citizenship to immigrants after two years' residence, several lawmakers argued for more liberal policy. One speaker even held that it would be inconsistent if, "after boasting of having opened an asylum for the oppressed of all nations, and establishing a Government which is the admiration of the world, we make the terms of admission so hard as is now proposed. It is nothing to us, whether Jews or Roman Catholics settle among us; whether subjects of Kings, or citizens of free States wish to reside in the United States, they will find it in their interest to be good citizens, and neither their religious nor political opinions can injure us, if we have good laws, well executed." [22] Even when, in 1794, the residence requirement was raised to five years, it was still relatively easy to become an American citizen.

In spite of the general welcome to newcomers of Continental

[22] Congressman Page of Virginia. *Annals of Congress*, Vol. I, columns 1148–1149.

origin many colonists feared that immigration might threaten the Anglo-American character of institutions and life. Irish-Catholics were an object of distrust, and some authorities threw barriers in the way of their coming. In Pennsylvania, Governor George.Thomas and other prominent men worried lest the Germans create a solid, unassimilated bloc which might in wartime endanger the general welfare. The idea spread that German children ought to be taught the English language and "the Constitution and interest of the Colony." Benjamin Franklin and William Smith, provost of the College of Philadelphia, entered actively into these plans. The program met with some support from the Lutheran and Reformed groups among the Germans but aroused the bitter antagonism of the Quietist sects. Christopher Sauer, their spokesman, led a virulent campaign against the whole business and little by little won the support of all the German groups. As a result the Germans, instead of becoming more fully knit into the Anglo-American population, developed a marked German self-consciousness and a determined effort to preserve German culture. Thus the first formal "Americanization" movement came to a bad end.

Yet the movement was significant for two reasons. In attempting to Anglicize German-Americans it challenged the idea that America's ethnic uniqueness and superiority sprang from its heterogeneous population. This early Americanization movement also rightly recognized the importance of the English language as an assimilating agent. In spite of opposition, English did make its way among non-English groups. DeWitt Clinton, speaking in 1814, hardly exaggerated when he said that "the triumph and adoption of the English language have been the principal means of melting us down into one people, and of extinguishing those stubborn prejudices and violent animosities which formed a wall of partition between the inhabitants of the same land." [23]

The antiforeign bias which had appeared in mid-eighteenth century Pennsylvania became a major tenet in the creed of many Federalists during the early years of the Republic. Quick to sense the fact that most newcomers, especially those from France and

[23] Clinton, *op. cit.*, p. 29.

Ireland, sided with the Jeffersonians in the bitter party conflicts of the day, Federalists expressed the fear that these immigrants might involve us in the wars of the French Revolution on the Jacobin side and undermine the American social order to boot. In 1798 the Federalists succeeded, with the Alien Act, in empowering President Adams to deport "objectionable" aliens and in extending from five to fourteen years the residence requirement for the naturalization of the foreign-born. With the victory of Jefferson all this was undone. The Naturalization Act of 1802 was no doubt partly inspired by the desire to catch the votes of newcomers as well as by sentiment and conviction. In any case it restored the five-year period of residence, and, save for its exclusion of Negroes and Indians from citizenship, laid down the policy which remained in force until 1906.

When Louisiana was bought in 1803 the issue of the loyalty of aliens was presented in new form. The transfer of this immense territory to the United States sharpened for the moment the conflict between the different national loyalties of the polyglot population in the New Orleans region. Since the Americans wisely did not interfere with the Catholicism and the Latin culture of the Louisianians, loyalty to the American nation developed with the passage of time. Die-hard Federalists who had been embittered at Jefferson's action in buying Louisiana and in thus augmenting the agrarian interests in federal councils, grumbled at the incorporation of an alien and Catholic population. But by and large the Louisiana Purchase did not kindle the antiforeign fires which had flared up in the Federalist regime.

Not until the 1830's did any notable group call into question the loyalty of newcomers to the nation and demand that the process of naturalization be made more difficult.[24] The nativist movement can best be understood in terms both of certain broad general tendencies in patriotic and nationalistic thought and of specific actualities in American life. Perhaps the ideological currents were the less important, but they were by no means negligible. One of the most

---

[24] The standard account is Ray A. Billington, *The Protestant Crusade, 1800–1860* (New York, 1938).

notable of these was the growing tendency to see in "race" a factor in the growth of American nationality. This was all the more striking since Americans had long held that the American nation exemplified, above all else, the contract theory of government. They had long believed that from the time of the compact which the Pilgrims had drawn up in the cabin of the *Mayflower* American experience had borne out the theory that government originates in agreements between governors and governed that are more or less formal in character.

Now, in the second quarter of the nineteenth century, various writings suggested that the concept of "race" as a factor in the growth of the nation was finding favor. George Bancroft's *History of the United States*, for example, accepted the contract theory but on more than one page hinted at the idea that some part of the glorious American achievement in self-government and freedom must be laid at the door of the English "racial" heritage. Sermons and Fourth of July orations frequently emphasized the role of race in nationality. Thus the Reverend Erasmus D. McMaster, a Presbyterian clergyman at New Albion, Indiana, speaking on the Fourth of July in 1856 and defining a nation as "a people permanently united together in certain relations," spoke of community of race as one of the most important of these relations.[25]

Other speakers and writers saw as the foundation stone in American nationality the dominance of the so-called Anglo-Saxon race. In developing the theme of loyalty to the American nation a Harvard Phi Beta Kappa orator in 1849 insisted that our immigrants had given to American nationality only a temporary diversity, that they had rapidly become assimilated, and that however much the mixture of bloods had provided a salutary influence, it had not impaired the supremacy of the Anglo-Saxon strain.[26] Others went still further in emphasizing the alleged superiority of the so-called Anglo-Saxon race. George Perkins Marsh, for example, attributed to its "Gothic" origins the excellence of the New England people,

[25] Erasmus D. McMaster, *The Nation Blessed of the Lord: A Sermon* (New Albany, 1856), p. 4.
[26] George W. Bethune, *An Oration before the Phi Beta Kappa Society of Harvard University* (Cambridge, 1849), pp. 12–13.

their institutions, their way of life.[27] In 1855 a pro-slavery apologist prepared the preface for the English translation of Gobineau's *Essai sur l'inégalité des races humaines,* a book which seemed to assert the innate superiority of the Anglo-Saxon race and the danger of progressive racial debauching unless the purity of races was kept intact. Such ideas, while as yet not widely held in any explicit form, nevertheless found enough champions to give some intellectual support to the nativist movement, which was by and large the result of new actualities in American life.

Back of the new nativist movement was the greatly increased Catholic immigration from Ireland and Germany. American Protestantism had long cherished a bitter distrust of Catholicism, and now the embers which had smouldered were fanned into a flaming hatred. The word spread that an Austrian missionary society, the Leopold Association, was pouring gold into America to undermine the national Protestant faith and also other indigenous institutions. Samuel F. B. Morse, artist and inventor, took up his pen and violently denounced Catholic immigrants, the papacy, and the hierarchy, and insisted that the very foundations of the republic were endangered. Riotous mobs assailed Catholic churches on the score that they harbored munitions and arms designed for a general Catholic onslaught. The nativists entered politics, demanded a twenty-one-year probation period before immigrants could become citizens and the exclusion of Catholics and the foreign-born from political office. In the 1850's the Know-Nothing movement, which began as a secret political society, carried on the crusade and for a time here and there captured enough public offices to threaten the older political parties.

Through the whole literature of the nativists and the Know-Nothings ran the argument that Catholic immigrants were not and could not be loyal to the nation. In *A Voice to America* (1855) Frederick Saunders, himself English-born, insisted that in so eclectic a nation as the United States it was of first importance to the integrity and security of American free institutions to make sure

[27] George Perkins Marsh, *The Goths in New England* (Middlebury, 1843), *passim.*

that foreign manners be carefully precluded from vitiating the national morals, that the spirit of American nationality rule in the councils of the government. Saunders excoriated the Catholic conception of the Sabbath and denounced the growth of parochial schools.

Protestantism was, in truth, a patriotic touchstone of the first order. The consciousness of Protestantism, the knowledge that Protestantism met with disapproval and even restrictions in Catholic countries, furthered the sense of American distinctiveness and, on occasion, an aggressive resolve to safeguard the rights of the American Protestant in Catholic countries. A writer in the *American and Foreign Christian Union* in 1854 declared with grave disapproval that Americans in foreign lands had been denied the right of a decent burial on the ground that they were heretics, that Protestant chapels were forbidden in Cuba, Mexico, and in other countries, that American diplomats kow-towed to Catholic governing authorities. In the identification of Protestantism with Americanism the Bible figured as a sacred patriotic symbol. One of the most dearly held beliefs among Protestant Americans of the old stock was, as John J. Miter of Milwaukee put it in a spirited address in 1844, that the Bible "is a comprehensive and safe manual for the Patriot as well as for the Christian." [28] Catholic opposition to its use in the public school appeared to pious Protestant patriots as little short of treason.

No less shocking to the old stock was the quite natural influence that priests exerted over their immigrant flocks. This smacked of clericalism, of the Old World. It went against the cardinal American doctrine of separation of church and state. When it was clear that urban immigrants were easy prey to corrupt politicians the outcry in Protestant quarters became all the more bitter. "We seek to banish all foreign domination, and all forms of foreign domination from our midst," exclaimed Erastus Brooks, a self-made New England journalist and politician.[29] Catholicism seemed to

[28] John J. Miter, *The Patriot's First Duty* (Milwaukee, 1845), p. 7.
[29] Erastus Brooks, *American Citizenship and the Progress of American Civilization* (New York, 1858), p. 19.

many Protestant patriots such foreign domination *par excellence*.

In the nativist literature anti-Catholicism was the major, though not the only, theme. Many tracts, sermons, orations, and periodicals regarded Protestantism and loyalty to the American nation as one and the same. Gift-books such as *Our Country; or, The American Parlor Keepsake* (1854) furnished readers with stories designed to show the evils of priestcraft and of foreign influence on the American home, on schools, and on public life. *Our Country* also included, however, patriotic poems and illustrations, with words of wisdom from the fathers of the country. Other nativist literature likewise rang with apostrophes to the forefathers, the national traditions, the sentiment of patriotism. "We cannot treasure too carefully all those peculiar features whether of character, customs, or opinions, that are so distinctively our own," wrote an outspoken nativist.

The nativist zeal for Protestantism, for the rule of the older stock, and for the safekeeping of traditionally American customs was strengthened by economic considerations. Fear for the American standard of life, which foreign workers threatened to debase, and dislike of the doctrinaire radicalism of a handful of outspoken newcomers fed the nativist fires. "The bringing of foreign ignorance in competition with American intelligence, in the several branches of ordinary labor; the pitting of brute force against strength wielded by education; the gradual encroachments of foreigners upon the heretofore occupied domains of the American laborer; and the usurpation by them, of the various kinds of employment, one after another, have a tendency to degrade labor that should be honorable; not only in the several branches so usurped and occupied, but in all others." So spoke Alfred B. Ely in an address in the year 1850.[30] In the proneness of some foreign workers to establish trade unions and other "fandangoes," in the whole movement of the "wicked antirenters" and "reform conventions," great evil lurked, Ely told his audience. Let the people rather be educated in the knowledge and fear of God, as they were in the days of the Puritan fathers, let them keep free from the ignorant, vicious foreigners,

[30] Alfred B. Ely, *American Liberty* (New York, 1850), p. 27.

let them exclude the most recreant among them, and the republic might yet weather the storms—loyalty to the nation might yet triumph.

Organized labor through its leadership favored shutting out immigrant workers but came to this position by a different sort of reasoning. Seth Luther, in an address to the working men of New England in 1832, called upon the federal government to protect labor from "the dreadful evils which manufacturers are bringing upon us. For we insist, that if Congress have power to protect the owners against foreign competition in the shape of goods, they have the same right to protect the operative from foreign competition in the shape of importation of foreign mechanics and labourers, to cut down the wages of our own citizens." [31] The labor press echoed these sentiments.

Although nativist sentiment did not die, as the rise of Know-Nothingism later proved, the movement scored no lasting victories. Here and there, in Massachusetts and in Maryland, for example, the delicate balance of political parties enabled the Know-Nothings to enjoy short-lived victories during the mid-1850's. But each effort to exclude foreigners or to lengthen the period of naturalization or discriminate against them in office-holding fell by the board. The sentiment of the majority was expressed by Alexander Duncan of Ohio, who in 1841 delivered a speech in Congress which no doubt pleased both those old-fashioned native-born citizens who regarded nativism as un-American and the recent comers themselves. "Sir," shouted Duncan, "the blood of every foreign patriot which was shed in the Revolution, as well as in our second struggle for Independence, cries aloud from the ground that drank it, and demands, as a matter of right, that *his* countrymen shall be admitted to the rights of an American citizen." [32]

William H. Seward, governor of New York, spoke for those who saw in the immigrant a source of labor for growing industry, an increase of buying power in the home market, and a settler of western lands which the speculator was anxious to have developed. He

[31] Seth Luther, *Address to the Workingmen of New England* (Boston, 1832), p. 39.
[32] *Congressional Globe*, Appendix, 2d Congress, 2d session, p. 269.

pointed out in his message to the legislature in 1842 that immigration was "an important and rapidly increasing element of national strength and greatness." Having no fear for the loyalty of the immigrant to the nation, Seward at the same time favored promoting through education and other agencies "the assimilation of their habits, principles, and opinions with our own." [33] His proposal for easing the naturalization laws did not enlist sufficient support to alter existing practice.

In one salient but indirect sense the presence of immigrants deepened loyalty to the American nation among the older stocks. When, as a Norwegian visitor, the scholar Ole Munch Raeder, remarked, anyone questioned the superiority of America over Europe, the native-born simply pointed to the fact that foreigners came to America in swarms, "with the traces of suffering unmistakably written on their faces and curses in their mouths at the tyranny they are escaping." [34]

In view of the nativist conviction that immigrants were not and could not be loyal to the United States without at least a long period of seasoning, it may be well to inquire into the attitude of newcomers themselves toward their adopted land. Let the immigrants of the second and third quarter of the nineteenth century speak. If those who wrote letters are representative and if the letters that have survived and have been brought to view are typical, then the overwhelming evidence points to the loyalty and even enthusiasm of the newcomers for the land of their adoption. This is not to say that now and then these men and women did not speak endearingly of the old country, but the weight of testimony in their letters leaves little doubt of their basic loyalty to America. Those who did regret their coming and who wished themselves back in the country of their birth were a minority.

"I believe that I will be satisfied in America," wrote a Swede who had but lately arrived in Milwaukee. "I am partial to a republican form of government, and I have realized my youthful dream of

[33] William H. Seward, Works, ed. by George E. Baker (Boston and New York, 1886), II, 278.
[34] Ole Munch Raeder, America in the Forties, ed. by Gunnar J. Malmin (Minneapolis, 1929), pp. 83–84.

social equality. . . . It is no disgrace to work here." [35] A Norwegian immigrant a few years earlier—in 1837—had written: "Here no restrictions are placed upon the right to earn one's living. Here no monopolies and privileges reign. . . . Religion is free as it was when the Creator made man." [36] Again and again immigrants spoke of the greater opportunities in America. "For my part, I have not missed Sweden much," wrote Hans Mattson from Moline in 1852, "I was long aware of the smooth way in which its less favored citizens were oppressed, of the too great power of the higher estates. . . . A Free country, where all had the same right to the advantages which the Creator had given them, this was all I sought, and also found." [37]

A German immigrant said in much the same vein, "I think I would rather be poor here in America than in Blakenheim. There one is obliged to do obeisance to the great, while here that is not necessary." [38] From Kaufman County in Texas a Norwegian immigrant wrote in 1852 to an old friend at home: "I have learned to love the country to which I emigrated more sincerely than my old fatherland, of which I can never think with any heartfelt longings. From my point of view I consider the old monarchies, aristocratic and hierarchical institutions as contemptible playthings of which the human intelligence ought to be greatly ashamed. I feel free and independent among a free people, who are not chained down with any old class or caste systems, and I am proud of belonging to a mighty nation, whose institutions will and must in time come to dominate the entire civilized world." [39]

In 1855 Thomas D'Arcy McGee, in his *History of the Irish Settlers in North America*, declared that "no people—not even the natives of New England—have a greater interest in the preservation of the Union, than the Celts in America. What we never got from England, we have here—equal laws and equal justice. . . . The Union gives us homes, suffrages, and wages; the Union gives

[35] Augustana Historical Society, *Publications*, VII (1937), 50–51.
[36] *Norwegian-American Studies and Records*, VIII (1934), 25.
[37] Swedish Historical Society of America, *Yearbook 1923–1924*, p. 98.
[38] *Wisconsin Magazine of History*, XX (June, 1937), 446.
[39] *Norwegian-American Studies and Records*, VIII (1934), 52.

us peace, plenty, and equality; the Union protects our altars, confers our lands, accepts our services in peace and war, and educates our children." [40]

That the fertility of the soil and its rich yield had much to do with the transfer of loyalties is borne out in many a letter. "Thank God we are here—the land of plenty in gold, silver and precious mines; the land flowing with milk and honey," wrote the enthusiastic Captain Thomas F. O'Malley Baines from California.[41] Another Irish spokesman declared that "for a thousand years . . . there will not be such opportunities in the world again as are now open to the Irish in America." [42] Nor were these sentiments confined to any one national group. "You must not think that America is a country which abounds in scenic beauty," wrote a German immigrant from St. Louis. "But if you come you will find a *good* country. Here the farmer who has established himself lives in almost unbounded wilderness, happy and contented like Adam in the Garden of Eden." [43] From Sauk City in Wisconsin, a Swiss immigrant in 1855 sent back to his mountainous homeland the message, "We can't thank God enough that we are in America. We have had a good harvest." [44] And a Norwegian immigrant confessed that "this is a very beautiful and fertile country. Prosperity and contentment are to be seen almost everywhere one goes. . . . We have gained more since our arrival here than I did during all the time that I lived in Norway." [45]

Much evidence suggests that if an immigrant wrote glowingly of the community in which he settled, of Wisconsin's beauty or of Minnesota's climate, he did so chiefly because he knew of what he spoke at first hand, and not for any lack of admiration for the country as a whole. Thus Ole Munch Raeder reported of the immigrants

[40] Thomas D'Arcy McGee, A History of the Irish Settlers in North America (Boston, 1855), p. 196.
[41] Thomas F. O'Malley Baines, My Life in Two Hemispheres (San Francisco, 1889), p. 97.
[42] McGee, op. cit., p. 185.
[43] Missouri Historical Review, XIV (January, 1920), 219.
[44] Wisconsin Magazine of History, VI (1922–1923), 327.
[45] Mississippi Valley Historical Review, IX (June, 1922), 73.

he saw: "There is nothing narrowly local about either their patriotism or their plans and enterprises. . . . All are Americans and
their nationalism is constantly increasing as they become more
conscious of a common history, with memories of common enterprises and common glory. This patriotism is more concentrated
and therefore stronger than it would be if people also bestowed their
affection upon some particular state or community as the best in
the Union and the Universe." [46]

To be sure even the immigrant who appreciated America and
gave his loyalty to it now and then inevitably thought of the homeland in affectionate, even in poignant, terms. A Wisconsin immigrant admitted that "at night, I am back in Germany occasionally
with you; but in the morning I am in the glorious land, America,
again." [47] From St. Louis a German immigrant, Hermann Steiner,
wrote in 1834 that continued good fortune made him and his fellow
newcomers hope that "when once this new country shall have become a new fatherland to us, we may indeed be able to fully value
and appreciate all the benefits which a loving Creator has so lav-
ishly bestowed upon the inhabitants of this fortunate continent." [48]
It was not unusual for an immigrant to declare that in spite of all
the hardships he would not choose to return to his native land,
were there the chance. "I can safely say," wrote one such recent
arrival, "I would not, nor would my Maisie, return to England on
any account whatever." [49]

One proof of the loyalty of countless newcomers to their adopted
land was their readiness to serve in the Union armies. What was, no
doubt, in the hearts of any number of immigrants was put into
words by a Bohemian in central Kansas who lamented the horrible
event but quickly added "this is the country of my choice" and
straightway enlisted.[50] There is no great point in piling up concrete
examples, but one more is worth the telling. Some Swedes in Min-

[46] Raeder, op. cit., pp. 148–149.
[47] Wisconsin Magazine of History, XX (June, 1937), 444.
[48] Missouri Historical Review, XIV (January, 1920), 219.
[49] Edith Abbott, Historical Aspects of the Immigration Problem; Select Documents (Chicago, 1926), p. 246.
[50] Kansas State Historical Society, Collections, XI (1913–1914), 469–472.

nesota had often been taunted by a native-born neighbor who, in the early days of 1861, demanded of Hans Mattson why, instead of merely protesting his loyalty, he did not enlist. Convinced that the differences "between us and the American will disappear so much the faster" by taking arms, Mattson volunteered. More than a hundred of his Swedish-American neighbors followed his example.[51]

It is true that immigrant letters now and again spoke of a father or a mother who could not or did not accept America; of dear prices and hard times; of mishaps and of the role of luck in the new land as in the old; of stumbling blocks in job-hunting; of the handicaps of scanty knowledge of English; of the obstacles that confronted anyone who tried to earn his living by means other than physical labor; of persisting homesickness for the old country. But those who felt misgivings were outnumbered by those who accepted America and gave it first place in their hearts.

More than one factor, of course, entered into the transfer of loyalty on the part of throngs of immigrants, a transfer which was generally gradual and unconscious. The attitude of the newcomer himself was naturally of great weight. Gottfried Duden, reporting on immigrants in 1827, spoke of the natural inclination of the immigrant to keep one foot in the fatherland. "As a rule," he wisely advised, "it will be well for every immigrant to make up his mind to forego his fatherland for the first ten years, and seriously fix his mind upon the resolve to make America his home. This will be the basis upon which many an advantageous understanding will rest." [52]

In making the transfer of loyalty, immigrants found much support in the attitude of at least an important segment of the foreign-language press. This has not yet been studied sufficiently to permit one to make sweeping generalizations. In the very first number of a secular newspaper which Claus Clausen, a Lutheran pastor in Wisconsin, launched in 1851, he wrote that it was "very important for the Scandinavians in America to have a newspaper in their mother tongue, whereby they may be informed of institutions and conditions in the country of their adoption; through it they will learn

[51] Swedish-Historical Society of America, *Yearbook*, 1923–1924, pp. 107–108.
[52] *Missouri Historical Review*, XIII (April, 1919), 279.

of their American privileges and responsibilities." [53] The Swedish church, especially the Augustana synod, as well as the Swedish-American press, was forced by circumstances into a genuine Swedish-Americanism. Disliking the term "foreigner," learning English relatively easily, and seeing how futile it was to resist the general tendency of the second generation to marry into families of other stocks, countless immigrants found that the years confirmed their Americanism.

In the process of Americanization the early nineteenth-century immigrants were also helped by what Ellen Semple has called "the most American of American conditions, abundant land." This quickened the evolution "from European peasants to self-reliant, enterprizing American citizens." The case was somewhat different in the cities, but until well after the Civil War, throngs of immigrants still sought the land.

Americanization was also eased by the fact that, save for the nativists, Americans by and large identified Americanism with a sort of live-and-let-live individual freedom. Perhaps no better example of this could be found than the words the editor of the *Overland Monthly* wrote in 1869 in response to the anti-Chinese agitation in California: "We have but one national characteristic, and that is freedom. The tendency of our institutions is not to make men alike. Our future glory and safety lie in this: that we do not undertake to harmonize all classes, and assimilate races, but to educate man." [54] True enough, this attitude of live and let live, of thinking of immigrants merely as individuals, had its drawbacks. These will be discussed subsequently in an analysis of the influence of industrialization and urbanism in bringing the problems of assimilation squarely to the fore.

Of all the immigrants one group alone came unwillingly. It came from an all but unknown continent. The culture of the west African coast differed profoundly from that of the Europe which fed the stream of immigration to the United States. Color and the

[53] Theodore Blegen, *Norwegian Migration to America* (Northfield, 1931), p. 307.
[54] *Overland Monthly*, III (September, 1867), 256.

chains of slavery still further set the Negro off from all other Americans. In these respects he was an alien of aliens. What can be said of his attitude toward America, of his loyalty to the land that enslaved him? Here again the evidence is scanty, and the problem of interpreting the little testimony at hand is one of the most difficult in American historiography.

Jefferson raised the question in his *Notes on Virginia* (1787). "For if a slave can have a country in this world, it must be any other in preference to that in which he is born to live and labour for another: in which he must lock up the faculties of his nature, contribute as far as depends on his individual endeavours to the evanishment of the human race, or entail his own miserable condition on the endless generations proceeding from him." [55] There is good evidence to bear Jefferson out. "I know," wrote one Negro, "this was the soil on which I was born; but I have nothing to glorify this as my country. I have no pride of ancestry to point back to." [56] A Richmond Negro, Bureell W. Mann, writing in 1849, made no bones of his sentiments. "I do not Weep to stay in any part of America, But to go home to my forefathers Land!" [57]

Yet relatively few Negroes, whether slave or free, did actually choose to go back to Africa. Even those who admitted that Liberia was the only real country for the colored man frequently refrained from recrossing the Middle Passage, whether from fear of the climate and the African natives or from reluctance to break all the ties they had. Many who did venture to return went as missionaries of a religion and of a culture they had come to know and love in the land of their bondage.

The fact was, the articulate Negro was full of conflicts, of divided loyalties. As a free man of color in the Illinois Territory put it in a letter dated July 13, 1818, "We love this country and its liberties, if we could share an equal right in them; but our freedom is partial and we have no hope that it will ever be otherwise here; therefore we had rather be gone, though we shall suffer hunger and

[55] Jefferson, *Writings* (Ford ed.), III, 267.
[56] Carter G. Woodson, ed., *The Mind of the Negro as Reflected in Letters Written during the Crisis 1800–1860* (Washington, 1926), p. 137.
[57] *Ibid.*, p. 42.

nakedness for years." [58] There was, nevertheless, the pull of the familiar, the growing feeling, especially among those who had tasted the limited sweets of "freedom," that America was after all their land, a land for which some of their fathers, at least, had fought and died, a land where they themselves were born, a land where they would die. This was what spelled the failure of the colonization movement.

Little by little free Negroes developed a positive devotion to America. In an address given at a mass convention of Ohio Negroes in 1852, William Day dwelt on the services and sufferings of colored soldiers in the Revolution and deplored the fact that no attempt had been made to preserve that record. Their history, he said, lay on the soil watered with their blood. "We can be, as we have always been," exclaimed this fervent orator, "faithful subjects, powerful allies: an enemy in your midst, we would be more powerful still. We ask for liberty, liberty here—liberty on the Chalmette plains, liberty wherever floats the American flag. We demand for the sons of the men who fought for you, equal privileges." [59] Thus dark-skinned Americans in convention assembled resolved that "all colored men in Ohio eighteen years and over should form military units for drill if they are not allowed in the white ones; for they should be ready to defend the United States in case of foreign invasion." [60]

Such sentiments were not exceptional. Alexander Crummell, writer and preacher, spurning the disunionism of the Garrisonian abolitionists, urged that Negroes "make some endeavours for the preservation and the strengthening of the nation. For the state is a part of one's personal self." [61] It was possible for free Negroes in Illinois in 1856, in deploring the prejudices which they encountered in their native land, to insist that nevertheless it was as dear to

[58] Woodson, ed., *The Mind of the Negro*, p. 2.
[59] *The Loyalty and Devotion of Colored Americans in the Revolution and the War of 1812* (Boston, 1861), pp. 3–4.
[60] *Proceedings of the Convention of Colored Freemen of Ohio* (Cincinnati, 1852), p. 6.
[61] MS., Address of Alexander Crummel, Schomburg Collection, No. 315 (New York Public Library).

them as it was to the white man. The gallantry and courage of the Negro troops in the Civil War bore witness to the truth of all these expressions of loyalty to the nation.

That the loyalty of the Negro to the nation was related to the opportunities the nation gave to the colored people was obvious to those having the wisdom to see it. But few, North or South, had that much wisdom. Even Jefferson, humane disciple of the Enlightenment that he was, framer of the Declaration of Independence with its ringing statement of the natural right of all men to freedom, did not share the extreme eighteenth-century environmentalist faith in the identity of "original human nature" and in the capacity of any people handicapped by unfavorable odds to achieve the level of the most advanced civilizations. As the nineteenth century advanced, as its intellectual leaders one after another rejected the eighteenth-century philosophy of natural rights and adopted the historical and institutional position, the abolitionists alone clung to the faith that under favorable conditions the Negro would prove himself worthy of the privileges of other Americans.

In justifying slavery, Southern apologists rejected outright all notions of potential equality and proclaimed the born inferiority of the Negro. Destiny itself, the argument ran, marked him for eternal slavery. Any idea that he might safely be given his freedom and admitted to citizenship was born of the Devil. The purity of the white race must be maintained at all costs. Such was the theme developed in countless volumes, sermons, and articles in the Old South and approved, tacitly at least, in many circles in the North.

Any such tenet hardly squared with the concept of a unique American people, homogeneous and constituting the racial basis of a unified nation. The Negro might be loyal to the nation or to what the nation might become; but so long as he remained a slave, so long as he was generally regarded as inferior and incapable of assimilation or even of sharing in the rights of other Americans, he was bound to be an alien in the heart of his own country.

Not until 1887 did the nation officially admit that another alien, long hated, long fought, might become a loyal American citizen. Throughout the first three quarters of the nineteenth century only a handful of missionaries and social idealists denied by word and deed the prevalent dogma that the Indian was, like the African, of an inferior race, alien, incapable of learning the white man's ways or of ever becoming an American. Numerically the red man was only a slight challenge to the concept that one nation, in one naturally determined physical domain, ought to be composed of but one people. But ideologically the necessity for justifying the general treatment of fighting him and seizing his land reinforced the idea of a superior white race. It also set apart a small minority of primitive people, defrauded of their culture, full of bitter memories, and devoid of any substantial reasons for giving their loyalty to a nation of conquerors and despoilers.

In the fateful year 1861 the American nation possessed a body of thought concerning the ethnic basis of loyalty to the nation. There were actual conditions that partly supported that body of thought and partly denied it. Only a negligible few believed that all the peoples within the national domain, men and women of old American stock, recent comers, Africans and Indians, constituted a potential ethnic unity—a new nationality in the making. At this point all such thinking bogged down in actualities. Nativists denied the desirability, even the possibility, of real amalgamation of immigrants with the old stock: they feared that the newcomers, unless restricted and subjected to a long period of probation, would jeopardize the American way of life, the very institutions and values that made America a unique and a superior nation.

In the South the word was being spread that the concentration of immigrants in the North only exaggerated the differences actually existing in the "racial" basis of two separate nationalities—Northern and Southern. The Northern race, declared a Southern spokesman in 1860, is bold, hardy, intelligent, free, proud, ready to receive into its embrace the heterogeneous spawn of Europe and mold it to its own shape. "The Southern people," on the other hand, "are brave, courteous and gentle, credulous and forbearing—loving friends, chivalrous to enemies, and good masters to whose strong and gentle hands alone the Almighty would entrust the tutelage of his most helpless and degraded children." [62] Another Southern nationalist declared that whereas the Northerners were descended from the Saxon stock of the seventeenth-century British population, Southerners sprang from the Norman element. The characteristics presumably differentiating those above and below the Mason and Dixon line were ascribed to these different racial heritages.

No wonder, in view of all this and more, that the German traveler, Friedrich von Raumer, wrote in 1846 that, while it seemed clear that whites and blacks could never amalgamate, "the nationality even of the white Americans is disputed." [63] Von Raumer himself did not take so clear-cut a position. He was content to wait for the verdict of the future. Meantime powerful economic ties were laying a tangible foundation for loyalty to the nation, a loyalty that transcended, or promised to transcend, the cleavages of localities and sections, of old stock and new, even of black and white—promised, in short, to give substance to faith in the loyalty of a new people to a new land.

[62] William H. Holcombe, *The Alternative: A Separate Nationality or the Africanization of the South* (New Orleans, 1860), p. 11.
[63] Friedrich von Raumer, *America and the American People* (New York, 1846), p. 145.

IV: THE ECONOMICS OF LOYALTY

The numerous republics [states] scattered through so wide a range of territory, embracing all the climates, and containing all the various products of the earth, seem destined, in the course of years, to form a world within themselves, independent alike of the treasures and the industry of all the other sections of the globe. Each year they are learning, more and more, to look to each other for all the various articles of food and raiment; while the third great human necessity, defence, they have been from infancy practised to furnish in common. The bonds of union, indeed, are more numerous and intimate than can be easily conceived by foreigners.

FRANCES WRIGHT, 1821

The patriotism that is a virtue, and that ennobles character, is a spirit of devotion to one's country, from a purified instinct and for purposes of enlightened benefit.

THOMAS STARR KING, 1851

IN FORGING political independence the Revolution did not bring that solidarity on which effective national loyalty depends. The multiplicity of peoples, the variety of climates, soils, and customs, and, particularly, local and regional interests and state pride and devotion, all seemed to work against national unity. To these divisive factors must be added certain economic tensions and conflicts of interest. Merchants and entrepreneurs were divided. Urban workers and their employers were often set against each other. Industrial and banking groups in the East were aligned against western and southern farmers, and, everywhere, debtors against creditors. In the conflicts of these groups the sentiment of patriotism played a part. Each group appealed to patriotism by identifying its position and program with the general interest of the country, with devotion to, and love of, the nation. On occasion such appeals and counterappeals sharpened antagonisms still further. Yet the sentiment of patriotism also sometimes softened ill-feeling. Even when conflicts did not yield to patriotic appeals the attempts of various groups to identify their interests with love of country were seeds from which, as we shall see, sprang fruit of consequence.

A case in point is the revolt led by Daniel Shays, Revolutionary veteran and champion of the indebted farmers of Massachusetts. In raising the standard of revolt in 1786 against the propertied class and governing authorities, Shays and his men believed themselves fighting for the spirit of '76, for the natural right of all men to the property represented in their mortgages which were being foreclosed by legally correct but creditor-minded courts. Were the common people, Shays demanded, to forfeit freedom, their rights, the very homes and hearts for which they had shed their blood in the War for Independence?

On the other hand, wealth and constituted authority looked on Shays' rebellion as a disorderly and entirely unjustified attack on the rights of life, liberty, and property for which the Revolution had been fought. Fear that the prosperity born of freedom might be jeopardized by domestic violence and by attacks on property lay back of many of the conservative appeals for casting party passions aside. At West Springfield, in the heart of the disgruntled area, the Reverend Joseph Lathrop insisted that the enjoyment of our good land and of all the blessings of national freedom depended not only on obedience to God and on the virtue and frugality of the people; it depended no less on "internal justice and peace." [1] Samuel Stanhope Smith of the College of New Jersey seconded the Massachusetts parson. In his eyes the putting-down of the rebellion was an act of true patriotism. Had not the insurrection threatened the very existence of the republic? Smith demanded. The false patriotism with which demagogues aroused the populace to fury stood in high contrast, he concluded, with that true patriotism which alone secures men in their property and their rights through obedience to law.

[1] Joseph Lathrop, A Sermon, Preached at West Springfield . . . December 4, 1786 (Springfield, 1787), p. 12.

Leaders of the movement for a stronger union of the states, for something like a national government, saw in the Shays affair good reason for prompt action. Shays, according to David Daggett, a New Haven lawyer, was an ignoble, contemptible fellow; but what if a greater than Shays, a Cromwell or a Caesar, should arise? Where were the bulwarks against such an evil? The convention sitting in Philadelphia, Daggett went on, was the answer: by constructing a more energetic and coercive power, it might insure both national unity and the integrity of property against violence. Nor was Daggett alone in calling for a stronger union to keep local agrarians from making onslaughts against property and to provide insurance against the horrors of anarchy.

On occasion conservatives frankly identified the suppression of the rebellion with upholding the rights of the creditor class—the basis of prosperity in any nation, the contention ran. Thus David Daggett denounced the Shays movement as a diabolical and unpatriotic effort to sever the bonds of society, to advance agrarian interests above the general good, and to flaunt demagoguery and indecency. "Where," demanded this spokesman for the well-to-do in taking to task the followers of Shays, "is your faith and honor in discharging obligations for money generously loaned you when in the deepest distress? Patriotism is fled; the days of 1776 we cannot recall." [2]

In the agitation for a stronger union the material advantages of the creditor class were associated by conservative orators not only with justice but with patriotism itself. How hurtful to the honor and dignity of America for the states to repudiate the financial obligations they had incurred in their efforts to throw off the British yoke, exclaimed the indignant Letitia Cunningham of Philadelphia, in 1783. Should the faithless republic pursue such a course, the writer went on, its baseness could best be compared to that of a common prostitute among chaste and reputable nations! Only the enemies of America could seduce her into committing such an un-

[2] David Daggett, An Oration, Delivered on the Fourth of July, 1787 (New Haven, 1787), pp. 14–15.

pardonable sin, that we might henceforth be a reproach and a by-word among the nations.[3]

The case was pushed further. In Boston, the Reverend Josiah Bridge declared that those who, in the days of the utmost perplexity and danger, asserted their country's rights not by mere flourish or words, but by risking their dearly earned interest, had every right to expect that government would honor its sacred agreements.[4] On the eve of the Constitutional Convention, Tench Coxe, a Phila-delphia publicist, likewise carried the argument further in con-tending for a new central government to nip in the bud any state repudiation. He appealed to national pride and honor in urging that the cancellation of debts dishonored our national character abroad, curbed immigration, and deterred those with capital from opening our lands, setting up manufactories, and multiplying the lines of trade which alone could make the country rich and powerful.

It now appears that the Confederation years were not in fact "the critical period" of tradition. Yet staunch advocates of a stronger union pictured, in the words of Simeon Baldwin, a New Haven lawyer, a state of general decay. "Oh my country!" he lamented in 1788 in a characteristically fervid Fourth of July oration. "Thy glory hath been tarnished by the consequences of a confederation totally deficient. The resolves of that illustrious body of men who form the nerveless council of our union [the Congress] are disre-garded at home and despised abroad. Our commerce languishes. Public credit is no more; and the glory of the United States—where is it? It expired with that patriot warmth which once united our councils, opened our purses, and strengthened our arms without the force of law." [5]

To such a dreary and grim overview, orators now and again added still other touches. Thus in 1795, the Reverend Samuel Stanhope

[3] Letitia Cunningham, The Case of the Whigs Who Loaned Their Money on Public Faith Fairly Stated (Philadelphia, 1783), pp. 26 ff.
[4] Josiah Bridge, A Sermon Preached before His Excellency, John Hancock, May 27, 1789 (Boston, 1789), p. 41.
[5] Simeon Baldwin, An Oration, Delivered on the Fourth of July, 1788, at New Haven (New Haven, 1788), p. 9.

Smith remarked that the founders had mistaken revolutionary patriotism for something peculiar and lasting in the people and had therefore made a government fit only for patriots and heroes, one which had not taken due account of the people's proneness to give way to selfish inclinations.[6]

Long after the Constitution had been adopted it was the habit of Federalist orators, and of Whig speakers after them, in reviewing the past, to perpetuate the sorry picture of domestic revolt, of barriers set up by one state against the commerce of another, of the refusal of foreign powers to treat with a government too weak to enforce its engagements, of public debts voided, of poverty and chaos casting their shadows over the land. In creating positive loyalty to a strong central government such orations may have played some part—though just how much it would be hard to say.

In arguing for the ratification of the Constitution, the authors of The Federalist, Jay, Hamilton, and Madison, had insisted that a strong central government would promote prosperity. They seemed at least partly right in their contention. The barely perceptible but nevertheless real prosperity which had begun to make itself felt before the Constitutional Convention met continued to mount in the years that followed. Just as it was usual for orators, especially those of the Federalist bent, to associate hard times with the ill-jointed Articles of Confederation, so it was equally common for them to identify the prosperity of the late 1780's and early 1790's with the Constitution itself.

The widely held verdict was well phrased by that staunch nationalist, Tench Coxe, who, in 1794, wrote of "the astounding prosperity of the country, in consequence of the restoration of the Union and order in 1789." [7] The theme found its orators. Countless thousands of men and women listened on every Fourth of July to such words of patriotic pride as those which the young Amherst student of law, Samuel F. Dickinson, poured forth at Belcherstown in 1797. "By steady adherence to the principles of the Constitution," the

[6] Samuel Stanhope Smith, The Divine Goodness to the United States of America (Philadelphia, 1795), p. 12.
[7] Tench Coxe, A View of the United States of America (Philadelphia, 1794), p. 501.

young collegian declared, "United America has become proverbial for prosperity, so far as she is known on the habitable globe. Her civil and commercial interests have increased beyond the most sanguine computations. Her arts and sciences have flourished without a precedent." [8] In the middle decades of the nineteenth century spokesmen of business associated commerce with patriotism in claiming that the merchant class had been responsible for the separation from England and for the federal Constitution.

The identification by antagonistic groups of their own interests with patriotism is apparent in the literature called forth by the Whiskey Rebellion some half dozen years after the assembling of the Constitutional Convention. Shortly after the federal government got under way, its authority was challenged by the refusal of Pennsylvania farmers to pay excise taxes on whiskey, their chief cash product. The Whiskey Boys regarded a direct tax as an unwarranted government encroachment on the principles established by the Revolution—the rights to life, liberty, property, and the pursuit of happiness. Federal authority nevertheless triumphed when superior force compelled the Whiskey rebels to lay down their arms and submit to the detested law of the central government. To conservatives everywhere the successful quelling of the insurrection was a clear proof of the ability and determination of the new government to look out for their interests. "May anarchy never again rear its hydra head in United America!" exclaimed the Reverend Samuel Kendall in Boston in a Thanksgiving sermon.[9] Speaking on the importance of preserving domestic tranquillity and union, the Reverend Abiel Holmes of Cambridge declared, in the same vein, that civil war, diminishing as it did the treasure and the strength of a nation, poisoned the very roots of national well-being.[10]

In Federalist eyes only a thin line separated opposition to the

[8] Samuel F. Dickinson, An Oration, Delivered on the Fourth of July, 1797 (Northampton, 1797), p. 19.
[9] Samuel Kendall, A Sermon, Delivered on the Day of the National Thanksgiving, February 19, 1795 (Boston, 1795), pp. 23, 30.
[10] Abiel Holmes, A Sermon on the Freedom and Happiness of America (Boston, 1795), p. 15.

excise tax from attempts to disrupt the nation itself. Thus Governor Caleb Strong of Massachusetts declared that so long as the people remained united they would "continue to increase in power and prosperity; but, whenever the ties, which connect them, are dissolved, they will probably decay, and fall to ruin by mutual jealousies and internecine feuds." [11] When local and agrarian interests opposed the Federalist policies and especially the Hamiltonian financial program, when this program was denounced as pro-British and anti-American, as aristocratic and plutocratic, Federalist writers reechoed Washington's condemnation of political partisanship as unpatriotic.

At the height of Federalist power in the 1790's almost any opposition was regarded as factionalism, as inimical to the unity of the nation, even as disloyalty itself. Candidates for offices held by Federalists met with opprobrium: they were labeled demagogues, wicked men lustful for power, propagators of lies designed to stir up jealousy among the people, to enrage the multitude, and so to clear the seats of honor for themselves. "Our country is threatened not from foreign invasion, but by domestic dissention," declared Luther Richardson in a Fourth of July oration near Boston in the year of Jefferson's election to the presidency. "By inflaming party discord we precipitate her downfall. In vain we supported an age of toils; in vain we fought and bled in the defense of freedom, if it is unworthy of preservation." [12] Hundreds of orators spoke the same language. No one can say how many Americans were actually influenced by such efforts to identify support of the *status quo* with patriotism, but the victory of Jefferson in 1800 shows that the effort was not altogether successful.

In any case the Jeffersonians, prior to the victory of their leader, resented the identification of loyalty to the nation with loyalty to the program of the party in power. Thus on the eve of Jefferson's triumph Abraham Bishop, a staunch New Haven Republican, denounced the effort of the Federalists to associate the *status quo* with patriotism. In his mind the laboring and subordinate people

[11] Caleb Strong, *Patriotism and Piety* (Newburyport, 1806), p. 60.
[12] Luther Richardson, *An Oration Pronounced on July 4, 1800* (Boston, 1800), p. 16.

throughout the world had been and were "deluded under the mask of religion, morality, and patriotism." Turning the tables, Bishop went on to identify conservatism of the Federalist variety with the profiteering of Federalists in the war against France which had just ended. "The great, wise, and rich men well understood the art of inflaming the public mind, and generally present at the outset, *the delusive bubble of national glory*, a thing in which nine-tenths of society have no kind of interest; but which well managed turns into crowns and diamonds in the hands of the blowers." [13]

Conservatives not only associated opposition to the government they controlled with disloyalty to the nation. Under Hamilton's leadership they also promoted a positive policy fraught with considerable significance for the economic foundations of patriotism. To say this is not to say that Hamilton and his associates conceived of patriotism merely in economic terms. Yet in the main Hamilton's program in the early years of Washington's presidency was twofold in purpose. It was meant to bind the commercial and financial classes to the new national government. It was also intended to create and expand a national economy. Such were the objects of his proposals for a tariff to protect infant industries, for a central bank to create national credit, for internal improvements to stimulate home markets, for a naval force to protect commerce on the seven seas. The great documents in which Hamilton argued for his program were potent instruments in the growth of loyalty to the nation.

The program of Hamilton, though only partly realized, was written in unfading ink. Other men took up the cudgels for it in the years that lay ahead. Later it was to become an actuality. The point to make here was well phrased by Hamilton's influential adviser, Tench Coxe, who foresaw that the program would be "cement of incalculable value" in promoting the unity of the nation and loyalty to it "by interchange of raw materials, provisions, fuel, and manufacturing among the several states." [14]

In upholding the program of economic nationalism as both de-

[13] Abraham Bishop, *An Oration on the Extent and Power of Political Delusion* (New Haven, 1800), pp. 6, 15–16.
[14] Coxe, *op. cit.*, p. 326.

sirable in itself and useful in consolidating the nation, patriots did not hesitate to associate material interests with moral values. The president of Rhode Island College, Jonathan Maxcy, in an address in 1795, pleaded for encouragement to manufacturers on the score that in war the nation would thus be equipped with a lasting fund of strength and skill for use in defense. Without the exertion demanded by industry, men would live so largely in idleness and effeminacy that they would fall prey, Maxcy feared, to the very first invader.[15]

Tench Coxe carried the argument further, appealing to national pride and interest in contending that a tariff was needed in order to encourage the making of munitions: foreign powers might choose to cut us off from bringing these into our ports, and on munitions from abroad the country must depend so long as it had no defense plants of its own. Coxe went on to say that European upheavals might also cut off American farmers from their world markets. Was it not sensible, then, to encourage the growth of a large manufacturing class at home which would provide a market near at hand for the surplus produce of American husbandmen? Was not such a policy a necessary basis for loyalty to the nation?[16] Thus government was to aid industrialists, and in some measure workers and farmers. Loyalty to the nation must rest, in other words, on firm foundations.

Patriotism was indeed often identified with economic virtues deemed useful to national welfare. In pleading for the encouragement of American industry through tariffs and subsidies, Coxe was by no means alone when he associated patriotism with American-made goods. In the eyes of many champions of American industry such extravagances as handsome clothes, buttons, pins, furniture, carriages, and other European fineries not only checked the growth of home manufactures but unsettled American morals as well. Noah Webster, schoolmaster, champion of an American language and culture as well as of an American economy, went even further

[15] Jonathan Maxcy, *An Oration Delivered before the Providence Association of Mechanics and Manufacturers* (Providence, 1795), pp. 9, 17.
[16] Coxe, *op. cit.*, pp. 49, 99.

than Tench Coxe in identifying American homespun with patriotism. "It is the authority of foreign manners," he wrote in the *American Magazine* in 1787, "which keeps us in subjection, and gives a kind of sanction to the follies, which are pardonable in Europe, but inexcusable in America." [17] Thus the famous orthographer and cultural patriot was describing as "American virtues" thrift, simplicity, and industry—traits useful in a society with little capital, with great potential resources, and with a shortage of manpower.

Others were not less forthright in their association of national well-being with the advance of industry and with the economic virtues functional to it. "No nation was ever more indebted to industry for its progress in improvements than the United States," wrote David Humphreys, Washington's former aide and a diplomat, industrialist, and poet. "National felicity commonly increases or diminishes, with the increase or diminution of national industry." [18] It was usual for writers and orators, in summing up the characteristics of patriotism and the duties of the patriot, to include economic virtues suited to the needs of a growing economy, as Professor Charles B. Hadduck of Dartmouth did long after Humphreys wrote. In addition to making much of the patriotic duty of military and civilian service, of obeying the laws and respecting the institutions of the country, of upholding religion and morality, the patriot was "to make the most of himself in every way," [19] to further the development of the country's resources.

Here was a definite basis indeed for patriotism. Tench Coxe, with a rare insight into human nature, expressed what was in many minds when in 1794 he declared that "the political concord and attachments, which grow out of mutual benefits are the most rational and permanent. To encourage these is the *piety* of American patriotism." [20] The plain implication of any number of similar

[17] *American Magazine*, I (December, 1787), 39.
[18] David Humphreys, A *Poem on Industry, Addressed to the Citizens of the United States of America* (Philadelphia, 1794), Preface.
[19] Charles B. Hadduck, *The Patriot Citizen: An Address* (Hanover, New Hampshire, 1842), p. 18.
[20] Coxe, *op. cit.*, p. 326.

homilies was that the American should be grateful and loyal to a land that blessed everyone with so many benefits. "The ease with which honest industry may acquire property in America, the equal distribution of justice to the poor as well as to the rich . . . call upon them to support their government and their laws, to respect their rulers, and gratefully to acknowledge their superior blessings," wrote Mrs. John Adams to a friend in the year 1787.[21]

At about the same time the Reverend Enoch Huntington of Middletown, Connecticut, developed the theme still further in declaring that "we are more upon a level as to wealth and the distribution of the good things of this life than any other people I know of upon the face of the earth and it is our peculiar privilege that we are so." [22] Ten years later the people of Billerica, Massachusetts, listened to a sermon of Henry Cumings in which he spoke as dozens of his colleagues were speaking elsewhere. "Every good citizen may avail himself," Cumings said, "of the profits of his own industry and economy, and may *sit down under his own vine and fig tree and have none to make him afraid*. And perhaps there is no other country on the face of the globe, where people of all classes and of every honest profession, are favoured with equal advantages for procuring a comfortable living and making a decent and reputable appearance among their brethren." [23]

Nor were such sentiments confined to one section of the country. A Fourth of July orator in Athens, Georgia, declared in 1809, "how happy are Americans if they would but weigh their prosperous situation." [24] In South Carolina, Robert Y. Hayne was by no means alone in declaring, as he did in 1814, that in the United States "every avenue is open to enterprise; genius and industry have no bonds to break, no obstacles to remove, no difficulties to surmount." [25] A few years later the Charleston *Courier* rejoiced at

[21] Charles Francis Adams, ed., *The Letters of Mrs. John Adams* (Boston, 1848), II, 184.

[22] Enoch Huntington, *Political Wisdom, or Honesty the Best Policy* (Middletown, Connecticut, 1786), p. 16.

[23] Henry Cumings, *A Sermon Preached at Billerica* . . . (Boston, 1797), p. 16.

[24] *Georgia Express*, July 8, 1809.

[25] Robert Y. Hayne, *An Oration, Delivered in St. Philip's Church, on Monday, the Fourth of July, 1814* (Charleston, 1814), p. 8.

the signs of industry and prosperity visible all over the land, at the white sails of commerce swelling every breeze from Maine to Mexico, at the boundless wilderness retreating before the pioneers and at the well-being and happiness incident to rich, cultivated fields and to growing towns and villages everywhere.[26]

Closely related to the identification of economic opportunity with loyalty to the nation was the stake-in-society principle of the economists—the tendency, in other words, to link the permanence of the union with the institution of private property. Thus Gouverneur Morris, writing in 1802, declared that it was not to be expected that "men, who have nothing to lose, will feel so well disposed to support existing establishments, as those who have a great interest at stake."[27] Jefferson gave this a democratic basis in maintaining that the very existence of the nation depended on the widespread diffusion of property in the form of agricultural freeholds. We shall see that the champions of the free-homestead idea urged this not only as a natural right of men but as a policy bound to strengthen attachment of the plain people to the nation that bestowed farms on them and their posterity.

The association of loyalty to the nation with economic interest was, then, a major theme. In the patriotic literature of the early Republic it was, in fact, so dominant that dissent only gave it greater force. Such a note of protest was struck by Tunis Wortman, an anti-Federalist radical, who deplored the tendency to identify the thirst for gain and the allurements of luxury with national well-being. In his address in 1796 in New York he went so far as to say that "the desire of affluence and the love of ease, have absorbed every honorable and patriotic consideration, have rendered us supine and indolent, and have nearly banished from our minds the sentiments of public virtue, destroyed the ardor of liberty, and diminished our attachment to the sacred interests of our country."[28]

Disapproval of identifying loyalty with material interest con-

[26] Charleston *Courier*, July 4, 1823.
[27] Jared Sparks, ed., *The Life of Gouverneur Morris, with Selections from His Correspondence* (Boston, 1832), III, 172.
[28] Tunis Wortman, *An Oration on the Influence of Social Institutions on Human Morals* (New York, 1796), p. 29.

tinued to find occasional expression in subsequent decades. Thus James K. Paulding, the Jacksonian novelist and essayist, satirized this dominant tendency in suggesting that the true patriot was spurred on to individual wealth inasmuch as this was the only legitimate foundation of national prosperity.[29] On another occasion, Professor William Nevin of Marshall College, in speaking of the role of domestic affections in laying the basis for patriotism, regretted the custom of sending young boys out into the world to shift for themselves at so tender an age that the experience set them apart in their feelings from the organism of society. The profit motive might thus militate against patriotism, which was only an expansion of the early domestic sympathies into the broader ones of society. "His country and himself he will think to be two opposite parties playing with each other for gain; and ever on the watch, like a Boniface spider from his den of dry lodgings, to catch and keep all that he can, will become the grand object of his life." [30]

It was also true that when hard times seemed to contradict the tenet that America meant abundance for all, it was desirable to qualify and reinterpret the dominant American faith. This the Reverend Thomas Starr King, a Unitarian minister in San Francisco, did when he wrote that "the poor man should not feel poor when he thinks that his humble roof and circumstances are sheltered by a canopy of ideas and sentiments such as never before arched over any palace in the world." [31]

At least one section of the poor rejected the suggestion that "ideas and sentiments" were an adequate compensation for the necessities of a decent life. With the rise of Jacksonian democracy and the labor movement in the late 1820's and early 1830's the issue of national loyalty and patriotism was interpreted in terms other than those common among the well-to-do and those who saw wealth just around the corner. In his *Address to the Working-*

[29] William I. Paulding, *Literary Life of James K. Paulding* (New York, 1867), pp. 56 ff.
[30] William Nevin, *National Taste: An Address before the Goethean Society of Marshall College* (Chambersburg, Pennsylvania, 1844), p. 15.
[31] Thomas Starr King, *Patriotism and other Essays*, p. 40.

men of New England, delivered first in 1832, Seth Luther boldly declared that "it has always been the policy in Imperial and Kingly governments, to talk much about *National* glory, *National* wealth, and *National* improvement. . . . To hide existing or anticipated and *inevitable* evils, of the like kind . . . our ears are constantly filled with the cry of *National* wealth, *National* glory, the *American* system, and American industry." [32]

That Seth Luther had a real point, exaggerated though his words were, seems clear from the position taken by lawyers and judges in the early labor-conspiracy cases. From 1806 to the middle 1830's it was common to associate the attempts of journeymen cordwainers to build trade organizations with disloyalty to the nation. The effort of the workers to deny any fellow toiler the right to labor for less than the wages stipulated by the trade associations was, declared Moses Levy, a Philadelphia lawyer who represented the employers, contrary to the spirit of '76. Citing the common law as the law of the land, Levy asked whether the spirit of '76 could possibly prompt journeymen, in regulating the value of their hire, to set up a rule contrary to the law of their country? General and individual liberty was the spirit of '76. It was our first blessing. It had been obtained, and, concluded Levy, it must be maintained. In defending Levy against the charge of undue subservience to the privileged employers, Henry Baldwin, prosecuting attorney, maintained that as a good patriot Levy was merely setting himself against an attempt to subvert the free constitution of his country. [33]

On another occasion the presiding officer in one of the labor-conspiracy cases, Judge Ogden Edwards, stigmatized the trade unions as of recent origin in America, as mainly upheld by foreigners, and as utterly opposed to American doctrines. "In this favored land of law and liberty," Judge Edwards declared, "the road to advancement is open to all, and the journeymen may by their skill and industry become flourishing master mechanics. . . . Every American knows, or ought to know, that he has no better friend

[32] Seth Luther, *An Address to the Workingmen of New England* (Boston, 1832), pp. 8, 16.
[33] John R. Commons and Eugene A. Gilmore, eds., *Documentary History of American Industrial Society* (Cleveland, 1910), III, 235.

than the laws, and that he needs no artificial combination for his protection." [34]

No one can say even roughly how many workers, confronted by such efforts to designate their struggle to improve their lot as disloyalty to the nation, wondered whether Seth Luther was not right in having insisted that patriotism was merely a delusion designed "to hide existing or anticipated and inevitable evils." In any case, certain devoted patriots were sufficiently impressed by the tendency of some radicals to associate patriotism with exploitation to make explicit denials of any such relationship. Thus the poet Cornelius Mathews, a man of broad social sympathies and democratic inclinations, denied in a speech given in 1839 at New York University that "patriotism, or love of country, is an airy bubble, raised by statesmen to dazzle and bewilder the multitude." [35] It was rather, Mathews insisted, a genuine reality resting on the constitution of human nature and as such a source of exaltation to the individual that cherished it.

By and large it seems clear that workers did not question the intrinsic worth of patriotism and loyalty to the nation. It was a sufficiently powerful force to be useful to workers in their struggles for what they considered merely their rights to a fair share of their toil. Thus the common law which regarded labor organizations as conspiracies was denounced as an instrument inherited from aristocratic England and ill-suited to American needs. Caesar Rodney, the able and forward-looking attorney who defended the Philadelphia journeymen, denied that the motives of the prosecution were patriotic. "We are told," he exclaimed, "that this prosecution is brought forward from public motives, and not from personal views; when you see a formidable band of masters attending on the trial of this cause, and some of the most eminent counsel in the city employed to prosecute it; and when you see, further, that it is not taken by any of their customers, it will require strong arguments to convince you, it is done out of pure patriotic motives." [36]

No less significant was the effort of workers to win the right of

[34] Commons and Gilmore, eds., *Documentary History*, IV, 330–331.
[35] Cornelius Mathews, *Various Writings* (New York, 1843), p. 299.
[36] Commons and Gilmore, *op. cit.*, III, 162 ff.

organizing for fair wages on the ground that equal opportunity for sharing the benefits of America was the essence of Americanism. "The mischief is," said one attorney for the New York workers in the conspiracy case of 1836, "that you will attempt to keep any one class down to old values and thus exclude them from a just participation in the general prosperity. . . . In our country the protection against such a partial operation of the laws, is to be found in our courts of justice, and though the remedy may be delayed for a while, the good sense and true patriotism which pervades our whole community, render it ultimately certain." [37] When the decision went against the workers, the New York union labeled the charge of the trial judge as contrary to the spirit of our republican government, as part of an aristocratic plot to take away the sacred heritage of the liberty won in 1776.

In demanding free public schools labor spokesmen insisted that education at state expense was not only a means by which workers were to climb the economic ladder, not merely a matter of justice and natural right. They also held with educational reformers that free public schools were necessary in order that workers might become more informed and, therefore, better citizens and patriots. If workers could properly understand the nature and advantages of the institutions of the country and the blessings the land itself afforded, if they could clearly see how beneficial these were to their own interests, then loyalty to the country would be strengthened. Thus labor associated free public education not only with natural rights and economic interest, but with patriotism, an association destined to enjoy a long history in American public thought.

Labor leaders were not alone among dissident groups in identifying their economic interest with human rights and with patriotic devotion to country. In 1838 an antimonopolist spoke for a considerable segment of opinion in holding that "Revolutionary republicanism and patriotism have given way to speculation and stockjobbing; love of country, to love of gold." Unless we arouse ourselves, continued this orator, unless we take seriously the trust imposed on us by the fathers of the Revolution, and relieve the coun-

[37] *An Address to the Cordwainers of the United States* (Philadelphia, 1836), p. 4.

try from a band of purse-proud swindlers, who make fortunes by speculation alone, "we shall hand over our posterity to chains and ignominy." [38]

In other humanitarian crusades the general tendency was to identify the program in question with human rights. Yet human rights were also associated with economic advantages. Thus critics of imprisonment for debt insisted not only that it imposed an unfair economic disadvantage on the poor, but also that it flagrantly violated the great principle of the Revolution—that all men are born free and equal, and that each and every one has unquestioned right to the enjoyment of life, liberty, and the pursuit of happiness.[39]

The general nature of the argument in much of the reform literature is well represented in the temperance propaganda. Economic advantages were linked with the patriotism of human rights in the contentions of the Charleston advocate of temperance, Thomas S. Grimké. "It appeals," he said, "to the sense of duty and the spirit of usefulness." [40] Explicitly identifying patriotism with the hoped-for results of temperance—the preservation of the health and property of the community and the promotion of industry and economy—Grimké attempted to prove that the truly loyal American must abstain from spiritous liquors. In an engaging appeal another temperance advocate, Samuel Nott, set forth a different economic interpretation of patriotism. In opposing the argument that distilleries, by providing markets for coarse grains, promoted economic prosperity and therefore deserved well of the Republic, Nott maintained that "the wealth of a country cannot be really promoted by any means which increases idleness, improvidence and vice." [41]

[38] Edward D. Barber, *An Oration Delivered before the Democrats of Washington County* (Montpelier, 1839), pp. 17–18.
[39] An interesting example is *The Debtors' Prison: A Tale of a Revolutionary Soldier* (New York, 1835), pp. 26–27.
[40] Thomas S. Grimké, *Address on the Patriot Character of the Temperance Reformation* (Charleston, 1833), pp. 6–7.
[41] Samuel Nott, *An Appeal to the Temperate on the Vice of Intemperance* (Hartford, 1828), pp. 109–110. Similar views were expressed in *The Southern Patriot* (Charleston), July 2, 1842.

The tendency in labor and reform circles to challenge the *status quo* by associating human rights with patriotism stimulated, in the first instance, the effort by conservatives to discredit radical programs. This was often done by identifying them with imported, alien, "un-American" ideologies. Thus, to cite an example, Edgar Snowden in an address at the Columbian College in the federal capital in 1837, condemned the "monetary excesses" of the Jacksonian regime as those of "foreign philanthropists." Snowden spoke for many others in declaring "we want none of foreign, imported, feverish doctrine, which engenders habits and views hostile to American ideas of regulated liberty—which saps and mines the foundations of society in order to effect a slight change in the superstructure." [42] Such indictments of reform programs as alien and un-American were frequently heard in the North, but they became much more general in the South, where proslavery apologists denounced as unpatriotic virtually the whole humanitarian movement.

The denunciation of reform as unpatriotic was not, however, the only response to the effort of champions of human rights to associate their position with loyalty to the fundamental ideals of America. The Hamiltonian arguments regarding the economics of loyalty were also reoriented. This reorientation was affected by the growth of political democracy—by the fact, in other words, that it became more and more necessary for groups asking for privileges from the government to convince the electorate that these privileges were for the general good. Thus it was that the early Hamiltonian identification of national wealth with private property was given a more democratic basis in the writings of men who fell heir to the economic philosophy of Tench Coxe and Alexander Hamilton.

The leader of the new group was the Irish political refugee, Mathew Carey, who became a prominent bookdealer in Philadelphia. Although he staunchly upheld internal improvements and pointed out the bearings of these on national solidarity and national loyalty, Carey is better known as the champion of protective tariffs.

[42] Edgar Snowden, *An Address Delivered before the Enoisinian Society of the Columbian College, July 4, 1837* (Washington, 1837), pp. 12–13.

in the interest of which he founded the Society for the Promotion of National Industry. Unlike Hamilton, who favored close economic ties with Great Britain despite his advocacy of protection, Carey, in true Irish fashion, developed the anti-British implications of economic nationalism. Carey's protectionist doctrines attracted the favor of the German visitor, Friedrich List, who formulated his high-tariff views in his *Outlines of American Political Economy* (1827).

In addition to exerting wide influence through his emphasis on the relations between tariffs and an economically motivated national loyalty, Carey helped in still other ways to develop the economics of loyalty. In his widely read *Olive Branch* (1814) he tried to reconcile the bitter political antagonisms incident to the War of 1812. Carey argued that loyalty to the nation involves mutual concessions on the part of every group, concessions which, in the long run, would redound to the advantage of the group making them, since the interest of every group demanded the perpetuation of the Union.[43] In emphasizing national loyalty as a concomitant of economic nationalism Carey was appealing to a broader constituency than Hamilton had reached.

The economic nationalism of Mathew Carey was systematized and developed by his son, Henry C. Carey, a convert from *laissez faire* to something like a planned economy. In his *Past, Present, and Future* (1848) the younger Carey gave economic nationalism a definitely democratic slant. Hitherto internal improvements, protective tariffs, and a stable currency had been largely associated with the class interests of entrepreneurs, speculators, bankers, and merchants. Carey, however, related them vigorously and positively to the interest of the whole people—an interest which rested on the harmony of all subordinate and contributing interests. Thus Carey's writings were a landmark in the development of an American economic nationalism. His influence reached far beyond Philadelphia, a focal point in the literary expression of economic nationalism. Carey's association with Horace Greeley, editor of the widely

[43] Mathew Carey, *The Olive Branch* (Philadelphia, 1814; 10th ed., 1830), *passim*.

read New York *Tribune*, strengthened the movement in the growing metropolis.

No one in the Middle States, not even Carey and Greeley, popularized the new type of economic nationalism so effectively as New England's impressive orator, Daniel Webster. His moving addresses in commemoration of the landing of the Pilgrims and the battle of Bunker Hill laid the foundations for his subsequent achievement by identifying New England traditions and virtues with nationalism. In 1830, in his magnificent reply to Senator Hayne of South Carolina, Webster cleverly associated national interest with all the policies which his opponents declared to be sectional in character—tariffs, internal improvements at government expense, and restriction of the disposal of public lands in the West. That, however, would in itself have been insufficient. What made Webster's great oration such a triumph was his remarkable skill in identifying with a particular economic philosophy and program, not only the well-being and even the loyalty of Americans, but, in addition, the principle of Union *and* Liberty. Newspapers reprinted all over the North the memorable sentiment, LIBERTY AND UNION, NOW AND FOREVER, ONE AND INSEPARABLE. Schoolboys learned by heart the passage of which the unforgettable phrase was the climax. Public speakers throughout the East and West made frequent use of the golden words in the toasts they proposed and in the orations they delivered. Webster's LIBERTY AND UNION entered into the folk-consciousness of Americans living above the Mason and Dixon line. A new point had indeed been reached in the development of the theory of economic nationalism.

Webster impressively associated national loyalty with an economic well-being dependent on tariffs and internal improvements, but he did not convince large segments of the population even in the North. In the South, despite widespread and genuine devotion to the nation, leading politicians "calculated the value of the Union" and invoked the theory of state rights and particularist traditions to defend agricultural interests against the rising tide of economic nationalism in the North. We shall see in a subsequent chapter the nature and extent of this train of thought.

Writing in the early 1830's, shortly after Webster made his reply to Hayne, Alexis de Tocqueville, the acute and well-informed French visitor, expressed his belief that patriotism was still directed mainly to the states and seldom to the Union itself. Tocqueville felt that all the interests, habits, and feelings of the people were bound to the soil, the memories, and the advantages of the states, and on them rather than the Union political activity and personal loyalties centered. In addressing individuals, Tocqueville remarked, both the states and the federal government spoke with authority; but in speaking to the states, the general government was for the most part temporizing. It explained its motives; it justified its conduct; it hesitated to act until reduced to the last extremity. But in addressing the nation, the states spoke with a bold, commanding voice.[44]

Even if the Union had inherent strength, the French observer thought, the physical extent of its territory, the vast distances, the scattered population, would have made it hard to exert that strength. In any case, he concluded, the states, in forming the voluntary Union, had in no sense forfeited their own sense of nationality. All this Tocqueville maintained in spite of his admission that the people of the United States constituted in a real sense a single people with many similar notions of governmental institutions and values. Innumerable foreign visitors shared the opinion of the gifted French aristocrat concerning the looseness of the federal union.

However much Americans resented the reports of visitors like Tocqueville, the very intensity with which they spoke and wrote about the achievement of true nationality and true unity suggests that the wish was father to the thought. Many Americans themselves, moreover, were in fundamental agreement with the foreign commentators. Looking back on the 1840's, a former Confederate, George Cary Eggleston, was to write, after the smoke had lifted from Appomattox, that no national life existed at all in the antebellum period. Communication between place and place was not easy, he recalled; each locality suspected every other. "We were all of us Americans, intense, self-satisfied, self-glorying Americans—but

[44] Alexis de Tocqueville, *Democracy in America* (New York, 1900), I, 392 *ff.*

we had little else in common," he maintained. "We did not know each other. We had been bred in radically different ways. We had different ideals, different conceptions of life, different standards of conduct, different ways of living, different traditions, and different aspirations." [45] Granted that Eggleston's mind was full of living memories of the Southern crusade for independence and that he was exaggerating to make his point, there was nevertheless some truth in what he wrote.

That truth was illustrated by the frequent doubts which Northerners expressed regarding the permanence of the Union and the actual existence of a genuine national solidarity. In an address delivered before the alumni of Waterville College in 1830 John Neal, a well-known figure in the literary circles of New England, brushed aside the complacency of many ardent nationalists who assumed that there was nothing to fear regarding the unity and permanence of the country. "Nothing to fear!" the orator exclaimed. "Look at the South and West, in array with the North and the East: the manufacturing—the commercial—and the agrarian interest—the people beyond the Alleghenies—all striving . . . each for itself: and then say that we have nothing to fear! Other empires have been destroyed by overgrowth—and what is there to hinder our acknowledged overgrowth from leading to similar consequences? . . . Let us not wilfully shut our eyes to the fact that nations like men are mortal—that commonwealths like Sovereignties are the growth as much of situation as of inquiry—perhaps more." [46]

Commerce and industry were, despite such dark predictions, laying the foundations for the unification of the various parts of the North and West. Staunch nationalists likewise believed that the South was coming increasingly into the national orbit. The sections, it was frequently said, were being forever knit together by commerce. Disunion, so the refrain went, had become an impossibility. "Our commerce is equally important to every section," declared George S. Boutwell in *Hunt's Merchants' Magazine* in 1850. "It

[45] George C. Eggleston, *Recollections of a Varied Life* (New York, 1910), p. 6.
[46] John Neal, *Our Country: An Address Delivered before the Alumni of Waterville College, July 29, 1830* (Portland, 1830), pp. 12–13.

knows no North, no South, no East, no West—but only a great people, *one and indivisible.*" [47]

Though qualified by the triumph of Jackson and by the influence of Southern representatives in Washington, the sphere in which the central government operated was growing larger. That growth reinforced or won the loyalty to the nation of various groups that profited or hoped to profit from its undertakings. The support of commerce through the coast survey; the navigation act of 1817 restricting coastwise trade to American-built and owned vessels; the exploring expedition which, under the command of Lieutenant Wilkes, charted useful routes in the Pacific from 1839 to 1841, largely at the instigation of New England whaling and other maritime interests; and the ship subsidies of 1846 and 1847—all these are important examples of the use of federal power and revenue for advancing the interests of seafaring America. It was no accident that maritime America looked more and more to the central government as the source of blessings and as an object of loyalty.

Closely related to all this was the sentiment for an enlarged navy commensurate with the requirements and ambitions of an ever-expanding world commerce. No more ardent voice was ever lifted for the navy than that of Lieutenant Matthew Fontaine Maury of Virginia, the pioneer in oceanography. Writing in the *Southern Literary Messenger* in 1840, Maury urged that the existing navy was too small to right a wrong and too feeble to protect American citizens and American commerce in the remote stretches of the globe.[48] What benefits an adequate navy could confer on the pelt traders of the Northwest, on the twenty thousand whalers and fishermen of the North Atlantic, on the clippers engaged in the China trade! In time of war, moreover, foreign navies might blockade the coasts of countries essential to our trade. Only an effective navy could make the flag both a shield and a sword. All in all, Maury made a strong case for both the renovation and the enlargement of the navy in the interest of substantial groups of Americans. The benefits conferred on these by naval protection and the po-

[47] *Hunt's Merchants' Magazine*, XXII (June, 1850), 611.
[48] *Southern Literary Messenger*, VI (March, 1840), 234 *ff*.

tentiality of even greater advantages provided a material basis for loyalty to the nation.

Domestic trade was also the object of federal solicitude. Among nationalistic thinkers Hamilton and Clay, as well as the Careys, led the way in pointing out the significance of internal improvements and better communications in weakening local ties and in promoting loyalty to the nation. Those given to emphasizing the idea that natural waterways tied the country together were forced to admit, at least by implication, that however generous nature had been in providing natural avenues of transit, that generosity had not gone quite far enough. As population from the eastern seaboard spread into the trans-Allegheny country, local interests in both the older and newer parts of the country clamored for better transportation facilities. Under private auspices and with government support, roads, canals, and railways were built and rivers were dredged. Distances began that shrinking process which at length, in our own time, was to make them all but negligible. The promotional literature of the movement for internal improvements at government expense emphasized the advantages which such facilities would bring to agricultural, commercial, and industrial interests and to particular communities. Much weight was also given to the national bonds of unity which internal improvements were, it was felt, bound to forge.

Thus in the agitation for internal improvements the argument was advanced that the Union would find its greatest safeguard in public support of transportation projects. In the flush of nationalistic enthusiasm that followed the War of 1812, Calhoun, not yet committed to state rights and sectionalism, urged the necessity of binding "the Republic together with a perfect system of roads and canals" which, like a protective tariff, would in his eyes "make the parts adhere more closely" and "form a new and most powerful cement." [49]

An increasing number of Southerners abandoned the Calhoun program of 1817, but in other parts of the country men continued to talk in similar vein. If the distance between Carolina and Con-

[49] John C. Calhoun, *Works* (New York, 1856), II, 190.

necticut were annihilated by railroads, declared Asa Child in a Fourth of July address in 1838, the citizens of these states could never be foes. "New bonds will be thrown around the Union, which shall grow stronger as we pursue our march onward." [50] Joseph Bradley, actuary, counsel for railroads, and jurist, spoke for a large constituency when in 1849 he asked:

What constitutes the indissoluble bond which unites and keeps us together as one nation, as one people? What, but the mutuality of interests produced by the great variety of our industrial productions, and the consequent exchanges which the mutual supply of wants requires? It is this which lays down upon the map of our country the complicated network of our canals, our railroads, and our telegraphs. It is this which interlocks and weaves together all our public lines of communication and transportation; which carries life into all the breathing engines of social prosperity that labor around us, on the sea and on the land, by day and by night, unceasingly.[51]

An extensive examination of the out-of-the-way literature of the middle nineteenth century shows that this theme was extremely popular. "Science has conquered space and bound down the wings of Time," declared Park Benjamin in a sermon entitled *True Patriotism*, which he delivered at Geneva, New York, on July 4, 1851. "Though our country covers the broadest area in the world, with the exception of the Russian despotism, capital and labor are bringing together her utmost borders into limits more accessible than were those of England and Scotland a century ago. Besides these grand bonds of the railroads and telegraph and the post, the tides of migration, flowing to and fro, from East to West, from North to South and backward, mingle together our people more and more, and make them one people, one people held together by fraternity

[50] Asa Child, *An Oration: Delivered before the Citizens of Norwich* (Norwich, Connecticut, 1838), p. 18.
[51] Joseph P. Bradley, *Progress: Its Grounds and Possibilities* (New Brunswick, 1849), pp. 14–15.

and duty and patriotism." [52] Others emphasized the idea that improved facilities of communication would break down localism by enabling even the laboring classes to widen the sphere of their knowledge by traveling and by observing personally the ways of life of their fellow citizens, an opportunity reserved in the Old World to gentlemen of at least moderate fortune.

Even well before the Civil War the conviction was growing that the elastic network of communications was making the various parts of the country so interdependent that any secession movement must fail. At the time of the bitter controversy over the Missouri question in 1820, a Connecticut orator declared that if the Northern states should be disposed to separate from the national union, they would quickly seek shelter again under the old flag in order to enjoy the material sweets of that affiliation.[53] This argument was heard in later crises. Thus when the issue of slavery in the newly acquired territory threatened the national existence in 1850, the necessity of the Union to each section received much emphasis. Henry Clay, the tireless champion of internal improvements, reiterated it in fervid pleas for compromise and harmony. In 1858 Caleb Cushing of Massachusetts, in commenting on the geographical basis of national unity, declared that Pennsylvania and the West could never afford to permit the breakup of the Union.

This was not the first time, of course, that the West figured in public discussions of national unity and national loyalty. With no little insight, Francis J. Grund, an Austrian who took up residence in the United States, expressed his belief that the West was the greatest safeguard of national unity that the American people possessed. In case of a quarrel between the North and South both sides, Grund predicted in 1837, would appeal to the Western interest. "In whose favor it would declare," he went on, "on that side would be victory." Even in this case, Grund believed that the union of

[52] Park Benjamin, *True Patriotism: A Sermon Preached at the Presbyterian Church, July 4, 1851* (Geneva, New York, 1851), p. 16.
[53] Henry G. Nixon, *An Oration, Commemorative of American Independence* (New Haven, 1821), pp. 8–9.

the West with either party would oblige the other to yield, sooner or later, or endanger its own independence. "Neither," he concluded, "is the West more independent of the North and South, than those states of each other." [54]

The trouble with Grund's prophecy in part was that in the 1850's railroads were to tie Northeast and Northwest together in a far greater degree than Northwest and Southwest were united by the Mississippi river and the new Illinois Central Railroad. In the second place, Grund did not see, as Tocqueville did, that economic ties, being subject to shifts in a highly dynamic society, might not be adequate in every crisis. Yet in the long run he was right. The growing interdependency of the sections, promoted by improved communications, provided a powerful cohesive force in the development of loyalty to the nation.

The point Grund made about the role of the West as a cementing agency might well have been elaborated. When Easterners of importance traveled, they were more likely than not to go abroad; but Westerners who left their homes generally went to the seaboard and thus tended, more than tidewater people, to become familiar with sections other than their own. But their sense of being American, their loyalty to the nation, rested on a firmer foundation than that. The new states across the Appalachians were better soil for the growth of national sentiment than the original thirteen. They had no long histories as separate political units. The federal government had created them. Peopled by folk from many states and lands, the West was a place where men and women rubbed elbows with fellow settlers whose traditional loyalties were altogether different from their own.

The needs of the new western country could, furthermore, often best be served by the federal government.[55] Local militias could help protect the borderland against Indians but the federal army was always the principal safeguard. Proximity to the frontiers of Canada

[54] Francis J. Grund, *The Americans in their Moral, Social, and Political Relations* (London, 1837), II, 361.
[55] Curtis P. Nettels, "The National Cost of the Inland Frontier, 1820–1830," *Transactions of the Wisconsin Academy of Science, Arts, and Letters*, XXV (May, 1930).

and Mexico likewise tended to give the federal army a place of some importance. The national government proved itself the most effective agent for pushing back the Indian into the distant hinterland and for wresting fresh territory from Spain, Mexico, and Britain that frontiersmen could clear and make their own. The federal government could also best subsidize agencies for transportation because it enjoyed title to the most extensive lands in the whole nation.

Most important of all, the federal government was the dispenser of lands to the pioneers who established homesteads in the West. Nothing played a more significant role in the development of loyalty to the national government than this fact. Americans commonly regarded title to the soil as a natural right, and the free-homestead argument loomed large in the patriotism of human rights. It was no less significant a factor in the economics of loyalty.

All these factors together tended to develop national loyalty in Western hearts. The turgid, flamboyant declarations of Western regionalism did not really weaken that devotion. The nation everywhere—and above all in the West—was coming, then, to be identified with the realization of the American dream of universal enjoyment of the goods of this world.

Yet for a time, at least, the West in certain respects also leavened loyalty to the nation by promoting disunity. The whole question of whether slavery or the free homestead was to dominate the expanding West heightened rivalries between Northern farmers and industrial workers on the one hand, and Southern plantation owners on the other. The one group favored opening up freely the immense public domain to the pioneer settler, the other, sensing the likelihood that such a policy would augment Northern strength in federal councils, was opposed. Nor was this all. Competition on the part of Northerners and Southerners for a grant of public lands deemed necessary to build a transcontinental railroad to the Pacific coast likewise whetted sectional rivalries. When at length in 1861 Southern leaders withdrew from Congress, both issues were settled in accordance with Northern and, as events proved, with national interests. The West was opened to the small farmer on terms of the completely free homestead and also to the business corporation, both being benefited by unhampered access to the national domain.

That access was facilitated by the decision in 1862 to grant sufficient lands and subsidies to the corporation which undertook to span the continent with steel rails. The chartering of the Union Pacific was, moreover, acclaimed as a national necessity, as indispensable insurance for preserving the loyalty of California to the Union. In the course of time other transcontinental railroads still further welded the East and West together. After Appomattox, Southern railroads not only multiplied but also, as they came to be integrated with Northern systems, provided material bonds between the once divided sections. At the same time the magic growth of telegraph systems also broke down distances and facilitated easy communication between the several parts of the land.

Thus it was that, the Civil War won, the danger of disunion quelled, thoughtful Americans could see in the vast network of communications a powerful force for national union and national loyalty. James Russell Lowell, better perhaps than anyone else, spoke what was in the minds of thousands of Northerners when he wrote in 1865:

The whole people have acquired a certain metropolitan temper; they feel everything at once and in common; a single pulse sends anger, grief, or triumph through the whole country . . . this simultaneousness, this unanimity, deepens national consciousness and intensifies popular emotion. Every man feels himself a part, sensitive and sympathetic, of this vast organism, a partner in its life or death. The sentiment of patriotism is etherealized and ennobled by it, is kindled by the more or less conscious presence of an ideal element; and the instinctive love of a few familiar hills and fields widens, till country is no longer an abstraction, but a living presence, felt in the heart and operative in the conscience, like that of an absent mother. It is no trifling matter that thirty millions of men should be thinking the same thought and feeling the same pang at a single moment of time, and that these vast parallels of latitude should become a neighborhood more intimate than many a country village.[56]

[56] James Russell Lowell, *Writings* (Boston and New York, 1890), V, 243.

If Lowell overemphasized his point that the newspaper, the railroad, and the telegraph had converted the whole nation into a vast town meeting (and he did exaggerate), what he wrote had point nevertheless.

The unity incident to the growth of transportation and communication was reinforced by the striking development of manufacturing, especially in the field of printing and reproductive art. "There is," as the authority on the subject, Victor Clark, has reminded us, "a culture of taste as well as thought that qualifies men for social cooperation by giving them common standards of judgment." [57] The great impetus to this important if unconscious basis of unity was to come, of course, in the post-Civil War years; but the foundations were being laid as industry developed in the northern and eastern sections of the country and as markets for industrial output were tapped all over the land.

Thus there developed a well-rounded, coherent philosophy and program of economic nationalism. At first widely diffused throughout the country as a whole, this pattern of thought came to be more and more largely sectionalized in the North and Northwest. Yet in becoming identified with those regions it did not forfeit its nationalistic ideology. We shall see that a quite different conception of national loyalty was becoming crystallized in the South, a conception which was at length to come into direct conflict with the economic nationalism of the North. Before considering that conflict, it is well to turn to the sustained and systematic efforts made to nurture national loyalty by argument, symbol, and sentiment.

[57] Victor Clark, *History of Manufactures in the United States*, 1607–1860 (Washington, 1929), I, 582.

V: THE NURTURE OF LOYALTY

But, O ye favoured countrymen of Washington! Your republic is
not yet lost; there is still hope. The arm that wrought your political
salvation, is still stretched out to save; then hear his voice and live!
Hear the voice of the Divine Founder of your Republic! 'Little
children, love one another.' Hear his voice from the lips of his
servant Washington, 'Above all things hold dear your national
Union!'

PARSON WEEMS, 1800

In his now all but forgotten *Sketches of the Principles of Government*, published in 1793, Nathaniel Chipman expressed in admira-
ble fashion the view of patriotism prevalent in the early decades of
the Republic. Original nature, explained this wise and learned
Federalist judge of frontier Vermont, includes certain passions or
appetites, to be thought of as mere capacities rather than as fully
developed traits. Among these is a capacity for the social sense,
the great gift which the Creator bestowed on man to check envy,
hatred, malice, and revenge—deep-rooted impulses involved in his
fall. Man's social sense or consciousness of a kind of "individuality
of himself in the aggregate" is, if not the very germ of every social
attachment, the thing that gives strength to attachments. Among
these, Chipman continued, love of community ranks high by reason
of its early appearance among primitive peoples. To fit man for
society and civil government the Creator has incorporated this
passion deep and strong in the very nature of man.[1]

Sixty years later, on the threshold of the Civil War, the Reverend
Caleb S. Henry, an erudite Episcopalian who had taken a prominent part in the peace movement, expressed a similar idea of the

[1] Nathaniel Chipman, *Sketches of the Principles of Government* (Rutland, Vermont, 1793), pp. 55 ff.

nature of pride in country. "Patriotism has its root among the elementary affections, in the social sympathies of our nature," he wrote. "It is a sympathy which, twined with a thousand associations, makes a man feel that his individual life is bound up with his country's life." [2] This view of patriotism as based on original nature, a view which Caleb Henry went on to elaborate, was in truth, still typical of American thought.

Inborn though the basic impulse toward patriotism seemed to be, it was nevertheless believed to require continuous nurture. American writers on the subject recognized that such nurture was in part unconscious—twined, as Henry said, with a thousand associations which made a man feel that his individual life was bound up with that of his country. But it was also widely believed that deliberate and conscious cultivation of the basic impulse was indispensable. The principles of the Enlightenment, which still exerted sway over American thought, the tenets of the Romantic movement, an ever-surging force, and Christian doctrine itself all reinforced the conviction that the "innate impulse" must be carefully and persistently fostered.

True love of country, wrote Thomas B. Fox in a typical oration in the centennial year of Washington's birth, is not a mere sentiment of the heart, but a calm, rational principle of the mind, directed by an enlightened conscience. "The mere feeling of attachment to the land of our birth is not patriotism," this Massachusetts orator declared. "When the love of our native land, so analogous to the instinctive love of the child for its parent, is cultivated and expanded, beneath the care of reason and religion, then, but not till then, it becomes patriotism." [3] One more sample of scores of similar pronouncements must suffice as illustration of the point. "When we say that the Bible justifies and encourages patriotism," wrote the Reverend Thomas Starr King in 1851, "we virtually say that it is a sentiment subject to the sway of the moral law, requir-

[2] Caleb S. Henry, *Patriotism and the Slaveholders' Rebellion* (New York, 1861), pp. 7–8.
[3] Thomas B. Fox, *An Oration, Delivered at the Request of the Washington Light Infantry Company* (Newburyport, 1832), p. 12.

ing, like all our natural instincts, guidance, Christian light, and training." [4]

Men of the time realized half-consciously that national unity and distinctiveness were still in the process of becoming, and they were led to put strong emphasis on love of country and loyalty. In and out of season patriots insisted on the necessity for both the rationalistic and the emotional cultivation of national loyalty. Noah Webster is a good case in point. "The citizens of this extensive Republic constitute a *nation*," he wrote pointedly, in 1794. "As a nation we feel all the prejudices of a society. These national prejudices are probably necessary, in the present state of the world, to strengthen our government. They form a species of *political bigotry*, common to all nations, from which springs a *real allegiance*, never expressed, but always firm and unwavering." [5]

Webster set to work to promote the national "prejudices" so necessary, in his eyes, to American well-being. His great dictionary of American English and his ubiquitous and profitable "spellingbooks" popularized some of the reforms in orthography which he deemed basic to the growth of a distinctively American language and literature. Such a language and literature would, he believed, inspire pride of country and foster loyalty to it by winning glory for the nation in the eyes of the world. His schoolbooks included American orations, plenty of them. Were they inferior in any way, he demanded, to those of Demosthenes and Cicero? Would they not kindle patriotism in the hearts of American youth? In countless contributions to newspapers and magazines, in lectures and conversations, in letters to the great and to the humble, Webster kept unceasingly at his effort to inculcate a widespread understanding of America and devotion to it. [6]

He did not work alone. Jedidiah Morse's school "geographies" spared no superlative in praising the American nation above all others. Caleb Bingham and John Pierpont filled their school texts with all sorts of patriotic sentiment. Other compilers assembled

[4] Thomas Starr King, *Patriotism and Other Lectures* (Boston, 1851), p. 34.
[5] Noah Webster, *The Revolution in France* (New York, 1794), p. 45.
[6] The standard biography is Harry R. Warfel, *Noah Webster, Schoolmaster to America* (New York, 1936).

in similar manuals stories of the American past, apostrophes to Washington and to the other fathers, patriotic speeches and maxims galore. "Peter Parley" and William H. McGuffey are the best known of these editors—but there were scores of them. All through the first half of the nineteenth century publishers and authors vied with each other in giving full play to the patriotic impulse. Even arithmetic textbooks tried to instil lessons of patriotism in youthful minds. At least two authors claimed special consideration for their handiwork on the ground that boys and girls would imbibe patriotism in the course of reckoning sums and calculating problems!

Imbued with the conviction that merely local loyalties and interests could be weakened and national enthusiasm engendered through education, an impressive number of scholars and public men boldly advocated a system of schools sustained by the federal government. Such schools could inculcate in youth understanding of America and devotion to it. But lower schools needed a supplement, the argument went, in the field of higher education.

The idea of a great national university thus found favor in various circles. Its champions maintained that such an institution would promote American scholarship by stimulating research and by applying its results to the needs of American life. More than that, a national university would train public servants for competent and loyal service to the nation. Such were the advantages pictured in notable essays written in a prize contest sponsored by the American Philosophical Society. The eminent Dr. Benjamin Rush, father of American psychiatry, supported the movement. Washington himself set his heart on a great national university and even bequeathed a legacy for that purpose. Americans by and large, however, had no intention of surrendering to the federal government the control of American minds: the sectarian colleges, various local interests, state loyalties, class prejudices and fears, all stood in the way.

Yet the idea was not downed. In the literature subsequently evoked by this proposal, emphasis fell on the usefulness of a national university in providing an understanding of America and in inculcating loyalty. Thus in advocating such an institution, a representative orator reminded his Phi Beta Kappa audience at Trinity College in 1856 that "if true patriotism seems at an ebb, and the foundation principles of our republic to be neglected, so much the louder comes the appeal to us to develop the mental resources of the new world." [7] Just as Leyden and Berlin had founded their universities in a period of invasion and deep national depression and had discovered that they gave an incalculable stimulus to a patriotic revival, so the American people might gain in national feeling through a national university.

As it became clear that a national system of education in the interest of national loyalty was likely to remain a dream, patriots put their shoulders to other wheels. Samuel Hall, pioneer in American teacher training, insisted in his widely read *Lectures on School-Keeping* (1829) that love of country and devotion to it could be inspired by making sure that every citizen knew something of his country's past, of its institutions, of the obstacles the fathers had overcome in winning the blessings of freedom. Every child was to be familiar with the Constitution of the United States. "The earlier children are made acquainted with this, the more likely will they be to respect the law, and yield cheerful obedience to it." [8] Educational conventions passed such resolutions as that of the College of Teachers in Cincinnati, which in 1837 went on record in favor of the permanent study in all American schools, academies, and colleges, of the elements of government as developed in the Constitution.

About the same time, Francis Lieber, a recent comer from Germany and a professional political scientist, wrote that if the purest patriotism were to be kindled in youthful bosoms, American boys and girls must be sufficiently well informed about their country to defend it against the attacks of European critics. They must also be imbued with such sound knowledge of their national history and

[7] Benjamin A. Gould, *An American University: An Oration Delivered before the Connecticut Beta of the Phi Beta Kappa Society, at Trinity College* (Hartford, 1856), p. 11.
[8] Samuel Hall, *Lectures on School-Keeping* (Boston, 1829), p. 39.

life that they could never forget that their country, far from being an accidental mass of men and women, was actually the embodiment of eternal principles, principles for which their fathers had lived and died.

The school textbooks in American history that appeared in the early decades of the Republic set the pattern in all matters of patriotism for those that followed.[9] Declaring that every Englishman paid five times more in taxes than an American citizen did, John M'Culloch in his *Concise History of the United States,* published in 1795, proceeded to demonstrate other ways in which America had surpassed the Old World. Later texts emphasized the corroding influence of the English king and his foolish and evil ministers in the pre-Revolutionary period and gave vent to much anti-British sentiment. Still others illustrated the theme, so well expressed by William Grimshaw in his *History of the United States* (1822), that "the annals of the world exhibit no previous example of so rapid a progress." All the school histories glorified the battles, bravery, and exploits of American soldiers and sailors.

All this was only part of the justification for teaching American history to American youth. Charles A. Goodrich, in a school history which went through many editions after the initial one of 1822, upheld the study of American history on the ground that it was the history of the first civil government ever established on the genuine basis of freedom, and that it furnished "lessons upon the science of civil government, social happiness, and religious freedom of greater value than are to be found in the history of any other nation on the globe." [10] The democratic foundation of much patriotic conviction was admirably expressed by the gifted teacher and Transcendentalist disciple, Elizabeth Peabody. In the preface to her *Chronological History* (1856) she maintained that our past was the first recorded history of a government depending directly on the

9 A good account of the contents of school texts in American history is Agnew D. Roorbach, *The Development of Social Studies in American Secondary Education before 1861* (Philadelphia, 1937).

10 Charles A. Goodrich, *A History of the United States of America* (4th ed., Bellows Falls, Vermont, 1824), Introduction.

mass of people, "every individual of whom becomes a creator of its events, in precise ratio with his personal energy." [11] Such democratic and civic patriotism paralleled and in some school histories—perhaps the majority—dominated that of the more vainglorious and chauvinistic variety.

Such was the background of the first laws requiring the study and teaching of American history. In 1827, Massachusetts and Vermont led the way, to be followed by other Eastern states. The Middle West stood aloof, and in the antebellum South only Virginia provided for instruction in the history of the United States, and Virginia coupled it with a requirement in the history of the state. California, still in the pioneer stage of her development, enacted a law in 1851 which was designed to inculcate loyalty to the nation through the proper instruction of youth in all schools whatsoever. After the Civil War the movement spread until it became general. Finally, in the years that followed the First World War and in the early stages of the Second World War, special demands were made in the name of patriotism for additional legislative requirements, both as to the extent and the character of the instruction in the country's past.

The faith that educators put in the power of the printed word in school textbooks and in the exposition of patriotic lessons by none too well equipped teachers did not exhaust the resources of those who devoted themselves to the nurture of loyalty. One of the great educational forces of the last century was oratory—the oratory of the pulpit, of legislative halls, of public meetings of all sorts. Much of the oratory was full of patriotic ideas and sentiments. The bearings of oratory on the cultivation of patriotism were interestingly commented on by John Drayton in his *Letters Written during a Tour through the Northern and Eastern States of America* (1794). "Should we trace the medium of patriotism, through all its different stages," Drayton wrote, "and follow it, from the hordes of savages who roam the wilds unrestrained by the fetters of law, to where we meet societies of politeness and civilization; we will find,

[11] Elizabeth Peabody, *Chronological History of the United States* (New York, 1856), pp. 6-7.

that nothing is better calculated to impress this *ardor patriae*, than the voice of recital and persuasion, in the face of one's country. The savage sings the deeds of his fathers; and round the sacred fire, incites the young men to glory." [12] Drayton was no lone voice in expressing faith in the power of oratory in all that pertained to the nurture of patriotism.

American patriotic oratory can be best analyzed by taking account of the celebration of the great national festivals which called it forth. Of course we have no measuring device for determining just what influence patriotic oratory had. We can well believe that in some cases it was merely an emotional outlet, in others, a source of recreation. In still others it probably had no observable effect whatever. We know that oratorical expressions of and appeals to patriotism were by no means always implemented—perhaps they were seldom implemented—by those disinterested acts of devotion to country which patriotism implies. Yet a form of expression so widespread, so enthusiastically cultivated, so long dominant, was certainly more than mere bombast, more than a means of rationalizing interests, more than a balm to conscience.

Closely allied to oratory in the upbuilding of national loyalty was the role of symbols. The development of symbols in democratic republics is more difficult than in monarchies, where the person of the sovereign is an obvious and useful objectification of the nation and of all for which it presumably stands. In poetic minds and even in those of the people at large patriotic feeling somehow becomes associated not only with the soil but with a country's symbols. The sanctification of national symbols was described in romantic terms by George William Curtis in an oration at Union College in 1857. It was, he declared, comparable both to the cross in religious worship and to the lover's rapturous caresses of the glove of his mistress or of the lock of her hair worn close to his heart.[13] The point was apt, but in the trying days of the early republic the whole

[12] John Drayton, *Letters Written during a Tour through the Northern and Eastern States of America* (Charleston, 1794), p. 35.

[13] George William Curtis, "Patriotism: An Oration Delivered before the Graduating Class of Union College, July 20, 1857," in *Orations and Addresses* (New York, 1894), I, 45.

problem of developing appropriate national symbols was, of course, often overshadowed by the pressing issues of the day.

Practical need dictated the adoption of a seal as the official sign of the independence that was proclaimed in the famous Declaration. Congress named Franklin, Jefferson, and Adams to prepare a device for the seal of the United States and on August 10, 1776, these sturdy patriots recommended the adoption of *E Pluribus Unum* as the national motto. It had long been familiar to all who read the *Gentleman's Magazine* and even those with no Latin knew what it meant.

By a subsequent act of Congress, the American or bald eagle was added to the national symbolism. As early as 1707, Massachusetts had placed the eagle on her half-cents and New York had made use of it on her pennies, and so there was precedent for adopting it for the national seal. *E Pluribus Unum* was inscribed near the eagle's beak, a bundle of thirteen arrows put in his left talon and a palm of olive branches in his right. Franklin, with his usual wit, remarked that the eagle looked more like a turkey than anything else and added that "in truth, the Turkey is, in comparison, a much more respectable bird, and withal a true original native of America." [14] But the eagle appealed to the classical fervor of the time and seemed to be, as it were, a reincarnation of the ancient Roman bird in a new setting. Besides, Congress specified, in truly patriotic pride, that the eagle was to be the *American* bald eagle! Moreover it symbolized such needed values as superior courage, power, and authority. The eagle defied storms and commanded the air and had no equal in keenness of vision and in strength. Americans became accustomed to the symbol of the eagle as they handled ballots and exchanged the coins bearing its imprint. In the years that followed the War of 1812, artists and craftsmen adopted it as the motif for magazine illustrations, the upholstery of drawing-room furniture, dinner and porcelain ware, and even the humble buttermold! [15]

[14] Benjamin Franklin, *Works*, ed. by John Bigelow (New York, 1887–8), X, 279.
[15] Clarence P. Hornung, "The American Eagle, Symbol of Freedom," *American Artist*, V (November, 1941), 10 ff.

However conventional the symbol thus became, thoughtful men on occasion, at least, recalled the deeper significance of the king of the skies. Thus in speaking on the continued support of the national mint, which since 1796 had been coining ten-dollar gold pieces bearing the eagle, Gouverneur Morris declared to Congress that he was willing to contribute to the support of the mint, even if it was merely "a splendid trapping" of government. Impressing on current coin the emblem of sovereignty might have, he remarked, "some tendency to encourage a national spirit, and to foster national pride." [16] Certainly the emblem became deeply associated with patriotic sentiment. A hundred years later St. Gaudens, the distinguished sculptor who had been commissioned by President Theodore Roosevelt to design new coins, attempted to leave out part of the traditional eagle design. In the name of patriotism indignant protests were made.

Far more important in the fostering of national symbolism than the eagle was, of course, the flag itself.[17] Long before Jamestown was founded, the flag everywhere in the European world had come to stand for dynastic and national sovereignty. Like the American nation itself, our flag evolved from foundations laid in the colonial era. Although various colonies possessed their own local emblems —the green pine tree found favor in Massachusetts—provincial Americans shared with the mother country the Union Jack and the Meteor Flag and, like Englishmen across the seas, regarded these as emblems of loyalty. Nothing was more natural than for the colonists to make use of the British flags during the pre-Revolutionary contests with the king and parliament. At the same time, new emblems of colonial unity in the struggles for American rights emerged. The rattlesnake design with the famous caption DON'T TREAD ON ME was one; the white flag with a green tree and the motto AN APPEAL TO HEAVEN was another.

Washington displayed for the first time on January 1, 1776, the Great Union flag which suggested the double loyalties of a period

[16] Stephen C. Carpenter, *Select American Speeches* (Philadelphia, 1815), II, 76.
[17] The best brief account is Milo M. Quaife, *The Flag of the United States* (New York, 1942).

of hesitation and determination. The traditional crosses of St. Andrew and St. George in the corner-field symbolized loyalty to the crown, and the thirteen red and white stripes stood for colonial union. Used in the infant navy and over forts and barracks ashore, the Great Union flag was neither flown on the field of battle nor adopted by Congress. Only on June 14, 1777, by a simple resolution of twenty-nine words, did Congress create a truly American flag by substituting thirteen stars for the crosses in the Great Union flag. Thus by one simple change the Stars and Stripes was created. But the new flag was intended for use in the navy; the armies con- tinued to fly their several regimental emblems. So vague was knowl- edge about the new marine flag that a year and a half after the adoption of the flag resolution by Congress, our emissaries abroad were unable to give an accurate description of the Stars and Stripes.

As late as 1793, discussions in Congress over altering the Stars and Stripes indicate that the emblem had not yet come to be re- garded with any reverence or even as having any particular sig- nificance. It was decided, in spite of the plain indication that many new states were bound to be created out of the western domain, to add two stripes to the original thirteen in honor of the admission of Kentucky and Vermont. Thus it was that a banner of fifteen stripes remained the national emblem for almost a quarter of a century. In 1818 it was apparent that the flag could not well sub- mit to an indefinite multiplication of its stripes, and the thirteen original ones were restored at the same time that provision was made for increasing the stars as new states entered the Union. Only in 1834 did the army adopt the Stars and Stripes as its emblem; not until the War with Mexico did American soldiers fight in the field under its colors.

The maritime function of the early Stars and Stripes was long associated in the minds of seafaring New England with the power to protect commerce. This is well illustrated by the comments that Josiah Quincy of Boston made in Congress in 1812. The flag is "talked about as though there were something mystical in its very nature," Quincy asserted, "as though a rag, with certain stripes and stars upon it, tied to a stick and called a flag, was a wizard's wand,

and entailed security on every thing under it or within its sphere. There is nothing like all this in the nature of the thing. A flag is the evidence of power. A land flag is the evidence of land power. A maritime flag is the evidence of maritime power. You have a piece of bunting upon a staff, and call it a flag; but if you have no maritime power to maintain it, you have a name and no reality; you have the shadow without the substance; you have the sign of a flag, but in truth *you have no flag.*" [18] True though this was, the flag did gradually come to symbolize not only the power which accrued to the nation but loyalty to, reverence for, and love of the nation.

The story of the growth of that symbolism has never been told, nor can it be more than roughly outlined here. In the War of 1812, the first authenticated elevation of the flag over a schoolhouse took place at Catamount Hill, Massachusetts; and, though the custom did not become general until the Civil War, the practice grew with the intervening years. As it grew, the national banner became associated in the minds and hearts of children with the nation itself. Sometimes a dramatic episode, crystallized in song or music, sped the process. Such was the outcome of the emotions felt near Baltimore in the War of 1812 when Francis Scott Key rejoiced to see the Star-Spangled Banner still floating triumphantly in the rockets' red glare that lighted up Fort McHenry. The song only slowly won the affections of the people, but in expressing the emotions of indignation at the spectacle of armed invasion of the homeland, it nourished loyalty to the nation. During the Civil War it became the unofficial national anthem.

Others contributed to the process by which the flag came to symbolize the nation and to evoke sentiments of love and loyalty. Joseph Rodman Drake's spirited anthem, *The American Flag,* which first appeared in the New York *Evening Post* in 1819, found a place in patriotic anthologies and school readers. The precedents thus set were followed by Oliver Wendell Holmes, by Julia Ward Howe, and by John Greenleaf Whittier, to mention only a few of the poets who apostrophized the Stars and Stripes.

[18] Josiah Quincy, *Speeches Delivered in the Congress of the United States, 1805–1813,* ed. by Edmund Quincy (Boston, 1874), p. 309.

The flag did not stand alone as a symbol of patriotism. Just as religion develops many rituals and symbols, so does nationalism. The Liberty Bell in Philadelphia mourned the passing of the last signer of the Declaration in 1832 when Charles Carroll was laid to rest; two years later, it tolled for the death of Lafayette. On July 8, 1835, the fifty-ninth anniversary of the day when it had proclaimed the nation's independence, it cracked—symbolically, some feared, for it was tolling the death of Chief Justice Marshall, the great bulwark of nationalism. In time, the Liberty Bell came to be so honored that men took off their hats in its presence and old and young alike reverenced it as no other bell in all the world has been reverenced.

National monuments never became so enshrined in the American heart, never symbolized in the same way loyalty to the nation. The erection of these was largely the work of a few devoted men and women bent on preserving the memory of the nation's heroes in the interest of promoting patriotism. The first great monument —that of Bunker Hill—was completed in 1843 and occasioned one of Daniel Webster's greatest patriotic orations.[19] Difficult though the task of collecting funds had been, that of bringing the Washington Monument in the federal capital to completion was even greater. When in 1848 the cornerstone was laid, the orator of the day took pride in announcing the contribution from every corner in the Union of two hundred and fifty thousand dollars. But zeal lagged, and on the eve of the Civil War the promoters painfully confessed that lack of interest necessitated indefinite postponement of the operations. Only in 1884 was the task finished.[20]

Meantime the Mount Vernon Ladies' Association was rescuing Washington's home from neglect and converting it into a national shrine—a precedent for scores of similar undertakings elsewhere. The hope of the promoters was that such memorials would inspire those who contemplated them with patriotic devotion. No one can say that such hopes were altogether vain. Few, however, would

[19] George E. Ellis, *The Bunker Hill Battle and Monument* (Boston, 1844), gives the main facts.
[20] The best account is Frederick L. Harvey, *History of the Washington National Monument* (Washington, 1902).

claim results at all commensurate with the hopes that fostered the monument-making, which at length came to be established on a habitual basis.

Students of nationalism have frequently compared the religious feast and fast days of the Christian calendar with national festivals and holidays. Of these, America has had her full share, but, like nationalism itself, their growth was gradual and faltering. Even before Washington's death his birthday was frequently commemorated, and after the plethora of orations which marked his funeral, it was not unnatural for the patriotic association to become almost institutionalized by the observance of his birthday with appropriate orations and other exercises. Before the Civil War the twenty-second of February was, apart from the Fourth of July, the only genuinely national holiday.

Thanksgiving Day grew out of the Puritan habit of designating various days as special religious occasions for expressing appreciation to the Deity for general and special blessings.[21] There was no single day universally observed, and only gradually did the custom develop of associating a particular day with the traditional Pilgrim feast described by Governor William Bradford in his *History of Plimoth Plantation*. By sheer accident or else for some reason deemed practical, President Washington proclaimed Thursday, November 29, 1789, as a special day for Americans to give thanks for having at last achieved a new and firmer union. Until the Civil War only two other presidents, John Adams and James Madison, appointed thanksgiving days, and these fell in April, May, and September. Even in New England there was no single autumn day designated annually as Thanksgiving Day: the states observed different days, and these varied from year to year.

One person deserves the chief credit for the establishment of Thanksgiving Day as a national festival. In 1846, Sarah Josepha Hale, editor of *Godey's Lady's Book*, initiated a campaign for a truly national Thanksgiving Day. "There is a deep moral influence in these periodical seasons of rejoicing," she wrote, "in which whole

21 W. deLoss Love, *The Fast and Thanksgiving Days of New England* (Boston and New York, 1895), is a standard account.

communities participate. They bring out . . . the best sympathies in our nation." Year after year she wrote impassioned editorials in the nationally read magazine; she wrote thousands of letters to all the state governors, to members of Congress, to presidents, urging them not merely to revive an old custom but to create a focus of loyalty to the nation by reminding the American people of a common, heroic past. "If every State would join in Union Thanksgiving on the twenty-fourth of this month," she wrote in November, 1859, "would it not be a renewed pledge of love and loyalty to the Constitution of the United States?" [22]

The Southern states were suspicious of any Yankee holiday, and individualistic Vermont wanted to give thanks on her own particular day. Hence the crusade met with only partial success. But in the midst of the Civil War Mrs. Hale succeeded in persuading President Lincoln to proclaim the first national Thanksgiving.

The significance of the event was not lost in thoughtful discussions. "Today, for the first time," the Reverend M. A. De Wolfe Howe noted in a sermon at Philadelphia, "the nation has forgotten, or ceased to object, that the Puritan instituted this solemnity." Overlooking for the moment the Confederacy, Howe went on to say that sectional lines "have been wondrously obliterated." [23] In any case, Lincoln's request for special thanks to God for the preservation of the Union captured many an imagination. The last Thursday in November came, with one or two exceptions, to be proclaimed henceforth as a national holiday. School children listened to Pilgrim lore, ministers preached special sermons associating religion and patriotism in the traditional manner, and the appropriate dinner became a national institution.

Thanksgiving Day, with its New England overtones and its relatively late appearance, has always been a minor national festival at least in comparison with the "nation's birthday." Independence, as a matter of fact, was actually agreed upon July 2, 1776. Writing

[22] Sarah J. Hale, *Fruits of American Life* (Philadelphia, 1835), p. 209; see also Ruth Finley, *The Lady of Godey's, Sarah J. Hale* (Philadelphia, 1931), p. 199.
[23] M. A. De Wolfe Howe, *Loyalty to the American Republic: A Discourse in St. Luke's Church, Nov. 26, 1863* (Philadelphia, 1863), p. 5.

to his wife the next day, John Adams commented: "The day is past. The second day of July, 1776, will be a memorable epoch in the history of America. I am apt to believe that it will be celebrated by succeeding generations as the great anniversary festival. It ought to be commemorated, as the *Day of Deliverance*, by solemn acts of devotion to God Almighty. It ought to be solemnized with pomp and parade, with shows, games, sports, guns, bells, bonfires, and illuminations, from one end of the continent to the other, from this day forward, forever more." [24] It was not to be this day; nor was it July 8, when the Declaration was first read publicly at Philadelphia, amid considerable rejoicing; nor yet August 2, when the members of Congress signed the document. It was rather July Fourth, the day that Congress adopted the Declaration. The following year on that very day Philadelphia Quakers lodged complaints over the windows broken in the midst of much festivity, which included music furnished by the Hessian band! In Boston the Fourth of July became an official holiday in 1783. About the same time it became the general custom to celebrate that day.

The recreational functions of the Fourth of July need not detain us—the public feasting, the cannon and firecrackers, the militia reviews, the picturesque parades, the indispensable barbecues, the bunting and display of flags. Everywhere the Declaration was read; everywhere, that is, save on a relatively few occasions when New England Federalists took exception to the Jeffersonian emphasis on the natural rights philosophy. The day was not without its headaches, its lawlessness, even its fatalities. In 1821 Thurlow Weed rebuked New York City for inadequate fervor and, on learning that the police were to arrest anyone for starting a bonfire, applied a match to a tar barrel in his dooryard as a protest against what he deemed to be modern degeneracy! [25] At least until the eve of the Civil War, when sectional antagonisms sounded with tragic overtones, Southerners celebrated the day with no less emphasis on patriotism and national zeal than Northerners, albeit they took oc-

[24] John Adams, *Works*, ed. by Charles Francis Adams (Boston, 1854), IX, 420.
[25] Thurlow Weed Barnes, *Memoir of Thurlow Weed* (Boston, 1884), p. 28.

casion to stress the dangers to the spirit of '76 which they saw in the growing consolidation of federal power.[26]

As Americans marched westward they took the Fourth with them. At Indianapolis in 1822 the single Revolutionary veteran was the object of much to-do, and the later disclosure that he had been a Hessian soldier occasioned good-natured mirth. There being no flag at hand, old Mrs. Ames supplied one with the help of a white sheet and a pair of blue breeches and some red flannels. In the far Northwest, Captain Ingraham celebrated the day in 1791 by roasting a seventy-pound pig, hoisting the colors, firing a salute, and drinking the president's health. Lewis and Clark, a few years later, made merry with "a sumptuous dinner of fat saddles of venison." In 1832, Captain John Wyeth had to satisfy his thirst with cold water; he fared better two years later, when there was abundant liquor; his men drank too much for the peace of his camp, and he himself indulged in a "pretty hearty spree." On their arrival in the Oregon country, Mr. and Mrs. Marcus Whitman preferred to kneel down and, with Bible and flag, dedicate the land as "the home of American mothers and the church of Christ." [27]

Far away in London and in the capitals of the Continent, small groups of Americans assembled to express their loyalty to the nation by merrymaking and by appropriate exercises.[28]

Although in the first decade of the new century political rivalries in New England were so keen that in some instances Federalists and Jeffersonians had rival celebrations, and although elsewhere special groups, the antislavery men, the temperance people, and the artisans sometimes tried to capture the day for their own ends,[29]

[26] This statement is based on an investigation of reports of the Fourth of July in a sampling of the Southern press. See, for example, the Augusta Chronicle and Gazette, July 7, 1798; Columbian Museum and Savannah Advertiser, July 8, 1800; Georgia Express, July 8, 1809; Charleston Mercury, July 4, 1855; Charleston Daily Courier, July 4, 1855.

[27] Washington Historical Quarterly, IV (July, 1913), 163–181.

[28] For examples, see Orie W. Long, Literary Pioneers; Early American Explorers of European Culture (Cambridge, Mass., 1935), pp. 124–125.

[29] See Charles Warren, Jacobin and Junto; or Early American Politics as Viewed in the Diary of Dr. Nathaniel Ames, 1758–1822 (Cambridge, Mass., 1931), p. 185; Abraham Bishop, An Oration on the Extent and Power of Po-

by and large the Fourth brought together Americans without reference to their differences. The Fourth of July, Edward Everett declared in 1835, was a splendid occasion for assembling Americans, without respect to party, as members of one common family.[30] In Washington, in 1851, Daniel Webster put into felicitous words what was still essentially true in spite of the late national crisis. "This anniversary animates, and gladdens, and unites all American hearts," he said. "On other days of the year we may be party men, indulging in controversies, more or less important to the public good . . . but today we are Americans all; and nothing but Americans." [31] As late as 1858, when Southern orators were declaring that it might be necessary to set up for themselves in order to preserve the true meaning of the day, Rufus Choate preserved the conventions by referring to it as "our great national love feast." [32] About the same time Abraham Lincoln, in debating with Douglas, told his listeners that the day should remind all Americans of all the good in the Declaration, that it should make everyone feel more attached to the others and to the country.[33]

Such sentiments, even when due allowance is made for the fact that they did not altogether square with realities, certainly contained some part of truth. "The Fourth of July! What magical sounds to an American ear! What associations do they not awaken of hard fought battle-days and nights of danger, toil, privation!" wrote an American resident in London in 1827.[34] In recalling memories of Independence Day, Dr. Thomas Nichols much later commented, as scores of other writers had done, on the meaning

litical Delusion (New Haven, 1800), p. 46; Jonathan Chapman, An Oration Delivered before the Whigs of Bristol County, at Taunton, July 4, 1839 (Taunton, 1839), pp. 7 ff.; Beloit (Wis.) Journal, June 29, 1848; The Man, July 4, 1834.
[30] Edward Everett, Oration Delivered on the Fourth of July, 1835 (Boston, 1835), p. 8.
[31] Daniel Webster, Address at the Laying of the Corner Stone of the Addition to the Capitol, July 4, 1851 (Washington, 1851), p. 7.
[32] Samuel G. Brown, ed., The Works of Rufus Choate (Boston, 1862), II, 416.
[33] Abraham Lincoln, Complete Works. ed. by John G. Nicolay and John Hay (New York, 1894), I, 258.
[34] American Sketches; by a Native of the United States (London, 1827), p. 95.

of the day to sensitive and imaginative young Americans. "We had no doubt that ours was the freest, most enlightened, and happiest country in the world; and, in spite of the envy of tyrants, we felt sure that all the rest of mankind would soon be of the same opinion, and only too glad to follow our example." [35] Even the thoughtful men who resented the partisan harangues, the repetition of stale commonplaces, the empty declamations, often believed with Jonathan Chapman of Taunton, Massachusetts, that the day did remind Americans of their duty and obligation to preserve the nation, to resolve with freshened enthusiasm that henceforth, at least, fewer should say that the day was more honored in the breach than in the observance.[36]

An examination of hundreds of Fourth of July orations delivered in the first eight decades of the Republic reveals a fairly common pattern of thought and feeling which, even when one makes allowances for rhetoric, no doubt both expressed and in some degree promoted loyalty to the nation. The typical oration began with a recital of American history in the colonial era and traced the hand of God at every point, emphasized the love of liberty of the early Americans, described the events leading up to the Revolution with considerable animus against the British, glorified the heroism of the struggle for independence, expressed reverence for the Revolutionary leaders, urged the importance of attacking existing problems in their spirit, took pride in the amazing material and social progress of the country, and expressed loyalty to the nation and faith in its future. Classical metaphors and Biblical quotations and embroidered figures of speech made the Fourth of July orations masterpieces of patriotic oratory according to the canons of the day.

In short, the Independence Day oration, for all its bombast and platitudes, epitomized the whole pattern of American patriotic

[35] Thomas L. Nichols, *Forty Years of American Life* (2d ed., London, 1874), pp. 20–23.
[36] Chapman, *loc. cit.*; Charles W. Upham, *Oration, Delivered at the Request of the City Authorities of Salem, July 4, 1842* (Salem, 1842), p. 6, and John Neal, *Our Country: An Address Delivered before the Alumni of Waterville College* (Portland, 1832), p. 30.

thought and feeling. Even when it was quickly forgotten, even when in their daily lives the men who had delivered it and the men who had listened to it forthwith indulged in profitmaking in public office, in outsmarting the government, in defying the national laws, in laboring for the advantage of state, section, and class, the Fourth of July oration was still an invitation to patriotism, still an inspiration for loyalty to the nation.

No symbol brought home to the American people so graphically their collective idiosyncrasies and virtues as Yankee Doodle and Brother Jonathan.[37] The origin of what was at first a mere good-natured and mildly derisive nickname for the Yankee as the American type is shrouded in obscure legends. It seems likely that British troops referred to colonial New Englanders as Yankee Doodle. In any case sometime during the Revolution loyalists called the patriots collectively Yankee Doodle, implying a shrewd, rustic fellow; and Yankee Doodle lived on, not as a true national symbol, but as the symbol of the New Englander whose type did gradually expand into an all but national figure. Certainly the Yankee Doodle concept contributed to the growth of Brother Jonathan, the first national symbol of the American people. Brother Jonathan was again the derisive label that loyalists attached to patriots during the Revolution. From that day in 1787 when Royall Tyler's play, The Contrast, first presented Brother Jonathan as the symbol of the triumphant American democracy, a crude, naïve, simple fellow, but withal shrewd and able to look out for himself, the American stage for decade after decade familiarized people with a type in which they readily recognized themselves.

No one can now say just how it happened that Brother Jonathan, the double-jointed, broad-footed, awkward fellow with ever so much good-natured Yankee cunning, became metamorphosed into Uncle Sam. Legend has made the prototype of Uncle Sam one Sam Wilson of Troy, a purveyor of supplies to troops in the War of 1812. It is now fairly well established that the sobriquet

[37] The best studies are those of Albert Matthews, "Brother Jonathan" in the Colonial Society of Massachusetts, Transactions, January, 1901, pp. 94–119, and "Uncle Sam," American Antiquarian Society, Proceedings, n.s. XIX (April 15, 1908), 21–65.

Uncle Sam, as a designation for the federal government, first appeared in the Troy *Post* on September 7, 1813, and that the nickname enjoyed considerable local usage in the anti-war papers, always with somewhat derisive overtones.

Certainly Uncle Sam did not at once come into general currency throughout the whole land. In his *Letters from the South* (1817) James K. Paulding, the Knickerbocker littérateur, referred to Uncle Sam as a generous, good-hearted old fellow, hospitable to all comers. A few years later the editor of *Niles' Weekly Register* in Baltimore identified Uncle Sam with all that kept the wheels of the federal government in operation, and a few years later Ann Royal reported that government employees in Washington frequently remarked, "I work for Uncle Sam." The first known cartoon, which appeared in the New York *Lantern* in 1853, reveals the metamorphosis of Brother Jonathan into Uncle Sam. Not until the Civil War did the figure we know become generally familiar to Americans through the cartoons of Thomas Nast.

By the time that national unity was being tested in civil war, the Uncle Sam symbol conveyed a very definite cluster of qualities expressive of both the American people in their collective capacity and of their government: a hearty, fraternal impulsiveness, an instinctive, rustic wisdom, an ability to laugh at one's own expense, tolerance, a readiness to listen patiently to all sorts of complaints, the will to see things through, the determination to look after soldiers and sailors, widows and orphans. Uncle Sam, while primarily the symbol of the federal government, also resembled the qualities ascribed to the American people, or at least to the old Yankee stock: courage, thrift, simplicity, an ability to carry more than a fair share of the load, a capacity to labor and to make lightning decisions, and an optimism not to be floored.

Even when special-interest groups attempted to identify their particular cause with the Uncle Sam symbol, there was a sort of subtle, stubborn resistance on the part of the American people. Sooner or later the type reemerged as the paternal figure who looked good-naturedly on his quarreling children with a live-and-let-live air, assuming that through competition the best youngster would win out, but always having an ultimate tough core that withstood sectional and class interests when they pushed their objectives so far that those of others were jeopardized. Such a symbol of the national type, of the federal government, and in a sense, of the nation itself, must have played a significant role in personalizing the nation as an object of affection and loyalty. Uncle Sam came in due time to have no rivals. Brother Jonathan disappeared and Liberty, even after she was enshrined in the statue in New York harbor, was too abstract, too impersonal, too aloof in didactic idealism ever to win the place in the American heart that Uncle Sam enjoyed. Uncle Sam had won his place in American affections, and especially in times of crisis he was the one to whom Americans turned as the symbol of their strength and their hope for the future.

VI: THE TESTING OF LOYALTY

How long, Columbians dear will ye complain
Of these curst insults on the open main?
In timid sloth shall injur'd brav'ry sleep?
Awake! awake! the voice of nature cries—
Awake to glory and to vengeance rise!
To arms! to arms! ye bold in giant bands!
'Tis Heaven'd inspired, 'tis God himself commands,
Save human nature from such deadly harms,
By force of reason or by force of arms!

DAVID HUMPHREYS, 1786

Oh Beautiful! my country! ours once more!
Smoothing thy gold of war-dishevelled hair
O'er such sweet brows as never others wore.

.   .   .

What words divine of lover or of poet
Could tell our love and make thee know it?
Among the Nations bright beyond compare
What were our lives without thee?
What all our lives to save thee?
We reck not that we gave thee,
We will not dare to doubt thee,
But ask whatever else, and we will dare!

JAMES RUSSELL LOWELL, 1865

IN THE PUBLIC MIND it is often hard to say whether a specific action is loyal or disloyal. Men are prone to confuse their private interest and larger patriotism, and the line between the two spheres is hazy. Certain situations, however, have provided fairly clear-cut tests. Of these, residence abroad has affected throughout our history a relatively small but highly articulate fraction of the population.

To absence from the homeland some responded in one way, some in another. A goodly number of missionaries found that their country became all the more dear to them as the years passed. Letters and reminiscences reveal the nostalgia with which the Fourth of July was celebrated or with which the visit home was anticipated. It was not unusual for Americans traveling abroad to be thrilled at seeing the Stars and Stripes or a Yankee ship or even a Connecticut-made machine or a bale of cotton. "If every American will look into himself at the moment he is glowing with patriotism," remarked Harriet Martineau, the brilliant English visitor, "he will find his sectional prejudices melted away and gone for the season. The Americans feel this in their travels abroad, when their country is attacked. They yearn toward the remotest dwellers in their country as if they were the nearest and dearest. Would they would always feel thus at home!" [1]

Other Americans who once scorned their native land or disparaged it learned to love it while living across the seas. Thus the historian, John Lothrop Motley, who had entertained a low opinion of his country, returned after a few years to confess to the man who had once taken him to task for his attitude: "You were all right; I was all wrong. It *is* a country worth dying for; better still, worth living and working for to make it all it can be." [2] It was something like this that Emerson had in mind when he remarked that "we go to Europe to be Americanized."

On the other hand, Americans, few in number in the Jacksonian era but increasing toward the turn of the last century, have also chosen to repudiate the land of their birth for some other country.

[1] Harriet Martineau, *Society in America* (New York, 1837), I, 186.
[2] Wendell Phillips, *Speeches, Addresses and Lectures, Second Series* (Boston, 1891), pp. 347–348.

Conscious decisions to reject American nationality have been, to be sure, relatively infrequent. On the contrary, America has provided her people with far more opportunities than the Old World, a fact to which the immense flood of immigrants has, of course, borne witness.

Expatriation, the reverse of immigration, has represented a criticism of American civilization, of America itself. Until almost our own day some have continued to seek the richer opportunities in the arts provided by the Old World. Some have become enamored of the picturesqueness of European life, more satisfying to their minds than the rawness and monotony in America. Whatever their reasons for leaving the United States, others have regarded it as the highest of compliments to be taken for Britishers.[3] In the latter part of the nineteenth century, when the snobbishness of those-on-the-make became marked, an ever larger number sought European titles by marriage or purchase or both. By no means all the expatriates were able completely to forget America or to identify themselves to their satisfaction with the land of their adoption: witness the pictures Henry James drew of uprooted and sterile American expatriates. In any case, however, their expatriation was objective evidence of a willingness to subordinate any loyalty they felt for America to other values, to another culture.[4]

Attitudes toward Europeans who emigrated to America and toward the much smaller number of men and women who abandoned the United States for the Old World have been influenced both by interest and ideals. Being a nation of newcomers and willing through most of her history to receive immigrants, America found it natural and advantageous to urge European governments to renounce the doctrine of perpetual allegiance which they stubbornly cherished. The prevailing assumption that all individuals are free to seek life, liberty, and happiness wherever these can be found likewise tended to reinforce the idea that free choice is an

[3] Francis J. Grund, *Aristocracy in America* (London, 1839), I, 114.
[4] See Henry James, *William Wetmore Story and His Friends* (Boston, 1903), I, 296, 298; Henry James, *Charles W. Eliot* (Boston and New York, 1930), I, 149; and Charles R. Leslie, *Autobiographical Memoir* (London, 1860), I, 122, 127, for typical comments on expatriation.

essential element in citizenship and in national loyalty. In other words, American citizenship has been regarded as a privilege, not as an imperative. In view of the American criticism of European governments for their reluctance to abandon the doctrine of the perpetual allegiance of emigrants, logic and consistency suggested that the federal government grant freely the right of expatriation to those citizens who abandoned the United States for Europe. In practice the way was often smoothed for the relatively small number of Americans who chose to forego the blessings of their native land. The federal government did not, however, explicitly recognize until 1907 the right of an American citizen to renounce his citizenship.[5]

The number of Americans guilty of overt treason has likewise been very small. In recognizing the right of the government to protect itself against treason the Constitution took care to prevent treason trials from becoming, as they often had become in England, political weapons by which officials could virtually outlaw criticism of their acts. The first test came in 1794 when ringleaders in the Whiskey Rebellion were declared guilty of treason and then pardoned. The precedent was followed later in Northampton County, Pennsylvania, when John Fries was set free after a court had convicted him of treason. The most sensational charge of treason was, of course, that which President Jefferson brought against his political foe, Aaron Burr. Whatever Chief Justice Marshall's motives as presiding judge may have been—there was certainly no friendship between him and Jefferson—he so interpreted the constitutional definition of treason that conviction in subsequent cases was not easy. President Jackson may have had that in mind when he dropped his threat to indict South Carolina's leaders in the nullification movement for treason. Compromise through political action settled the issue, at least for the time.

In the midst of the Civil War, Congress passed more stringent treason acts, but little was done to enforce them even though many

---

[5] The best accounts are I-Mien Tsiang, *The Question of Expatriation in America Prior to 1907* (Baltimore, 1942) and Richard Flournoy, *The Nationality Act of 1940* (New York, 1941).

felt that the occasion warranted drastic action. The "rebellion" and the widespread defeatism in the North nevertheless brought home to countless Americans the meaning of treason. The consciousness of treason, and its negation of patriotism, also owed much to Edward Everett Hale's "The Man without a Country," a stirring fictional account of Philip Nolan—the American whose expressed wish that he might never hear again the name "The United States" brought him such bitter suffering.

Since wars in one way or another involve the whole population, they have been highly significant tests of national loyalty. The troubled decade before the War of 1812 provided constant reminders that America might be pulled into the European maelstrom. In every section, leaders associated the military spirit, the necessity of defense, and the actualities of war with patriotism. Sermon after sermon testified to the close tie-up between religion and warlike patriotism. "In contending for our liberties," declared the Reverend Abiel Holmes in 1795, "He *taught our hands to war*, and our *fingers to fight*." [6] The common prejudice against a standing army only heightened the praise bestowed on the militia, which was generally deemed sufficient both to put down domestic revolts and to crush any invader.[7] Veterans of the Revolution at the meetings of the Society of the Cincinnati identified the military virtues with patriotism and insisted that the precarious world situation called for vigorous defense. Thus David Humphreys in 1804, at Hartford, declared that "to inspire our nation with military ardour and enthusiasm appears essential to our existence. Effeminacy, cowardice, and dissension," he went on, "in a country marked for invasion by its weakness, leaves everything to be apprehended from aggression." [8]

President Jefferson in trying to avoid war through economic pres-

[6] Abiel Holmes, *Sermon on the Freedom and Happiness of America* (Boston, 1795), p. 25.
[7] Examples are Peter Thatcher, *Sermon, Preached before the Ancient and Honorable Artillery Company, June 3, 1795* (Boston, 1795); Thomas Welsh, *An Oration, Delivered in Boston on March 5, 1783* (Boston, 1783); and Barnard Whitman, *National Defense, A Discourse* (Boston, 1829).
[8] David Humphreys, *A Valedictory Discourse, Delivered before the Cincinnati of Connecticut, in Hartford, July 4, 1804* (Boston, 1804), p. 21.

sure on the European belligerents looked on his course as one singularly patriotic, designed to preserve peace and thus to advance the national interest. His foes regarded it as cowardly subordination of American interests to false pacifism. Contrary to a common impression, this attitude was by no means confined to New England. It was, in fact, especially marked at Charleston, South Carolina, a commercial city dominated at that time by Federalists. In view of Charleston's subsequent role in nullification and secession, generally regarded as highly antithetical to national loyalty, it may be well to choose from that city, which regarded itself as patriotic, illustrations of opposition to Jefferson.

By tolerating French and British interference with our shipping, we had, according to the Charleston *Courier*, degraded ourselves until we were the laughingstock of the world. The French had made the Chesapeake a nest of pirates, the British had persisted in swooping down on American ships and pressing American sailors into the Royal Navy. "Are these the blessings for which our fathers fought? . . . Forbid it, Heaven!" [9] A Palmetto orator declared that it was high time to rescue from oblivion the services and virtues of the fathers. "If the time should ever come, when our rights shall compromise our interest, when the Spirit of '76 shall become a spirit of calculation, when our commerce shall be the prey of picaroons, and our name be disregarded among nations, we shall have mournfully degenerated. The heroes of the Revolution will have toiled in vain, our liberties will be tamely sacrificed, and America become again a vassal province." [10] The Charleston *Courier* voiced a widespread sentiment in demanding immediate and thorough preparation for war.[11]

New England Federalists joined hands with their South Carolina brethren in denouncing the peace policy of Jefferson. Josiah Quincy of Boston put the matter bluntly in his excoriation of the embargo in 1808:

[9] Charleston *Courier*, July 4, 1807.
[10] Hext M'Call, *An Oration, Delivered in St. Michael's Church, on the Fourth of July, 1810* (Charleston, 1810), p. 12. See also Benjamin Markley, *An Oration Delivered on the Fourth of July, 1811* (Charleston, 1811), pp. 8, 22–23.
[11] Charleston *Courier*, July 4, 1808.

Sir, you call upon patriotism for sacrifice to which it is unequal; and require its operation in a way in which that passion cannot long subsist. Patriotism is a great comfort to men in the interior, to the farmer and the planter, who are denied a market by your laws, whose local situation is such that they can neither sell their produce, nor scarcely give it away, and who are made to believe that their privations will ultimately redound to the benefit of their country. But on the seaboard, where men feel not only their annual profit, but their whole capital perishing, where they know the utter inefficacy of your laws to coerce foreign nations, and their utter futility as a means of saving our own property; to such laws in such a situation, patriotism is, to say the least, a very inactive assistant. You cannot lay a man upon a rack and crack his muscles, by a slow torment, and call patriotism to soothe the sufferer.[12]

Thus boldly was the doctrine avowed that patriotism had its limitations, that there are material sacrifices too great to be made even in the name of national loyalty. Americans had become accustomed to the idea that life might and must be forfeited for country; they were a long way from believing that property might and should be sacrificed.

Despite the deep gulf between those who favored and those who opposed the Jeffersonian embargo as a means of avoiding war, the dramatic firing of the British man-of-war *Leopard* on the *Chesapeake* off the Maryland shore aroused the whole nation to a high pitch of indignation. Had Jefferson so chosen, he might have had a united country back of a declaration of war. Henry Adams has probably not exaggerated in writing that "for the first time in their history the people of the United States had learned, in June, 1807, the feeling of true national emotion." [13] Yet, when the crisis was passed, the old cleavages again stood starkly naked.

At last, thanks to a variety of factors—the appetite of Westerners for expansion into the Floridas and Canada important among them—war was declared amid much patriotic fervor on the part

[12] Edmund Quincy, ed., *Speeches Delivered by Josiah Quincy in the Congress of the United States* (Boston, 1874), pp. 67–68.
[13] Henry Adams, *History of the United States* (New York, 1890), IV, 27.

of the "War Hawks" from beyond the Alleghenies. Yet it was fought by a divided people. Daniel Webster, destined to become the great nationalist, now from the floor of Congress decried the war and adamantly set himself against conscription proposals. New England governors refused to allow militia to cross state boundaries, even when the foe was at the door and when military defeat seemed in the immediate offing. It is enough to call attention to the military disasters of the war itself. National loyalty seemed to have reached a new low.

Yet the war brought forth notable expressions of patriotism, especially in the West and South. In view of the tendency of Americans to label antebellum Southerners as antinationalists, it may be well to draw illustrations from below the Mason and Dixon line. "We are at war now," declared somewhat testily a Charlestonian, "and united—practically. One little speck alone is seen on our otherwise unclouded horizon. The wily serpent of discussion has stolen into the cradle of the Revolution [Massachusetts]. But fear not, it contains an infant Hercules. Soon will the sounds arouse him from his slumbers, and the strangled monster writhe his folds in vain." [14] Other Carolinians expressed sentiments of high national loyalty. One spoke thus forthrightly: "When the great body of the country stands in need of the contributory aid of every citizen, to throw off one's national character is a desertion of his country—a pusillanimous compliance with selfish and interested dictates, and not the just and honorable exercise of a natural right." [15]

Robert Y. Hayne, to become in time the leader of the antinationalists, now took to task a member of the senate of Massachusetts for declaring he was ready to exchange the American government for the British constitution, monarchy and all. "Can that war be unjust," Hayne asked of the New England Federalists, "which was waged for the preservation of our commerce, the honor of our flag, and the liberty of the citizen? They purchased with their blood the independence of their country, and shall we surrender it with-

[14] William Johnson, *An Oration, Delivered in St. Philip's Church . . . by Appointment of the '76 Association* (Charleston, 1813), p. 17.
[15] Joshua W. Toomer, *An Oration, Delivered in St. Michael's Church, on Monday, the Fourth of July, 1814* (Charleston, 1814), p. 17.

out a struggle?" [16] Thus in the several regions expressions of patriotism and of loyalty to national policy shifted with changing interests and situations.

Despite the cold-shouldering of the war, despite the sectionally conscious and anti-war Hartford Convention, the struggle was hardly over when orators were proclaiming its contributions to the unification of the nation and to the growth of patriotism. In the words of a South Carolinian, the war as a time of danger was not without its use, inasmuch as it served "to develop the real talent and patriotism of the country, test the sincerity of many a clamorous partisan, and elect from obscurity many a statesman and soldier, whose poverty was an obstacle to his advancement, or whose ambition was content with being unknown." [17] Another Charlestonian grandiloquently insisted that "the War has given strength and splendor to the chain of the Union. Every link exhibits the lustre of the diamond. Local feelings are absorbed in the proud feelings of being an American." [18]

This was not mere wishful thinking. True, the navy failed to wrest control of the seas from the enemy and America did not win at the peace negotiations its contentions concerning neutral rights. The tradition was nevertheless established that the struggle secured freedom of the seas to America as the Revolution secured freedom of the land. The war also became a concrete focus of patriotic pride. "Our navy," declared a South Carolinian in 1813, "has become the rallying point for the affections of the nation; and when men regard, esteem, and love the same great and meritorious object, from that moment they begin to regard, to esteem, and to love one another. Is there aught in which America, from New Hampshire to Orleans, is more united, than in the love and admiration of our infant navy?" [19] American naval victories were indeed long cele-

[16] Robert Y. Hayne, *An Oration, Delivered in St. Philip's Church, on Monday, the Fourth of July, 1814* (Charleston, 1814), p. 13.

[17] William Crafts, *An Oration, Delivered in St. Michael's Church on the Fourth of July, 1812* (Charleston, 1812), p. 24.

[18] Christopher R. Greene, *An Oration, Delivered in St. Michael's Church, on Tuesday, the Fourth of July, 1815* (Charleston, 1815), p. 11.

[19] J. S. Richardson, *An Oration, Delivered in St. Michael's Church, on Monday, the Fifth of July, 1813* (Charleston, 1813), p. 22.

brated. Rhymesters sang with considerable spirit of battles won, of glories achieved, of splendid memories. In taking four bulky volumes to tell in epic verse the story of American achievements in the war, Dr. Richard Emmons was only more verbose than dozens of fellow patriots.

Most of the accounts of the War of 1812 rang with a bitter Anglophobia. Of long standing, hatred of Britain was strengthened not only by memories of the second war for independence but by the harsh descriptions of America that filled the pages of English travel books. Anglophobia seasoned the programmatic pleas for cultural independence from intellectual chauvinists and the flamboyant Fourth of July oratory of the ensuing decades. It also colored the more sober thought of Americans of almost every section and class.

Such patriotic sentiments were accompanied by the triumph— for the time being—of policies long deemed nationalistic. The sometime state-rights Jeffersonians, with Calhoun in the vanguard, now came out for rechartering the Hamiltonian bank, for a protective tariff, for a standing army, for internal improvements. During a few years the Era of Good Feeling suggested that a new national unity had sprung from the recent war.

But the ebb was greater than the flow. Within half a dozen years the Missouri crisis loomed up ominously and provoked dark forecasts from statesmen. Compromise, all-important in the growth of national unity, saved the day. A new crisis nevertheless developed a few years later when South Carolina nullified a national tariff law she now regarded as hostile to plantation interests. In a spirited oration Robert Y. Hayne declared that the American Revolution had its origin, "not so much in the weight of *actual* oppression, as in the great principle, the *sacred duty*, of resistance to the exercise of unauthorized authority." The fathers, Hayne recalled, had fought against tariffs and centralization: God forbid that the Union be now dissolved, though tyranny in the new form it had assumed in Washington must be resisted—if need be to the death.[20] Denounced as traitors to the nation, the nullifiers stoutly contended that, loving their country dearly, they were rebels only against op-

[20] Robert Y. Hayne, *An Oration, Delivered in the Independent or Congregational Church, at Charleston* (Charleston, 1831), pp. 2–3.

pression, traitors only to injustice, champions only of the Constitution and the Union in all their purity.

Once compromise provided a formula, the Charleston *Courier*, in an editorial on the Fourth of July, 1832, rejoiced at the spirit of conciliation that had appeared at Washington, but confessed that ominous clouds still hovered over the horizon. "We are a united people, but not a harmonious nation." [21] The Charleston *Mercury* likewise insisted that the state-rights party had acted, as the fathers of '76 had done, not on the aggressive, but on the defensive. "Who, indeed, are the true friends of the Constitution," the *Mercury* queried, "but those who resist its infractions . . . those who would remedy the evils which threaten to dissolve it?" [22]

Such interpretations of the Revolution called forth by the nullification controversy did not, it is true, go unchallenged in the South itself. The Savannah *Georgian*, for example, insisted that the state-rights men were setting themselves against Washington, Franklin, and Madison in trying to overthrow the Constitution. "And will Georgians, citizens of one of the Old Thirteen, aid them [the state-rights party] in this? No! the light of the 4th of July will stream across their path, to remind them that Liberty was not won in a day, but was acquired by their patriotic ancestors after a seven years' struggle, after unexampled patriotism and suffering." [23]

The war with Mexico, like the second conflict with Great Britain, was fought by a divided nation. Those who opposed the war, and they were numerous, did not regard themselves as disloyal to the United States: on the contrary, they deemed the war an inexcusable, aggressive attack on a weak neighbor, designed to swell by aggrandizement the nation's already vast domain. Such opposition was by no means confined to antislavery forces in the Northeast, who foresaw with disapproval both extension of slave power as a result of conquest and relative weakening of the East in the

---

[21] Charleston *Courier*, July 4, 1832.

[22] Charleston *Mercury*, July 4, 1832.

[23] *The Georgian* (Savannah), July 3, 1834. The same views were expressed by Thomas S. Grimké, *An Oration on the Principal Duties of Americans, Delivered before the Washington Society, and Other Citizens of Charleston* (Charleston, 1833), and by other South Carolina Unionists.

Union. In Illinois, young Abraham Lincoln had no heart for the war, and said as much. Far from being united on the war as a crusade for the acquisition of slave territory, the South itself was divided, and those who opposed the war had no notion of being disloyal. Thus, Henry Gray, whose Fourth of July oration in Charleston in 1847 expressed Southern opposition to the war, called attention to the facts that our armies were bringing grief and desolation to Mexico, that in the eyes of Europe we were playing the role of a bully and that in our own eyes our achievements could give us no genuine pride. "This wretched greediness for land and for extended sway," declared the orator, "will be our ruin." [24] In opposing the war, the South Carolinian, like the hero of Lowell's *Biglow Papers*, regarded his position as truly loyal to the best interests of the nation.

Yet historians may be too prone to emphasize the opposition to the war with Mexico and the divisive effects of the quarrels over the spoils. Like the second contest with England, the Mexican War did demonstrate the ability of the nation to conduct a foreign war, and this achievement must not be underestimated as a force in building faith in the nation's power. The relatively easy victory over their southern neighbor encouraged many Americans to think that their country "could lick anything under creation." The acquisition, moreover, of a vast domain for exploitation reinforced the economics of loyalty among those eager to speculate in virgin lands or to pull up stakes and move westward. And animus toward an outside foe did, for a time, lend some cohesiveness to the varied interests within the nation.

The war itself gave specific point to an idealistic nationalism and patriotism as well. Hundreds of newspapers in the West and the South put before their readers sentiments comparable to those of the Savannah *Georgian:* "Seventy-one years have passed away, and the spirit of Liberty breathes over more than twice as many independent states and is piercing through the mountains of Mexico,

[24] Henry Gray, *An Oration, Delivered before the Fourth of July Association, on the Fifth of July, 1847* (Charleston, 1847), pp. 9–10. See also Nelson Mitchell, *An Oration, Delivered before the Fourth of July Association* (Charleston, 1849), p. 25.

to teach another people the prowess of American arms—the puri-
fying progress of civil and religious liberty." [25] Compilers brought
together patriotic songs inspired by the war, songs expressing the
same feelings the War of 1812 had evoked: the war was fought
with God's blessing; it was a contest for freedom; it was waged
against tyrants; it was in defense of the native soil which Mexico
had violated. Spirited ballads commemorated particular battles
and celebrated favored heroes. The flag, under which American
soldiers now fought for the first time, was the subject of many an
apostrophe, typical of which was this one:

Then up with our flag! Let it stream on the air!
Tho' our fathers are cold in their graves,
They had hands that could strike, they had souls that could dare,
And their sons were not born to be slaves.
UP! UP! with the BANNER, where'er it may call,
Our millions shall rally round,
And a nation of FREEMEN that moment shall fall
When its stars shall be trailed on the ground.[26]

The contest did, to be sure, call forth pacifist denunciations of
war. Against these must be set the glorifications of the appeal to
the sword. One, typical of many others, found a place in Nahum
Capen's *The Republic of the United States* (1848). Strongly
nationalistic, insisting on the strength and permanency of the union,
Capen declared that the great evils of war are insignificant from
the point of view of eternity—that most of the expenditures, after
all, enriched the people of the nation waging the war; that wars are
often the only means for advancing freedom and civilization; that
war destroys only to renovate, and that, in any case, the support of
war is a plain patriotic duty.[27] So in the minds of many men the
association between war and patriotism was strengthened.

[25] *The Georgian* (Savannah), July 5, 1847.
[26] William McCarty, *National Songs, Ballads, and Other Patriotic Poetry* (Philadelphia, 1846), p. 22.
[27] Nahum Capen, *The Republic of the United States* (Boston, 1848), pp. 37–
38.

In the years that followed the Mexican War, extremists in both North and South professed a readiness to see the nation broken up. The left-wing abolitionists, many of whom were pacifists, demanded the rupture of the Union by peaceful means. To at least some Southern fire-eaters, on the other hand, an appeal to the sword was a justifiable, perhaps a necessary instrument for the defense of Southern rights. Yet these ardent spokesmen spurned any allegation of disloyalty to the Constitution or to the Union: they even continued to speak of the American nation to which they gave the deepest loyalty. But in their eyes the essence of the American system was not a consolidated nation. It was rather the federal concept—the balance of power between sovereign states and a federal agency responsive to their will. In their minds the more rapidly growing North was threatening that system. The consolidation of the nation in the interest of one section was to them an outright betrayal of all the fathers had fought for in the Revolution.

During the heated discussions over the disposal of the territory taken from Mexico in 1848 extreme words continued to be spoken. The Charleston *Mercury* said that the crisis was at hand. "The South, for the first time, perceives the insecurity and ignominy of her situation in the Union. . . . We should don the casque and buckle the armor." [28] A Fourth of July orator made his audience feel, according to the same newspaper, that South Carolinians were "prepared to count the cost" and to "peril all" in defense of their rights under the Constitution, "if blindness and fanaticism should continue to usurp the place of reason and patriotism." [29] Another speaker demanded, "Carolinians! will you quietly and without a determined struggle allow the seal of infamy to be set upon you? Will you allow this stab to be made at the great principle of constitutional liberty, for which our fathers struggled so hard for eight long years, and not throw your whole moral weight and force as a guard against it?" [30] Other voices, it is true, were raised for the

[28] Charleston *Mercury*, July 4, 1850.
[29] *Ibid.*, July 9, 1850.
[30] William P. Miles, *An Oration Delivered before the Fourth of July Association* (Charleston, 1849), p. 15.

Union,[31] and compromise again provided a formula which permitted the storm to be weathered.

Despite continued assertions of loyalty to the nation, the extremists did not hold their peace. "The seductive dream of *national unities*," declared a Georgian in speaking of the movement to unify the European peoples under monarchical auspices, was not only preventing the success of the republican leaders across the seas; it would likewise destroy the liberties of any people. "For," he continued, "the Revolution changed Georgia from a colony bound to a *foreign* authority, into one of the sovereign commonwealths, to *whom* a central authority owes allegiance; and she has ever fought, as of right she ought, against a colonial, central, preponderating power." [32] In 1857, a Fourth of July orator declared, in proof of the loyalty of Southern rights men to the Union, that if the issue were forced on them, they would claim, as their portion, the Star-Spangled Banner; they would adopt it as their own; they would save it from apostate hands.[33]

In the acute and growing tensions, the political parties, like elastic bands, served a worthy function in holding together the discordant sections. The political party was a mere entente of local machines, but without it the Union might have been broken before the North was sufficiently united and strong to crush secession. No wonder there was alarm when the Whig party, which had attached so much verbal importance to national unity and power, began to disintegrate. But the Democratic party still provided a focus of loyalty to the national union. Speaking in Boston in 1858, Jefferson Davis of Mississippi, ardent Democrat, admitted that "the waves of sectional antagonism" were "dashing themselves against the granite patriotism of the land." Strong though the material and moral ties were that bound the sections, they were, he admitted,

[31] Charleston *Courier*, July 4, 1850; *The Daily Georgian* (Savannah), July 4, 1850; Lewis M. Ayer, *Patriotism and State Sovereignty: An Oration, Delivered before the Two Societies of South Carolina College* (Charleston, 1858), pp. 13–15.

[32] Alexander Franklin Hill, *The Glory of Georgia* (Athens, 1859), p. 18.

[33] Fleetwood Lanneau, *An Oration Delivered before the Cincinnati and the '76 Association* (Charleston, 1857), p. 6.

inadequate; the State Rights Democracy alone—the only surviving national party—could at this belated hour save the nation.[34]

Two years later that party had also been broken on the shoals of sectional conflict. The Mississippian had been right. All the voices, North and South, that were raised in the name of national loyalty and patriotism—and countless voices were indeed raised— were of no avail.[35] Some of the very men who had denounced the New Englanders of 1814 for disloyalty to the nation were now supporting disunion in the name of the fathers of '76, under the banner of American patriotism. The great test of loyalty to one, undivided nation was at last at hand.

The North was ill prepared to meet the test. The country had developed as a federation of small units, and local traditions and prejudices had left their imprint. In the late months of 1860, Northern newspapers frequently spoke of "the United States of the Confederacy" and many in both East and West opposed the war on the ground that it was occasioned and conducted by a party false to the federal conception of the Union. The East was jealous of the West, the West suspicious of the East. If nationality was a common word it often represented, as Professor Fred Shannon has insisted, an enthusiasm which could have been accurately translated into class and sectional interest. Well might George Bancroft, the historian of militantly American nationalism, call on the men of Massachusetts in the autumn of 1861 to cease being men of Massachusetts, of New England, of the North, and to be Americans instead.[36]

The fact that an untold number of Northerners failed to share the sentiments and convictions of such thoroughgoing nationalists as Bancroft was evidence that loyalty to the United States was not unstinted. All sorts of special groups cherished some loyalty above the nation. In the case of Lydia Maria Child and her fellow aboli-

[34] Dunbar Rowland, ed., *Jefferson Davis, Constitutionalist: His Letters, Papers, and Speeches* (Jackson, 1923), III, 327–329.
[35] For an example see Robert L. Dabney, *The Christian's Best Motive for Patriotism: A Sermon Preached in the College Church, Hampden Sidney, Virginia, on a Day of General Fast, November 1, 1860* (New York, 1860).
[36] New York *Tribune*, October 10, 1861.

tionists, to cite an extreme example, a nation that tolerated slavery was altogether unworthy of affection and respect. The flag itself inspired her soul with sadness. "Unless it ceases from this iniquity, I say, deliberately and solemnly, 'May the curse of God rest upon it! May it be trampled in the dust, kicked by the rebels, and spit upon by tyrants . . . When it [the United States] treats the colored people with justice and humanity, I will mount its flag in my great elm tree and I will thank you to present me with a flag for a breastpin; but, until then, I would as soon wear the rattlesnake upon my bosom as the eagle." [37] Only with the Proclamation of Emancipation did Mrs. Child throw her full support to Northern arms and the preservation of national unity.

Although the Proclamation inspired patriotism in the abolitionists, it dampened the enthusiasm for the war in countless soldiers and civilians. Many humble folk who earned their livelihood by manual labor feared that the freedmen would become economic competitors. This fear, together with the feeling that the plain people were being sacrificed by conscription in order to protect the profits of the "shoddy aristocracy," in large part explained the anti-draft riots which for three days in the midsummer of 1863 swept New York City with demonstrations against Negroes.

Soldiers' letters also expressed outright antagonism to the war once it had taken, in their eyes, the character of a struggle for abolition. "I have only nine months to serve," wrote a New York cavalryman to his sister, in the autumn of 1863; "and Uncle Sam may get all the nigger soldiers he can raise and scrape." Another New York fighter wrote, "The soldiers are down on the President's Proclamation, and our reg. is getting thinned out pretty fast by deserters . . . The soldiers swear they will never fight by the side of the damned Niggers." [38]

Other factors also diluted patriotic nationalism. In the early months of the war it was common to call attention to the barriers which material values imposed on patriotism. "Making haste to be rich has been the universal mania of our people," Charles E. Fitch

[37] Lydia Maria Child, *Letters* (New York, 1883), pp. 150–151.
[38] "War Relics and Reminiscences," David E. Cronin Manuscript Collection, New York Historical Society.

lamented. "We worshipped the Golden Calf. When the warning voice of patriotism came down from Pisgah Heights of thought into the busy haunts of commerce, bidding us take heed of the swift maelstrom of destruction, toward which we were hurrying, we have dubbed it an idiotic ebullition of fanaticism." [39] Even as he pronounced these words in that Fourth of July oration in the first year of the war, many New York businessmen were still luke-warm toward the national cause as they counted the loss of their Southern trade.

The plain truth was the nation had often been taken for granted or associated with economic advantages and opportunities. A writer in the *Continental Monthly* declared—and he was not contra-dicted—that "to one, the Nation exists that he may make wooden clocks and sell them. To another, to get good crops to market, to another, to make money in stocks." [40] As profiteering mounted, new warnings were issued in vain. "I fear," declared a Presbyterian minister in New York in 1863, that "too many frame their pre-dictions and shape their conduct from the fluctuations of the Stock Exchange, and the report of the daily bulletin." [41] What his com-ment would have been could he have heard the remark Judge Mel-lon is reported to have made to his son, James, one can only im-agine. "I had hoped my boy was going to make a smart, intelligent business man and was not such a goose as to be seduced from duty by the declamations of buncombe speeches," admonished the judge. "It is only greenhorns who enlist. You can learn nothing in the army. . . . In time you will come to understand and believe that a man may be a patriot without risking his own life or sacri-ficing his health." [42]

At the end of the war, James Russell Lowell, in praising heroism and patriotism inspired by the war, did not neglect to speak of the fortunes made in war contracts which provided soldiers with shoddy blankets and clad them in uniforms which fell apart in the first heavy rain. He did not forget to take to task "the speculators in

[39] Charles E. Fitch, *The National Problem: An Oration* (Syracuse, 1861), p. 14.
[40] *Continental Monthly*, IV (October, 1863), 602–603.
[41] William Adams, *Christian Patriotism* (New York, 1863), p. 7.
[42] Harvey O'Connor, *Mellon's Millions* (New York, 1933), p. 24.

patriotism" who had "striven to make the blood of our Martyrs the seed of wealth." [43]

The knowledge that many Americans continued to advance themselves while the fighting forces endured privation and risked their lives had an effect on the soldiers which is in some cases a matter of record. It is impossible to say how many shared the views of Samuel Budd, a New York soldier. Writing to his brother on October 25, 1863, he blurted out: "I see by your note that there is considerable patriotism in you, but if you should serve one year in the ranks of the country's defenders, your patriotism would be at a low ebb. We no longer look on it as a war for country but as a great speculation in which each one is trying to make as much as he can." [44] Nor was resentment expressed merely against profiteers. Elias Modlin, a workingman, a professed Christian, and a good neighbor who was not disillusioned about the war, wrote from Fort Pillow on March 29, 1863: "I would like to see those of my friends that are going to California: though it seems that they want to 'flee in time of trouble.' If a man is able to emigrate to California, it seems to me he might do something for the old flag." [45]

The Americans who felt as these two soldiers did were parting company with the traditional belief in the free play the state gives to the individual. Yet the idea that loyalty to the nation is tested by sacrifices was not easy to learn. That was made clear by resistance to conscription. It was equally evidenced by the attitude of many who admitted that the nation might ask men to forfeit their lives but would not concede that the same nation might require men to empty their pockets or submit to a modification of property rights.

The complexity of motives that led Americans to volunteer is abundantly illustrated in the letters of soldiers. All sorts of allowances must be made, of course, for it is not natural for men to reveal their innermost motives, even when they are aware of them. Yet the record is worth something. One soldier, Leander Stillwell of Otter Creek, Illinois, recalled that "it was simply intolerable

[43] James Russell Lowell, *Writings* (Boston and New York, 1891), V, 212.
[44] "War Relics and Reminiscences," David E. Cronin Manuscript Collection, New York Historical Society.
[45] Leonard Brown, *American Patriotism* (Des Moines, 1869), p. 341.

to think that I could stay at home, among the girls, and be pointed at by the soldier-boys as a stay-at-home-coward." [46] Letters also reveal that in some cases the need of a job explained the shouldering of arms, in others the desire to see the world. When conscription became the rule, some men served because they could not afford a substitute, others went into the army to profit from the bounties offered, and still others went in as substitutes, accepting gold to take the places of wealthier men in the ranks.

In any case, by and large, soldiers seem to have had little liking for the high patriotic verbalism of zealous civilians. They might listen, indeed, to the patriotic poems which the actor, James E. Murdoch, read to them in camp or to the words of national loyalty spoken by ardent chaplains. But among themselves they said little of such matters. As Charles Benton, a New York volunteer, reported, "whoever announces that he enlisted because he loved his country is sure to become the target for the shafts of ridicule." [47] Soldiers seldom sang patriotic songs spontaneously. The songs cherished most were profane ditties or simple melodies that eased the performance of routine duties, or else the songs that identified home with the cause for which they fought. When a popular song of home and loved ones did not explicitly identify these values with the war, it might, of course, be forbidden. Thus "When This Cruel War Is Over" was proscribed in the Army of the Potomac.[48]

The attitudes of soldiers toward patriotism fluctuated according to the situation. Edward Parker of a New York cavalry regiment, to cite an instance, on one occasion wrote home that if the government did not increase the pay of soldiers and cease treating them "like brutes," if it did not stamp out bounty jumping, the whole army would desert; but in other letters he was full of patriotism and all for seeing the fight to a finish.[49] The case of James Lockney, an Irish farmer of Wisconsin, is probably representative

[46] Leander Stillwell, *The Story of a Common Soldier* (Erie [?], Kansas, 1920), p. 10.
[47] William Matthews and Dixon Wecter, *Our Soldiers Speak*, 1775–1918 (Boston, 1943), p. 143.
[48] James Stone, "War Music and War Psychology in the Civil War," *Journal of Abnormal and Social Psychology*, XXXVI (October, 1941), 543–560.
[49] "War Relics and Reminiscences," David E. Cronin Manuscript Collection, New York Historical Society.

of a great many soldiers. Because he believed that the life of the nation was at stake, Lockney's loyalty and willingness to make sacrifices were real. At the same time, he was not without a goodly fund of practical sense and self-interest, and by and large, he managed to harmonize these with his patriotic zeal. When this was beyond him, the patriotic generally gave way to the practical.[50]

In the case of some soldiers—how many none can even estimate —patriotic idealism seems to have been a sustaining if not a dominant motive. Young Charles B. Bardeen of Wisconsin was a case in point. For him the war was a holy crusade for human rights; no personal sacrifice was too great for promoting victory.[51] And there is recorded evidence of deep patriotic feeling, particularly in the shadow of death. Chaplains and nurses are witnesses to the fact that two cases, cited here by way of illustration, were not isolated examples. As one soldier lay mortally wounded, he requested that a passing band play the *Star-Spangled Banner*. He asked the results of the battle. Told that it was a victory, he exclaimed, "Oh, it is glorious to die for one's country at such a time as this!" Another hoped that he might see from Heaven "the glorious old flag wave again over the undivided Union." [52]

In the South the story did not differ greatly. Many Southerners never abandoned their loyalty to the Union and made brave sacrifices in its behalf throughout the struggle. Others still cherished a love for the Union but, like Robert E. Lee, chose to follow their states. Of these some, like Lee himself, remained to the bitter end loyal to the Confederate cause and proved in countless ways their devotion to what they deemed duty and right. Others, whose state loyalty far exceeded their devotion to the Confederacy, led or supported virtual boycotts against the government at Richmond. The patriotism that had been so marked in the early months of the war dwindled as military reverses, hardships, and frustration became

[50] Elizabeth Ann Bascom, Why They Fought: A Comparative Study of the Impact of the Civil War on Five Wisconsin Soldiers, University of Wisconsin Masters' Essay, 1941, pp. 117–118.
[51] *Ibid.*
[52] Horatio B. Hackett, *Christian Memorials of the War* (Boston, 1864), pp. 32–33.

common. Desertions became alarming. Homesickness, complaints of the negligent treatment of the soldiers, discontent at profiteering and at the exemption of many large planters from military service crept into the letters of soldiers and kinfolk. Yet in some, patriotic morale was sustained through thick and thin.

It was customary for Confederates to talk of their country, to emphasize its unique history, its distinctive and superior people, its particularized mission to save modern civilization from the materialism of the industrial age. It was common to identify many of the old national symbols with the Confederate cause. Thus the Charleston *Courier* on the Fourth of July, 1863, declared that the day belonged to the Confederates, that their cause was identical with all its essential and permanent lessons. "We challenge the world to approve of the Declaration of Independence, and to show wherein the secession of the South fails in finding fuller and larger justification." [53]

The accepted pattern of Confederate patriotic sentiment was well represented in an address made to young women in Mississippi in 1864 by Colonel Duncan K. McRae, a North Carolinian. According to the custom in such addresses, the speaker began by emphasizing the idea that patriotism is a basic human instinct. In antebellum days it had inspired loyalty to the nation of which the South was part. But within that "gigantic frame, in apparent health and ripening vigor, there were the seeds of its own dissolution." Evil men in the North contributed to the dissolution of the nation, but natural and ineradicable causes of decay also helped to bring about the inevitable destruction. "Not until disgrace and slavery stared our people in the face, did they yield to the necessity of separation." Only the intense fire of persecution could have melted the golden chain of memories and associations which had tied North and South together. But all the loyalty that Southerners had felt for the old nation was now bestowed upon the new—their very own. "The world," continued the orator, "hath never conceived, history hath never recorded examples of patriotism more illustrious than the subordinate officers and private soldiers of the Confederacy have fur-

[53] Charleston *Daily Courier*, July 4, 1863.

nished to the cause of independence." [54] Even after bitter defeat proved that independence had been only a dream, thousands of Southerners clung stubbornly and loyally to that dream.

In the North the testing of national loyalty called forth anew the familiar patterns of patriotic thought, particularly religious ones. Thomas Starr King endeavored thoroughly to "Northernize" California, working, as he wrote a friend, within an inch of his life "speaking, preaching, nationalizing, traveling, organizing, etc." [55] He reasserted his timeworn contention that "Providence has ordained that out of identity of race, a common history, the same scenery, literature, laws, and aims,—the wide family feeling, the distinctive virtue, patriotism should spring." Where patriotism was shallow, continued Starr King, a sacred affection was absent, an essential element of virtue wanting, and religion was barren of one prominent witness of its sway. [56] Religion, declared the Reverend Henry N. Hudson, Shakespearian scholar and Episcopalian clergyman, imposed on men the duty of obedience inasmuch as government is plainly bound upon men by the law of nature. [57] Such was also the message of Catholic priests to their flocks. "A Catholic that loves not his country does not understand his religion," was the way one of the clergy put it. [58] Another preacher asserted unequivocally, "*We are a nation.* In these words we read the Divine commission, the promise of our strength . . . the lease of perpetuity." [59] The Reverend A. D. Mayo spoke for many of his clerical brethren in declaring "there has indeed been a Divine Intelligence guiding the destiny of our republic by the 'higher law' of

---

[54] Col. Duncan K. McRae, *Love of Country: An Address, Delivered before the Young Ladies of the Clio Society, of Oxford Female College, July 2 1864* (Oxford, 1864), pp. 10–11.

[55] Thomas Starr King to James Fields, October 29, 1862, Fields Collection, Henry E. Huntington Library.

[56] Thomas Starr King, *Substance and Show, and Other Lectures* (Boston, 1877), p. 391.

[57] Henry N. Hudson, *Christian Patriotism: A Sermon* (New York, 1861), p. 9.

[58] Joseph Fransioli, *Patriotism, a Christian Virtue* (Loyal Society Publications, no. 24, New York, 1863), p. 3.

[59] James Ludlow, *A Sermon Commemorative of National Events* (Albany, 1865), p. 14.

the progress of a free society toward a Christian democracy. . . . We believe that God Almighty is shaping a free and exalted civilized nation out of this republic." [60]

Other familiar strands in the pattern became more prominent in the emergency. Geographical determinism loomed large in the argument. "Physically speaking," declared our greatest nationalist, President Lincoln, "we cannot separate. We cannot remove our respective sections from each other, nor build an impassable wall between them." The same conviction—so widely felt—was developed in the annual message of 1862. "A nation," insisted the President, "may be said to consist of its territory, its people, and its laws. The territory is the only part that is of certain durability. One generation passeth away, and another generation cometh, but the earth abideth forever. It is of the first importance," he continued in introducing the theme that geography predetermined national unity, "to duly consider and estimate this ever-enduring part." [61]

The economic disadvantages of the breakup of the Union were in these arguments commonly related to geographical unity. Tariffs, standing armies in the European fashion, burdensome taxes, future wars, shrinking markets, all these would follow in the wake of an independent South, it was said. Besides, since the South was deemed to stand for the doctrine that all labor may rightfully be trodden into the mire, the great working mass of Northerners could not but be pushed to a lower level if Slavocracy carried the day.

The reassertion of traditional patriotic thought also included the idealization of a unique American past and the doctrine of the American mission to promote liberty in the world. Disunited, enfeebled, how could two jealous, armed camps accomplish such an end? Gilbert Haven, the prominent Methodist preacher, went so far as to declare that the triumph of the free North was a necessity because America must one day carry liberty all over the world. The

[60] A. D. Mayo, *The Progress of Liberty in the United States* (Boston, 1864), p. 496.
[61] Abraham Lincoln, *Complete Works*, ed. by John G. Nicolay and John Hay (New York, 1894), VI, 181; VIII, 110.

earth had become too small for the two conflicting ideas, aristocracy and democracy. "All peoples are fast becoming one people. They can have but one system of government. It must be that of ourselves. We are its divinely appointed representatives and defenders. We may be its divinely armed and appointed propagandists. . . . Our influence will renew and unite the world. Thus and then will wars cease to the end of the earth." [62]

Partly old, but partly new in the application given it, was the idea that the war merited loyal support inasmuch as it was a war for the most essentially American value—the dignity of human life, the democratic participation of all men in the decisions that governed their destiny. The North, it was asserted again and again, had been tolerant of slavery because it feared that only toleration could preserve the nation. But now it had become clear that far from being the tie that kept the nation together, this attitude had in reality all along been the knife that was cutting it to pieces. "This war," declared one democrat in commenting on the Census of 1860 and in attributing secession to the challenge of Northern strength, "had the same origin and necessity of every great conflict between the people and the aristocracy since the world began." [63] The passion for the country, declared another patriotic democrat, was "also and chiefly the passion for Liberty. We fight for empire," he continued, "because empire means democracy." [64] A. J. H. Duganne, whose high patriotism was charged with the warmth of democracy, expressed the same idea:

> Oh Northern Men! when will ye learn
> 'Tis labor that these tyrants spurn!
> 'Tis not the blood or skin they brand,
> But every Poor Man's toil-worn hand.
> And yet who serve them—knowing this,
> Deserve the slave-last that ye kiss! [65]

[62] Gilbert Haven, *National Sermons* (Boston, 1869), pp. 471, 472.
[63] Mayo, *op. cit.*, p. 481.
[64] Haven, *op. cit.*, pp. 382, 383.
[65] A. J. H. Duganne, *Utterances* (New York, 1864), p. 220.

How, demanded that kindred spirit, Thomas Starr King, could the true meaning of the struggle be obscured when so plainly it was a "war of mass against class, of America against feudalism, of the schoolmaster against the slavemaster, of workmen against the barons, of the ballot-box against the barracoon"? [66] This was, of course, the burden of Walt Whitman's moving war poems.

Thus it was that the war inspired a deep feeling of loyalty in the hearts of innumerable Northerners. To say this is not to deny the fact that in the war, especially in its early phase, there was in the North as in the South much display of superficial sentiment, of shouting, flag-waving folk watching troops file past, of women wearing rosettes in their hair, of gentlemen adorned with red-white-and-blue neckties or Stars and Bars.[67] To say that the war inspired a new and deep feeling of loyalty is not to deny the disheartening desertion or the demoralizing profiteering. Nor is it to deny the widespread defeatism and covert treason—gently dealt with because of its extent no less than because of the American tradition of civil liberties. Yet Emerson, so often the sensitive barometer, still spoke correctly when, in 1864, he wrote: "Before the War our patriotism was a firework, a salute, a serenade for holidays and summer evenings. . . . Now the deaths of thousands and the determination of millions of men and women show that it is real." [68]

James Russell Lowell developed this theme with great insight and feeling. In 1861, in an essay entitled "E Pluribus Unum," the gifted critic and essayist wrote that apparently God willed from time to time to test the manhood of nations by great dangers and great opportunities. "The occasion is now offered us of trying whether a conscious nationality and a timely concentration of the popular will for its maintenance can be possible in a democracy, or whether it is only despotisms that are capable of the burden and selfish energy of protecting themselves from destruction." [69]

[66] King, op. cit., p. 411.
[67] Charles C. Coffin, Four Years of Fighting (Boston, 1866), pp. 2–3.
[68] Ralph Waldo Emerson, Journals (Boston and New York, 1909–1914), X, 79.
[69] Lowell, Writings (Boston and New York, 1890), V, 63.

Four years later, at the end of the contest, Lowell wrote a commentary that deserves to be quoted at length:

If we have not hitherto had that conscious feeling of nationality, the ideal abstract of history and tradition, which belong to older countries, compacted by frequent war and united by memories of common danger and common triumph, it has been simply because our national existence has never been in such peril as to force upon us the conviction that it was both the title-deed of our greatness and its only safeguard. But what splendid possibilities has not our trial revealed even to ourselves! What costly stuff whereof to make a nation! Here at last is a state whose life is not narrowly concentered in a despot or a class, but feels itself in every limb; a government which is not a mere application of force from without, but dwells as a vital principle in the will of every citizen. . . . Loyalty has hitherto been a sentiment rather than a virtue.

But loyalty, he concluded, had now become, for the first time, identical with patriotism; nationality had ceased to be a dead abstraction; it had become a living and operative virtue in the heart, had enlivened the dullest soul, had lifted to higher levels of vision those most bogged down in petty concerns.[70] And Lowell was both right and wrong—right so far as certain immediate situations went, wrong to generalize in so sweeping a way. Patriotism did not take full and lasting possession of all who felt it deeply in particular circumstances. Yet loyalty and patriotism nevertheless did take on new meaning for innumerable Americans.

During the war itself, and especially in the years that followed, an additional theme was developed which exemplifies the impact of the struggle on conceptions of national loyalty and patriotism. It was the ancient idea of sacrifice—the inspiration in the cult of the dead heroes who had given their lives for their country. Such was the theme of Pericles in commemoration of the dead of the Peloponnesian war. Such was Lincoln's never-dying message at Gettysburg. In turn, Lincoln himself, by the fact of his assassination, became a symbol of those who had given their lives for the

70 Lowell, *Writings*, V, 211–212.

salvation and rebirth of the nation. The death of Lincoln, in the words of one commentator at the time, aroused the whole North, united hearts and hands of the people, and "made them resolve, and swear on the altar of their country, and over the mangled body of their dead President, to maintain this Union, one and inseparable." [71] Walt Whitman's *When Lilacs Last in the Dooryard Bloom'd* expressed the same symbolism in poetry of the highest order. But many an American who never read his beautiful tribute may well have felt, as Horace Morgan did, the "first thrill as a patriot" on hearing that Lincoln, too, had given his life for the nation.[72]

The mystical implications of the death sacrifice, not alone of Lincoln, but of all the Northern dead, permeated the innumerable Memorial Day addresses given year after year over the length and breadth of the North. Countless speakers put in their own words the sentiments of the distinguished Congregational leader of Hartford, Horace Bushnell. Speaking to the Yale Alumni in 1865 on "Our Obligations to the Dead," Bushnell declared: "from that shedding of blood have come for us great remissions and redemptions. In this blood of our slain our unity is cemented and sanctified. The sacrifices in the field of the Revolution united us but imperfectly. We had not bled enough to merge our colonial distinctions, and let out the state-rights doctrine, and make us a proper nation. . . . We have now a new and stupendous chapter of national history." [73]

Such was the basis for insistence on the duty of cherishing the memory of the dead. Some speakers emphasized the idea that such devotion would alone inspire in youth a similar readiness to make the supreme sacrifice for country should they so be called upon. Others expressed the fervent hope that by honoring the dead, whose memory was kept alive by the existence of the nation as well as by countless monuments, young and old alike would be inspired to

[71] Justus T. Umstead, *A Nation Humbled and Exalted: Discourse on the Death of Lincoln* (West Chester, 1865), p. 14.
[72] *The Western*, n.s., IV (January, 1878), 17.
[73] Mary Bushnell Cheyney, *Life and Letters of Horace Bushnell* (New York, 1880), pp. 486–487.

live generously and wisely for the nation. Hundreds of thousands of Americans listened to orations full of such thoughts.

Southerners, too, in honoring their war dead, kept alive memories of the Confederacy and loyalty to its values and ideals. That this fact militated against the growth of loyalty to the American nation as a whole is obvious. Gradually, however, a growing number of Southerners came to feel that loyalty to the Confederate memory and to the soldiers who died under the Stars and Bars was not incompatible with loyalty to America.

The Civil War accelerated and probably greatly stimulated among Northerners, especially among intellectuals, a new conception of the nation. To this new conception, with its many implications for patriotism, we now turn.

VII: THE RECONSTRUCTION OF
LOYALTY

*The Nation is to work as one whose achievement passes beyond
time, whose glory and honor are borne into the eternal city.*

ELISHA MULFORD, 1870

*A struggle, begun to tear the stars from our flag, we have reason to
believe, has only fixed them more securely. It is in mutual concessions of honest purpose we are to look for restored unity and completed nationalism in the hearts of our whole people.*

THE INTERNATIONAL REVIEW, 1874

*I believe sincerely that no European country knows a patriotism of
such fervor and explosiveness. . . . Yet no other nation has so much
needed high-strung patriotic emotion for the fulfillment of its mission as America.*

HUGO MUENSTERBERG, 1913

IN THE ERA that stretched from the end of the Civil War to the
First World War the voluminous literature of patriotism was full
of the traditional ideas and sentiments already formulated and
widely disseminated before 1861. The so-called instinctive basis of
patriotism; its religious foundations and associations; the invitation
to loyalty implicit in the economic resources, strength, and unity
of the nation; the awareness of a unique geography and people, of
a unique past and a unique future—all these continued to find full
and fair expression. Thanks to new agencies of popularization such
patterns of patriotic thought now were even more widely displayed
among the people than before. The expansion of the cheap newspaper and the cheap magazine, the mushroom development of the
chautauqua, the multiplication of schools and libraries, the vogue

of the dime novel, which devoted generous attention to patriotism
—all these brought to the people in great force the arguments, values, sentiments, and ideas associated with antebellum discussions
of national loyalty.

Relatively new developments also characterized patriotism in the
United States between Appomattox and the First World War. The
period saw, in the first place, a marked shift in emphasis away from
the older legalistic concept of the Union to the organic theory of
the nation. It also witnessed—and this aspect will be explored in
the next chapter—thoughtful protests against the organic theory
and its implications, together with reevaluations of patriotism and
concepts of national loyalty. Both the theory and the protest were
known in pre-Civil War days; but by reason of political, social, and
economic changes, both were later elaborated and given new and
sweeping applications. The contest was like the argument going on
in Europe, but each side differed somewhat from its European
counterpart.

The nation, according to the organic theory, is a living organism,
a superperson that has gradually developed much as other organisms and individual personalities grow. Back of this notion was the
European historical school of thought represented by Montesquieu,
Burke, De Maistre, and Von Haller, all of whom held that institutions develop gradually and in accord with natural conditions.
Savigny, Maine, and Bluntschli had applied the chief tenet of the
historical school to the state, which they viewed as the outcome
of a gradual growth rather than the result of a contract entered
into by men sometime in the dim past to insure their natural rights
to life, liberty, property, and security. In philosophical circles the
absolute idealists, especially Hegel and Fichte, had added a mystical element to the historical school in claiming that the state is
the organic expression of both a national will and a national spirit.

The literary Romanticists developed still further the concept of
national personality. Finally the evolutionists, especially Comte
and Spencer, invoked the sanctions of natural science for the laws
they formulated concerning the natural growth of the organic

state. Such, broadly speaking, were the ideological backgrounds of American writings.

The main approach to the problem of American nationalism in the antebellum period had been the legalistic or constitutional one that marked the writings of Marshall and Story and the orations of Webster. They had thought of the nation, it is true, in historical terms, but they were under the spell of the social-contract theory and tended to view the Union as a legal creation of contractual rights and obligations. The most self-conscious nationalists did, to be sure, now and then look upon the nation as if it were a living organism, an actual personality, endowed with a body and a soul that transcended the aggregate of individual bodies and souls.[1] This view was implicit, as we have seen, in the national symbols, especially in "Uncle Sam." It was also suggested in much patriotic poetry, which referred to the Union not only as a bulwark, a temple, a fortress, a ship, a golden chain, or a seamless web, but also as a closely knit family or even as a single individual.

During and after the Civil War, Northern intellectuals developed the incipient organic theory, which at first did not reach the rank and file even in the North. In the Old World the organic theory was likewise serving the integral type of nationalism that had largely replaced the older, humanitarian variety of the early nineteenth century. In time the newer conception of nationalism tended, in the United States as in Europe, to overshadow the older, humanitarian one.

In America the doctrine of organic nationalism lay back of many of the words and acts of public men: at times Lincoln himself came close to it; and Wade, Julian, Stevens, and Sumner thought and acted within its general outlines. In his widely heard lecture, "Are We a Nation?" (1867), Charles Sumner moved from his antebellum emphasis on the limited powers of the national government to an essentially organic theory of nationalism. The doctrine also influenced a group of political theorists, academicians, lawyers,

[1] For example, Daniel D. Whedon, *The Man-Republic: Phi Beta Kappa Oration Delivered at Wesleyan University* (Middletown, Conn., 1850), *passim*.

clergymen, and educators. Of these, the most outstanding were John C. Hurd, Sidney Fisher, Elisha Mulford, Francis Lieber, William T. Harris, Robert Ellis Thompson, and John W. Burgess. Not all the ideas making up the organic theory were avowed by each of these men, but their writings as a whole presented the doctrine fully.

These champions of the organic theory of the nation did not abandon the older idea that the nation is a homogeneous people speaking one language and living in a well-defined geographical area, politically unified for mutual defense against forces from without and for the maintenance of justice within. But there was a new idea. The nation was also thought of as a living organism, not a contractual relationship: a personality and an entity, composed of body, mind, and soul, not a mere voluntary association of political communities. "The historical nation," wrote the economist Robert Ellis Thompson of the University of Pennsylvania, "is an organism, a political body animated by a life of its own. It embraces not one generation but many, the dead and the unborn as well as the living. It contemplates its own perpetuity, making self-preservation the first law, and being incapable of providing for its own death or dissolution. There is in its own nature no reason why it should ever cease to exist, and the analogies often drawn from the life and death of the individual are fallacious." [2]

In almost all the writings on the subject no idea enlisted more enthusiastic support than the concept of the nation as a living organism with moral will and purpose. The nation, as Elisha Mulford, an Episcopalian clergyman and a disciple of Hegel, put it, "has its foundations in God . . . and subsists in no compact of men, but in the everlasting Will." [3] And being an organism, the nation is never static: it has as its end its own moral perfection through continuous moral conflict and endeavor. "Its advance lies through unceasing wrestling with evil. The moral being of the nation is its essential principle." Mulford concluded that the nation, having all the characteristics of a moral personality, is the realization of moral

[2] Robert E. Thompson, *Political Economy, with Especial Reference to the Industrial History of Nations* (Philadelphia, 1875), p. 34.
[3] Elisha Mulford, *The Nation* (New York, 1870), pp. 16, 392.

freedom. Thus in the nation are thesis and antithesis resolved in a growing synthesis.

In the organic theory, the nation was looked upon as the highest form of human association. It was an indispensable element in the achievement of a truly great civilization. This idea was much publicized by Francis Lieber, the German immigrant who taught political science at Columbia.[4] Closely associated with this doctrine was the emphasis on the nation as the greatest creative force and regenerative agency of mankind. William T. Harris, an interpreter of Hegel and a prominent St. Louis educator, and Professor John W. Burgess of Columbia took especial pains to familiarize Americans with this tenet.

The identification of the nation with moral principle, moral will, moral struggle and regeneration, led to the conviction that only through the nation can the individual realize his own moral freedom. Every man and woman was thought of as an embodiment of the nation itself. Hugh Miller Thompson, an Irish-born Episcopalian minister of the Middle West, was a champion of this idea. In a very Hegelian essay, appearing in 1862, he wrote: "We are Americans because we have been made so by the national influence. . . . Every great, distinct type of human nature grown in the Nation becomes forever a mould in which to cast man."[5] Patriotism, he went on, lifts a man out of his lower nature and "makes his heart beat with the hearts of heroes." Inasmuch as the nation's aims are loftier and wiser than those of the loftiest and wisest individual, or of any one generation, the "great nation grows slowly upwards to its perfect proportions, as the parent and teacher of man."[6] Mulford and Harris developed this concept in great detail.

The argument was elaborated. Although as living organisms all nations share with each other the principle of moral being and moral freedom, each nation also has, as does every well-developed organism, "its own distinctive Force or Idea." In true Hegelian

---

[4] Merle Curti, "Francis Lieber and Nationalism," *The Huntington Library Quarterly*, IV (April, 1941), 263–292.
[5] Hugh Miller Thompson, "The Nation," *Continental Monthly*, IV (December, 1863), 608 ff.
[6] *Ibid.*, p. 610.

fashion, William T. Harris taught that the Greeks had stood for beauty and individual freedom; the Romans for contract, property, law, and organization; the Anglo-Saxons for local self-government and freedom. The great American branch of the Anglo-Saxons represented, he believed, the self-activity of individuals and groups not only in government but in education, religion, and industry as well.

In his analysis of the several national Ideas, Harris spoke for many exponents of organic nationalism, but not for all. Robert Ellis Thompson, for example, held that the United States stood for "realizing and making positive those natural rights which inhere in man's nature." [7] In so doing, he synthesized the older natural-rights philosophy and the organic theory.

In the United States, the exposition of the organic theory had to come to grips with the tradition of federalism as well as with the problem of just what made up the American Idea. Subscribers to the organic theory agreed in holding that the nation is older than the states—is, in fact, their creator. Only in the nation do the states have their being, the argument generally went. Thus it was unthinkable for the states to disrupt the nation. "A revolution to destroy the fatherland," declared one writer, "is a monstrous absurdity —a parricide." [8] Sovereignty is indivisible and can therefore hardly be shared by the states. It proceeds, not from the Constitution, but, as one of the most able thinkers of the group, John C. Hurd, argued, from the whole complex of social, economic, and ethnic facts that have shaped the national spirit. And the indivisible sovereignty of the nation does not proceed from laws and institutions; rather, it creates them. The nation as a living organism is more closely related than any contractual constitution could be to the homogeneous and distinctive people that constitute the national will. Thus was the Hegelian dialectic applied.

As sensitive residents of a border state in the troubled Civil War era, the St. Louis Hegelians gave a special twist to federalism in

[7] Robert E. Thompson, *op. cit.*, p. 34.
[8] Joseph Fransioli, *Patriotism, a Christian Virtue* (Loyal Society Publications, No. 24, New York, 1863), p. 7.

their discussions of the organic theory of the nation. According to William T. Harris and Denton Snider, leading figures in the group, the conflicts within the country of state with state, and in the world of nation with nation, must somehow be overcome. Federalism provides the key. Snider, who saw in federalism the cardinal principle of the Constitution, called it "the state-producing-state." [9] Such a principle did not mean the dissolution of the single-state. It was rather the affirmation of all particular states in a larger whole which recreates them and which they in turn continually recreate. Such a process might well end in the development of a world-state corresponding to the World Spirit. The American federal system was to point the way.

Various political, social, and economic factors help to explain the militant assertions of organic nationalism, of national strength and solidarity. This period saw the expansion of business over state lines, the rise of a national labor movement, the organization of almost countless national societies of scholars, scientists, reformers, sportsmen, businessmen, women, and even children. New problems, national in scope, virtually demanded the national, rather than the local or the state, approach: railway regulation, trusts, currency, conservation, tariffs, control of political corruption. In consequence, every leading group, conservative and radical alike, tended to look to the central government for a solution, according to its own preference, of all these and various other issues. Thus the old fear of concentration of power in the central government became less marked than it had once been. This development provided a general setting for an organic theory of national loyalty.

The particular exigencies of the Civil War and Reconstruction also account for the popularity of this abstract and quasi-mystical theory. It was an instrument better suited for solving many of the problems at hand than was the older contractual theory. If the contractual, legalistic theory remained dominant, then it was awkward to disregard the Constitution even when its provisions plainly impeded the conduct of the war. But the organic theory, holding as it did that the moral unity and freedom of the people are su-

[9] Denton Snider, *The State* (St. Louis, 1902), pp. 151 *ff.*

perior to any constitutional technicality, enabled those conducting the war to ignore the Constitution if and when it hampered the military program. It was of similar service a bit later when the Radical Republicans were all for depriving the states of their customary control of such matters as poor relief, education, police regulation, elections, and landownership. A concentration of powers in the national government also seemed to the more idealistic Republicans necessary to protect the fruits of emancipation: if the Southern states were brought back into the old contractual Union, what would prevent them from reenslaving the Negroes and from uniting with Northern Democrats to cast aside the Republican saviors of the nation?

A concentration of powers in a truly national government also appealed to men of substance as highly desirable. A supreme national government, controlled by Republicans friendly to industry and finance, could insure favors to corporations, protective tariffs, a centralized banking system, the redemption of government securities, and subsidies to railroads. A national government could also provide the rank and file with free homesteads on the public domain and insure for the clamoring veterans of the late war adequate pensions from the exchequer.

Still other factors help explain the appeal of the organic theory. Certain sensitive men and women of an intellectual bent felt the need for something that could promise social unity in the chaotic post-Civil War years, when North was pitted against South, when East and West were still antagonistic, and when industrial and agrarian unrest seemed to be taking the country by storm. Platonism, emphasizing as it did the harmony of true reality and the elimination of conflict as man approached that reality, provided a philosophy of union. This explains in some small part, at least, the vogue of Platonism in various circles, in both the East and the Middle West. Likewise Hegelianism, with its reconciliation of opposites, also supplied an emotional sense of unity. Expounded with skill and even charm by the well-known educator, William T. Harris, Hegelianism thus enjoyed considerable favor both among school people and elsewhere.

The implications of the theory of organic nationalism for the concept of devotion and loyalty to the country are plain. The citizen's loyalty to the nation must be both implicit and explicit—he must keep in mind, according to the theory, the truth that there can be no genuine conflict between the individual and the nation inasmuch as man cannot possibly exist in the modern world apart from the nation. He must never forget that in the nation, and the nation alone, he realizes himself. "The nation and the individual, in their relations, exist each in a real and integral moral life and each as an end," wrote Mulford.[10] The nation's law, being the manifestation of a righteous will, must take precedence—save in cases of conscientious conviction that the government is in the wrong—over individual caprice and individual interest. The whole people is included; no one can be excluded from the nation by reason of differences of race or wealth. Nor can any individual sacrifice himself for the nation in vain. The patriot who dies for his country actually realizes life in the fullest sense. A favorite maxim was the Biblical injunction, "He that loseth his life shall find it."

The implications of the theory are more concretely clear when one recalls that abundant facts contradicted the theory of national integration. In the first place, the theory was not taken to heart by a great portion of the people. Nor could anyone deny the sectional antagonisms between North and South, the bitter legacies of warfare and Reconstruction among former Confederates, the actual economic hardships in the old Cotton Kingdom, and the inclination of Southerners to blame these on the triumph of national supremacy. The problem of finding a place for or assimilating the Negro and the immigrant, the existence of class differences and of rural and urban conflicts—all these had to be somehow resolved. As late as the 1880's James Bryce reported that at a recent triennial convention of the Episcopal Church a suggestion for incorporating in the liturgy a prayer, "O Lord, bless our nation," was rejected on the score that the word "nation" was too definite a recognition of national unity: the prayer in the form, "O Lord, bless these

10 Mulford, *op. cit.*, p. 259.

United States," proved, however, acceptable.[11] Other evidence pointed the same way. In the Democratic party the great majority still clung to the familiar federal union in which the rights of sovereign states were deemed inviolable, although this stand occasioned, of course, forthright denunciations on the part of certain Republican patriots who regarded the nation as a living organism.

Nor did the Supreme Court lend itself to an out-and-out organic conception of nationalism. Thus in *Texas v. White* (1869) the Court held that "the indestructible Union" was, after all, one of "indestructible States." In 1873, the Court rejected in the Slaughter House cases a constitutional interpretation which in effect would have reduced the states to the position of counties. It is true that a minority favored such a view and that by the 1880's highly nationalistic theories were more and more influential. Yet such a tendency in the Supreme Court was often qualified by state-rights doctrines, especially when the protection of property interests seemed to require such a reassertion. Thus exponents of organic nationalism sought to implement their theory by a specific program of action.

The problem of minority peoples was posed more sharply than ever before by the organic conception of nationalism. The keenly felt need for ethnic unity roughly paralleled a similar desire in certain European countries to impose upon minorities the culture of the dominant ethnic group. By and large, Americans supporting the organic theory held that the predominant strain in the American stock was "Anglo-Saxon," and to this they attributed innately superior qualities—above all, capacity for self-government and for dominion over politically backward peoples.

The missionary activities of various English intellectuals, notably the historian E. A. Freeman, who visited the United States in the early 80's, did much to endear this idea to influential Americans. Herbert Baxter Adams, from his history seminar at the Johns Hopkins University, sent out over the country many scholars imbued with this view, while the Congregational minister, Josiah Strong, reached a far greater number in his widely read *Our Country* (1885). This influential little book stressed the notion that Anglo-

11 James Bryce, *The American Commonwealth* (New York, 1889), I, 15.

Saxons are innately superior in all moral and political matters. Further, it preached that a militant national integration under "Anglo-Saxon" Protestant auspices was necessary. To insure the dominance of the American ethic in the world at large the book emphasized the evangelical obligation of missionary enterprise and imperial expansion.

Save by a few idealistic humanitarians, the Indian had seldom been regarded as capable of becoming a full-fledged citizen. Having at last been worsted and shoved into reservations, the red men, many held, now could be integrated into American life through missionary, educational, and governmental means, made over into good Americans and trained in loyalty to the nation. The Dawes Act (1887) laid the ground for this policy. But since it overlooked the whole rising anthropological concept of culture, the attempt, of course, fell far short of success.

On a much bigger scale than the Indian, the Negro also defied the ideal of a homogeneous nation. Organic nationalism offered no generally acceptable formula for the Negro. Elisha Mulford held that the "nation is lifted above the divisions and distinctions of race." [12] Many maintained that the Negro could and should be integrated into the main stream of American life. William T. Harris believed this could best be done by converting the Negro as fast as possible into a landowner and a capitalist and by inculcating in him the national virtue of self-direction. Those who held that the Negro could thus be absorbed into the national life viewed with disapproval the tendency of the federal government to hand over to the Southern states the supervision and general subordination into a special caste of the whole colored people. But it was natural for those who identified the American people with the Anglo-Saxon elite to look on the Negro as the thorny exception to that racial solidarity so dear to their hearts.

A national faith often needs an adversary, especially when the problem of internal ethnic unity proves stubborn. The post-Civil War decades witnessed a marked increase of immigration in which the Catholic element bulked large and a new wave of nativism and

[12] Mulford, *op. cit.*, p. 397.

anti-Romanism broke in the late 1880's and the 1890's. All the hackneyed arguments about the un-Americanism and disloyalty of the "Papists" were again broadcast over the land. The parochial school, which had been keeping pace with a growing Catholic population, was the object of bitter attacks. Spokesmen of the American Protective Association, the new organization of anti-Catholic nativists, demanded that Catholics send their children to the public school, which was commonly thought of as the training ground for patriotism. Nativists further contended that, if Catholics displayed their disloyalty to American institutions by refusing to patronize the nation's schools, then at least the parochial institutions must be made to teach the English language and the lessons of American history. Above all, the nativists violently denounced the Catholic agitation for public subsidies for church schools, which was deemed a flagrant threat to the precious American principle of separation of church and state.

Leading prelates such as Archbishops Ireland and Spalding and Cardinal Gibbons denied that Catholicism was unpatriotic and un-American. Next to God, Cardinal Gibbons declared, country should have the strongest place in man's affections. "It is a sacred duty for every American to do all in his power to perpetuate our civil institutions and to avert the dangers which threaten them." [13] Catholics told their adversaries that their priests and people had loyally rallied to the nation in all its great crises, that Catholics in the United States accepted as necessary and wise the separation of church and state. They argued that the divorce of secular instruction from religion in the public school was in itself a departure from traditionally American practice.

Closely related to the new flood of nativism and anti-Catholicism and implicit in the doctrine of organic nationalism was the increasingly insistent demand for the close identification of the immigrant with American life. But this was an even more difficult problem than it had been in earlier times. Pre-Civil War immigrants had, for the most part, immigrated in family groups and the chil-

[13] James Cardinal Gibbons, "Patriotism and Politics," North American Review, CCIV (April, 1892), 392.

dren had proved to be effective missionaries of American ways. But now an ever larger number of immigrants came without families. And some stayed merely long enough to accumulate savings in order to return to their homeland. Those who stayed often settled in closely knit colonies in great urban areas and remained isolated from old-stock Americans. No less important was the fact that immigrants came less and less, after the 1880's, from northern Europe and more and more from the radically different cultures of southern and eastern Europe.

When some of the most thoughtful and articulate immigrants, whose love of America none could question, confessed to the difficulties of becoming truly American in thought and loyalty, the odds which the rank and file of newcomers faced can be imagined. One immigrant, the Syrian Abraham Rihbany, spoke of the virtual impossibility of becoming Americanized while living in a colony of his own kinsmen but at the same time emphasized the hardships of breaking with them. A Rumanian Jew, M. E. Ravage, wrote that the mere taking-out of citizenship papers and giving-up of allegiance to a state was one thing; but that "renouncing your priceless inherited identity and blending your individual soul with the soul of an alien people is quite another affair. . . . To be born in one world and grow to manhood there, to be thrust then into the midst of another with all one's racial heritage, with one's likes and dislikes, aspirations and prejudices, and to be abandoned to the task of adjusting within one's own being the clash of opposed systems of culture, tradition and social convention—if that is not heroic tragedy, I should like to be told what is." [14]

William T. Harris had emphasized both the need of the immigrant for a sense of continuity with his past and the contributions his presence made to tolerance and to regard for the personal liberty of others. Such wisdom, however, was hardly the logic of the organic theory of nationalism. The growing tendency was to emphasize rather the need for a wholesale and thoroughgoing effort to Americanize the immigrant, the faster the better. The formula offered by the old-stock Americans of this persuasion was fairly simple. The

[14] M. E. Ravage, *An American in the Making* (New York, 1917), p. 200.

social settlement house provided a realistic, although a limited, approach to the problem. It won increasing support, to be sure, but never became the central tenet in the Americanization program. The chief reliance was on formal education. It was believed the public school would Americanize immigrant children. The evening sessions, where foreign-born adults might lay the foundations for loyalty to the nation by learning English and the basic facts of American history, also found favor.

To speed the transfer of loyalties, the immigrant was urged to take out citizenship papers. All sorts of inducements—including economic gain—were held out to him, if he would slough off his Old World ways and thoroughly identify himself with America. When the First World War threatened to involve the United States, it was clear that the national interest might suffer great harm from the throngs of un-Americanized immigrants who felt no loyalty to America and in some cases cherished great devotion to their fatherlands. The Americanization movement became the order of the day.

It is indeed true that the crusade—for such it was—achieved a good deal and that, whatever the cause, the great majority of immigrants proved their loyalty to the United States. But after several years of intensive effort, it was clear that the great masses of immigrants had not yet been assimilated—that the melting pot was not functioning adequately.

The causes were not far to seek. In some cases agents of Americanization tactlessly tried to thrust upon immigrants incomprehensible conceptions of American ways and values, only to arouse resentment and to cement old loyalties. Thoughtful workers in the movement confessed that it was no easy thing to change the culture, including subtle loyalties, of a transplanted people. Even second-generation immigrants, while having no especial allegiance to the native land of their parents, nevertheless often failed to strike roots, and to be accepted as Americans in such a way as to develop a complete loyalty to the United States.

The Americanization movement, comparable in a rough way to

similar efforts in Europe to impose the language and customs of the dominant ethnic group on minorities, was but one expression of the belief that the most loyal element in the American population was the "Anglo-Saxon." In support of this belief all sorts of arguments were brought forth: the "old" American stock was, after all, the only downright American element in the country; it was superior to more recent stock; it was free from the subservience to political machines that so stigmatized non-Anglo-Saxons; it alone, therefore, possessed that inherent capacity for self-government that was basic in the American faith. In consequence of all this, the argument went, the immigrant was not and could not become loyal to American institutions. The fate of the American way was deemed to be in the balance.

In the name of loyalty to America, other indictments of unrestricted immigration were forthcoming. Workers of old-stock background resented the circumstance that newcomers could be employed at lower wages than they thought worthy of toil. In spite of the fact that the employing class as a whole welcomed cheap labor from abroad, now and again a spokesman of American capitalism expressed the fear that immigrants were swelling the ranks of socialists and anarchists. Thus in the name of loyalty to America the demand for setting up bars against further immigration often cloaked group interests.

Within the framework of the theory of organic nationalism and of associated political and economic factors, the program of Radical Reconstruction of the South was given up and a movement, partly conscious, partly unconscious, for the reconciliation of North and South was launched. Insofar as the movement was a planned one it was intended to wipe out Southern loyalties to Confederate memories. Thus journalists, politicians, ministers, teachers, novelists, essayists, publishers, and even some veterans in the North promoted the reconciliation of the two sections. Thanks to Northern philanthropy, public schools were promoted in the South; thanks to Northern publishers, Northerners read the engaging memoirs of Confederates or the sympathetic, sentimental novels of reconciliation; thanks to investors, promoters, and industrialists, the Northern pattern of capitalism and urbanism began to make headway in the South.

Nor was the movement all on one side. Duff Green of North Carolina in 1866 gave evidence that Southerners themselves, in many cases, were ready and anxious to forward reconciliation. "For the competition, in the progress of civilization, in commerce and finance," he wrote, "is not between the North and the South, as rival and opposing interests, but it is between the North and South united, under a common government, organized as one people, for the promotion of their common welfare, happiness, and prosperity, and for the protection of their common rights and interests." [15] A decade later, Gilbert C. Walker, governor of Virginia, declared in an address, "That we are becoming a nation, according to the real signification of the word, I am proud to assert." [16] The support that Henry Grady, Robert E. Lee, and other exponents of "the New South" gave to the movement was telling in effect.

By the end of the century, despite the die-hards and the nostalgic zeal of the Daughters of the Confederacy for keeping alive old loyalties, the aspiration which the Southern poet, Sidney Lanier, had expressed in 1876 was at least approximated:

> Heart and Brain! no more be twain
> Throb and think, one flesh again!
> Lo! they weep, they turn, they run;
> Lo! they kiss: Love, thou art one! [17]

No great furor was occasioned when the superintendent of public education in Louisiana urged the schools to teach the national songs and the lessons of national patriotism. "The children should be taught that this beautiful national emblem," he declared in speaking of the flag, "represents the freedom, power, and glory of a government, the grandest and best in all the world, and that its honor and its safety must in a short time be committed to their

[15] Duff Green, *Facts and Suggestions* (New York, 1866), pp. v–vi.
[16] Gilbert C. Walker, *National Landmarks* (New York, 1876), pp. 4–5.
[17] Sidney Lanier, *Poems* (New York, 1884), p. 135.

hands." [18] Certainly the patriotic response of the South to the Spanish-American War left no doubt regarding the loyalty of its people to the nation.

In thinking of the past, the great majority of men and women tend to believe it is best that things come out as they do. Thus, as the years passed, Southerners relinquished little by little old loyalties and ideas. As the economic and social hardships of the Reconstruction years receded and as the promise of the benefits inherent in participation in the national life loomed ahead, Southerners more and more accepted the creed that the nation *per se* is a transcendently great value—that, heroic and gallant though their Confederate fathers and mothers were, they had in truth been mistaken.[19] Thus in spite of the fact that regional devotion was more intense in the South than it was, probably, in any other section, loyalty to the nation triumphed even in the region which had only yesterday repudiated it.

To insure the highest loyalty to the nation, to integrate sections, classes, and peoples into the living organism the nation was thought to be, the most ardent nationalists believed it necessary to endow the federal government with greater influence over the minds of Americans. In Congress, Senator Henry Blair of New Hampshire valiantly battled for federal support of public schools, especially in the educationally backward South. This he did on the score that such a policy would both extend the great American doctrine of equality of opportunity and integrate the South into the nation by inculcating the values of patriotism. The measure failed. Too many Americans still jealously cherished the older American fondness for local control of education. But the idea did not die.

The kindred determination to use the school as an instrument of patriotism led to victory after victory. More and more educators subscribed to the idea expressed in 1866 at the Indianapolis meet-

[18] Wilmot H. Goodale, "Patriotism," *American Magazine of Civics*, VI (April, 1895), 361–362.
[19] This idea is developed in Richard Shryock's "The Nationalistic Tradition of the Civil War; a Southern Analysis," *South Atlantic Quarterly*, XXXII (1933), 294–305. See also Paul H. Buck, *The Road to Reunion, 1865–1900* (Boston, 1937), *passim*.

ing of the National Education Association that "our schools must teach our children that patriotism is not genuine which is bounded by corporate limits or state lines, but that that only is genuine which holds as its own and would fight to protect every foot of land belonging to the United States of America." [20] William T. Harris, then United States commissioner of education, preached in and out of season the patriotic responsibility of educators to develop in every school child an appreciation of the nation and the deepest loyalty to it. Nor was he alone.

In accordance with the American belief that everything can be learned and taught, manuals of patriotism appeared. Educators such as Mary Sheldon Barnes of the Oswego Normal School emphasized the importance of presenting vividly and attractively to children the glorious deeds of American heroes, the sacrifices and bravery of our soldiers and sailors in wartime, the personalities of the presidents, who might properly be regarded as symbols of the nation in the manner in which royal personages in Europe were regarded. By the 1890's, state after state was requiring by law that subjects deemed peculiarly fitted to inculcating patriotism, such as American history and civics, be taught on every educational level below the college. Textbooks presented in general an anti-British and highly pro-American view of the Revolution and of the leading events in our early national history. The Grand Army of the Republic took pains to see that textbook writers presented what to them was a true, national, and patriotic view of the Civil War.[21]

The attempt to foster national loyalty by the ritualism of patriotism led to several innovations in the 1880's and 1890's. Senator Burrows of Michigan in 1890 suggested at exercises at West Point that the head be uncovered when the national anthem was played. The same year saw North Dakota and New Jersey enacting by law

[20] *National Education Association's Proceedings and Lectures of National Teachers Association* (Indianapolis, 1866), p. 40.
[21] This subject has been studied by the pioneer in the field, Bessie L. Pierce. Her *Civic Attitudes in American School Textbooks* (Chicago, 1920), *Public Opinion and the Teaching of History in the United States* (New York, 1926), and *Citizens' Organizations and the Civic Training of Youth* (New York, 1933), are standard accounts.

the requirement that the flag be flown every day from every school-house; other states quickly followed this example. After the flag had been exploited for partisan purposes by the Republicans in the presidential campaign of 1896 New York took legislative measures to prevent such usages of the national emblem in the future. This and comparable laws cloaked the flag with an almost religious sanctity—it was not to be treated disrespectfully or used in advertising for commercial profit. In 1897 the American Flag Association was launched in New York City. This organization did much to spread the idea of the sanctity of the flag. Within a decade, Flag Day was widely observed as a special occasion for reverence to the national banner.

Closely associated with flag ritualism was the frequently heard protest that the national holidays were no longer properly observed. Ex-President Cleveland was only one of many who lamented that Thanksgiving Day had largely lost its patriotic and religious significance, that Washington's Birthday hardly evoked appropriate memories of devotion, and that the Fourth of July had come to be given over to trivialities, "to senseless noise and dangerous explosions." [22]

Deprecating the neglect of patriotic observance, Cleveland encouraged a more intensive and extensive cultivation of the ritual of patriotism. He deplored the lack of harmony among the people, especially in industrial life; he decried what he declared to be the relaxation of the old virtues of frugality and the dominance of new values of extravagance. Are we sure, he asked, that we are doing all we ought to keep America in vigor and health? "Are we keeping its roots well surrounded by the fertile soil of loving allegiance, and are we furnishing them with the invigorating moisture of unselfish fidelity?" [23]

Closely related to the tendencies and needs of which Cleveland spoke was the appearance, in the period beginning in 1875, of more than a half-hundred new patriotic societies, the great majority of which were launched in the 1890's. The immediate occasion for

[22] *North American Review*, CXXCIV (April, 1907), 685.
[23] *Ibid.*, p. 692.

the formation of these was the series of centennials which celebrated the major events of the founding of the Republic—Concord and Lexington, the Declaration of Independence, the adoption of the Constitution, and the inauguration of Washington. All these centennials, especially that of 1876, had served to remind the American people of their past and of the nation's achievements. Self-conscious nationalists nevertheless believed that the glories of the past had not been adequately or systematically kept before the people, that the memory of the fathers must not again be allowed to fade. In forming patriotic organizations based on the principle of descent many leaders in the new movement expressed a certain snobbish pride in ancestry and sought to publicize their social prestige. This fact, however, does not mean that they were lacking in genuine devotion to the advancement of national loyalty.

Patriotic organizations of an hereditary character were not new. The Order of the Cincinnati had been launched by officers of the Revolution and in spite of ups and downs had continued to function. Its refusal in 1876 to admit to membership descendants of ordinary soldiers in the Revolution was the immediate occasion for the founding of the Sons of the Revolution, the first of the new societies. In addition to the Cincinnati, organizations of the officers and descendants of officers in the War of 1812 and in the Mexican War had been established. Only shortly after Appomattox, the Loyal Legion, designed to preserve the bonds between officers in the Northern armies, was organized. The Grand Army of the Republic, which included the rank and file in the Federal armies, came to be a powerful force in politics, especially in matters affecting pensions, and in the preservation of patriotic memories connected with the Civil War. It was easy and natural for veterans to emphasize the comradeship and the more satisfying memories of camp and battlefield and to regard themselves as the special custodians of patriotism.

The new organizations—and they multiplied in part because of internal divisions concerning the exact basis of hereditary membership—included societies composed of women descended from officers and soldiers in the colonial wars, the Revolution, and the War of 1812. Of these, the Daughters of the American Revolution, established in 1890, was by far the most influential. At first the new patriotic societies busied themselves chiefly with preserving documents, records, and those traditions of the war which particularly concerned them. Monuments were erected on battle sites, publications were launched, meetings and exercises were held. Through bringing together men and women from all sections of the country in the common cause of patriotism, the societies softened local and sectional loyalties.

While many societies kept their eye chiefly on the veneration of ancestors and historical activities, others, notably the D.A.R., broadened their program to include quasi-controversial public problems, such as child welfare and the inculcation of a particular conception of patriotism in schools through prize essays and the revision of textbooks in American history. By the time of the First World War interest in the Americanization of immigrants, in military preparedness, and in combating liberal and radical ideas was also clearly in evidence. It was only then that the patriotic societies, which had shown themselves adept in pressure politics, aroused any considerable criticism and opposition.

Although the economic aspects of the new organic, integral trend in nationalistic and patriotic thought by and large received little explicit emphasis, the exceptions to this general tendency are significant. Thus champions of a protective tariff sometimes associated economic nationalism with ideas closely akin to the new organic theories. "True Americanism," wrote Senator Burrows, "demands an industrial policy which shall be intensely American— in a word, true Americanism demands that this nation shall resume its place in the van of industrial nations of the world." [24] Occasionally some point was made of the time-honored concept that the national domain, despite the rapid depletion by great corporations, could still provide "limitless development and riches, relief to a crowding population, and homes to thrift and industry." [25] It was

[24] William D. Orcutt, *Burrows of Michigan and the Republican Party* (New York, 1917), II, 72.
[25] George F. Parker, ed., *The Writings and Speeches of Grover Cleveland* (New York, 1892), p. 429.

customary to insist that the strength, perpetuity, and destiny of the nation rested on mutual faith and confidence, on unity of aim and purpose, on the avoidance of anything like a class stand on controversial issues. Frequently this insistence veiled a position which in its definitely conservative overtones could properly be regarded as a class interest.

Certain examples will illustrate the quality and bearings of some of these ideas. Speaking before a military organization in Brooklyn in 1885, the Reverend Charles Hall not only associated military preparedness with loyalty to the country but urged the usefulness of a rejuvenated national guard in putting down unpatriotic strikes and labor unrest. Other spokesmen for the more conservative interests denounced as class legislation and as the negation of patriotism the demands of laborers and farmers in the 1890's for the redress of what they deemed grievances. Thus in an address at the University of Georgia in 1895, Marion J. Verdery urged in the name of national loyalty that Southerners steer clear of "isms," that they be "sound" in economics, that they resolutely stand out against an income tax and free silver, and above all against an alliance with the "mushroom" West—that "stronghold of socialism and anarchy." [26]

Nor was this all. In the midst of pleas for regarding the flag as sacred and for other types of patriotic ritualism, Elroy Headley declared that "it is an element of patriotism to reverence the successful business men of America, and our nation must request and heed the advice and admonitions of men experienced in affairs." [27] More characteristic, however, of the explicit and implicit bearings of the new type of patriotism and national loyalty on economic conflicts was the position expounded by the Episcopalian Bishop Doane of Albany. "The agitations of labor to depress capital or of capitalists to oppress the laborer," he declared, "together with all antagonisms . . . of different classes and conditions are unpatriotic because they hurt the country." [28] We shall see, too, that liberals

[26] Marion J. Verdery, *The Doubts and Difficulties of National Unity* (Augusta, 1895), pp. 11–12.
[27] Elroy Headley, *Patriotic Essays* (Newark, 1916), p. 11.
[28] William C. Doane, "Patriotism: Its Defects, Its Dangers, and Its Duties," *North American Review*, CLXVI (March, 1898), 320.

and radicals on occasion continued, as they had in times past, to identify their own interests and progress with national loyalty and with a greatly expanded conception of national functions and powers.

The newer type of nationalism and patriotism carried with it not only economic implications for domestic issues but for foreign relations as well. It is fairly clear that the Spanish-American War was the result less of direct economic pressure from interested business groups than of other forces. These included the belief of certain Republican politicians that a foreign war would divert attention from internal cleavages and thus lengthen the control of the Republican party over national life; the more important feeling that national interests were jeopardized by the continued control of Cuba by an unsympathetic Spanish monarchy; the widespread, though irrational, conviction that national honor had been insulted and violated by the sinking of the *Maine* in the harbor of Havana; and the exploitation and intensification by a competitive, profit-making "yellow press" of the patriotic conviction that only a war with Spain could free Cuba and thus fulfill the American obligation to spread freedom and end Old World tyranny in our dooryard. The riotous, often meretricious expressions of patriotism that accompanied the declaration of hostilities, the news of our victories, the return of our soldiers and of the war hero, Admiral Dewey, were only slightly dimmed by the critics of the war and of the imperialism which issued from it.

The movement for imperialism found its early champions chiefly among navalists, missionaries, idealistic intellectuals, and politicians rather than among businessmen. Yet the argument for colonial expansion was seldom entirely divorced from economic considerations. Colonies, it was said, would absorb the surplus produce from American mines and factories; they would provide the national economy with much-needed raw materials; they would offer an opportunity for adventure and for individual enterprise much needed now that the frontier chapter of American history had virtually ended; they would afford naval bases and coaling stations which would profit our carrying trade by insuring it full protection.

Such arguments were accompanied by the contention that over-

seas expansion was the fulfillment of the American mission to bestow our superior institutions on the backward portions of the globe
—our schools, churches, law, governmental arrangements, our ideas
of individualism and of political freedom. These arguments, which
had been brought into play again and again during the earlier debates over our "manifest destiny" to take over contiguous territories possessed by France, England, and Spain, were permeated
with a definitely organic conception of the nation. All living things,
the argument ran, began to die as soon as they stopped growing.
Only so long as the United States proved its vigor through geographical expansion could it assuredly be regarded—by analogy
with other living, organic entities—as immune to decay and death.
Advocates of the retention of Puerto Rico and the Philippines therefore insisted that expansion was the imperative of patriotism and
that the anti-imperialists were in fact devoid of true love of country.

Perhaps no single figure, certainly none in the public eye, so well
exemplified the organic theory of nationalism, of world power, and
of imperialism, as Theodore Roosevelt. In his mind—especially
during the presidential campaign of 1912—the nation's powers must
be enhanced in order to insure social justice to the rank and file.
But the idea of benefits bestowed by the nation on the individual
was always the minor note in Roosevelt's conception of patriotism.
In his mind, patriotism, which he defined as love of country tran-
scending devotion to any section or to any individual or class interest, was an elemental virtue, like love of home, or honesty, or
courage. Nevertheless, he knew, of course, that "scoundrels play
upon it for their own selfish ends." [29]

Without benefit of present-day knowledge of the role of such
unconscious factors as rationalization in motivation and in behavior,
Roosevelt never suspected that honest, righteous men, least of all
himself and those agreeing with him, might be identifying their
own predilections with patriotism and the national good. He could
indeed declare that he had no patience "with the man, whether a
multimillionaire or a wage-worker, whether the member of a big

[29] Theodore Roosevelt, *Works* (Memorial edition, New York, 1923–1926),
XV, 15.

corporation or the member of a labor union, who does not recognize the fact that as an American citizen his first loyalty is due to the nation, and to his fellow citizens no matter what position they occupy as long as those fellow citizens are decent men." [30]

There is no clear-cut evidence in all his comments on patriotism that Theodore Roosevelt ever developed an adequate criterion for testing policies he himself leaned toward by reason of temperament, class affiliations, or political expediency. He did not ask whether in reality they were, as he maintained, in the national interest. Both in domestic and in foreign policies the course of action he deemed truly in the national interest naturally tended to correspond to his own assumptions, values, and preferences, or to those of his associates.

Yet Theodore Roosevelt was indeed forced to come to grips with the relations of the individual to the government and to the nation itself. Like more conscious exponents of the organic theory of the nation, he believed that the relations between the individual and the country were reciprocal. The individual realized his capacity for happiness through the nation and in turn was obligated to serve it disinterestedly in peace, and in war to defend it to the death not only with courage but with technical military skill. His own words call for quotation: "There can be no genuine feeling of patriotism of the kind that makes all men willing and eager to die for the land, unless there has been some measure of success in making the land worth living in for all alike, whatever their station, so long as they do their duty; and on the other hand, no man has a right to enjoy any benefits whatever from living in the land in time of peace, unless he is trained physically and spiritually so that if duty calls he can and will do his part to keep the land against all alien aggressions." [31]

The difficult problem of the patriot's duty toward the government, as distinct from the nation, Roosevelt never adequately solved. On one occasion he declared he had never understood those who objected to the old navy toast of Stephen Decatur, "My country right, my country wrong; but right or wrong, my country."

[30] *Ibid.*, XV, 634.   [31] *Ibid.*, XX, 518.

Yet he found it hard to believe that anyone differing with him regarding what was right for the country could in truth be right. As a critic of President Wilson he therefore regarded it as unpatriotic not to oppose him "to the exact extent that by inefficiency or otherwise he fails in his duty to stand by the country." [32]

A harsh critic of pacifists and internationalists, whom he regarded not only as shortsighted and mistaken but often as cowardly, Theodore Roosevelt believed that war released or evoked the manly virtues without which the individual did not truly experience life and without which no country could remain a vigorous organism. Having no doubt that all the wars America had engaged in were righteous wars, he could not envision one which would not be righteous. Only through force could the nation command respect from others and realize its righteous and legitimate ends. Thus he was a supporter of Mahan's theory of sea power, an ardent champion of a larger navy, an earnest advocate of a more efficient and modern army, and an outspoken pioneer in the preparedness movement during the early months of the First World War. As president, he exemplified both the imperialism into which the organic theory of the nation easily carried its adherents and the idea that a great nation must play its role as a great power in world politics.

Roosevelt saw nationalism and internationalism as complementary; international law, the basis of internationalism, could be effective only if nations were unified, self-confident, and firmly allied. But nations could enjoy no lasting well-being in a chaotic world, and hence stable relations, governed by law and justice and sanctioned by force, constituted in his mind the reality of internationalism. In the Nobel Peace Prize address which Roosevelt gave shortly after retiring from office he supported the idea of an international organization with police power, an organization in which the United States would presumably play a leading role. Yet he would have nothing to do later on with Wilson's League of Nations. His partisan bitterness against the war president and the political party he stood for made it easier for Theodore Roosevelt to see in the pro-

[32] *Talks with T.R. from the Diaries of John J. Leary, Jr.* (Boston and New York, 1920), p. 177.

posed League the surrender of national values and interests allegedly
in behalf of a "vague, sentimental humanitarianism" of which he
was always suspicious.

To Roosevelt the gulf between the ideal and the actual in matters of patriotism and national loyalty always seemed deep. He condemned the tendency of labor and capital to put class interests
before the national good. He belittled the "sentimental humanitarianism" of those who gave their ultimate loyalty to "the vague
concept of mankind." He deplored what he believed to be the divided loyalties of many immigrants, castigated "hyphenated-
Americans" with much harshness as "the foe within the gates,"
and insisted on one-hundred-per-cent devotion to the nation on the
part of all newcomers. Although he believed in the superior virtues of the so-called Anglo-Saxon race, he did not question the contributions, the abilities, and the good citizenship of the various
ethnic strains in the population. He even had faith that ultimately, through opportunity, education, and fair play, the Negro
might become "a good American," and he went out of his way to
encourage those members of the race he believed to be leaders in
the uphill struggle.

Such, in brief, were the essential ideas of nationalism and patriotism that Theodore Roosevelt embraced with an emotional intensity that only his own words can convey. Those words reached
countless ears. Indeed, no one did more than he to bring before the
American people the idea of the supreme duty of loyalty to the
living, growing, vital nation that was at once an organic actuality
and that seemed to possess a manly, authentic personality. But
Theodore Roosevelt represented only one conception of American
patriotism.

VIII: THE CRITIQUE OF NATIONAL LOYALTY

What solemn nonsense it all is! Men loved the flag before they called it Old Glory; men died willingly for their country without special instruction in color symbolism; statesmen gave their lives to the public service without repeating a flag pledge every-day. . . . Reading drivel to children and making them sing doggerel can hardly have any effect except to vulgarize them.

THE NATION, 1900

True patriotism, from the American point of view, does not consist in a flourish of trumpets, in shouts of acclaim, in professions of loyalty, nor in national boasting; it is rather the result of a just appreciation of what our country is in its spirit of freedom, its institutions, its laws, its customs, its guarantees, its form of government, its splendid domain, its natural scenery, its status among the nations, and in its triumphant onward march.

HOMER E. PERRIN, 1900

We Americans do indeed need iron in our blood, but it is iron that shall make us do our dull, plodding, tiresome duties day by day. This alone is the patriotism to be taught in schools: and unless these ideals of duty toward one's country are made vital in the school-life, the flag-salute, the singing, the national self-glorification will result in a nation of swashbucklers, not of patriots.

JAMES PHINNEY MONROE, 1912

THE PATTERN of patriotism in the first half of the nineteenth century was in no sense confined to the spread-eagleism which justified the expansion of American institutions over the hemisphere on the score of their superiority, which brooked no criticism of the United States, and which sang the praise of nativism. These very tendencies met with much criticism. Nor did the critics regard themselves as in any sense disloyal to America. On the contrary, they pictured themselves as thoroughgoing patriots in the true sense of the term. The heritage of their thought was far too real to be ignored in the post-Civil War decades when integral nationalism of the organic type and a somewhat chauvinistic patriotism marked new currents of thought and feeling. That older heritage is well illustrated by the ideas of Ralph Waldo Emerson about the American nation and patriotism.

The Concord lyceum lecturer and philosopher shared many of the ideas common to expressions of American patriotism. To him, as to so many others, the land "wants no ornament or privilege which nature could bestow." Here, he wrote, "stars, woods, hills, animals, and men abound, and the vast tendencies concur of a new order." [1] Every foot of its soil, he felt, has its own proper quality, just as the grape on either side of the same fence has its own flavor. The Americans are indeed the Chosen People, led to this Promised Land by Providence itself. Like every other people, the Americans have their own genius. That genius, he continued, is expressed in the intellectual quickness, resourcefulness, and boldness of the people, in their inventiveness in the use of language— an inventiveness that in time may well result in a uniquely American tongue. When Americans forget their own distinctive quality, as they sometimes do, declared Emerson, they should go to Europe to learn there the full import and proper glory of their country.

At this point Emerson failed to share the sentiments which some fellow countrymen considered to be the essence of Americanism. True patriotism, "which would find a brother in a whole nation,"

[1] Ralph Waldo Emerson, *Complete Works* (Boston and New York, 1890), I, 372.

Emerson accepted as a noble if expansive sentiment; but he hated "the narrowness of the Native American Party," a mere dog in the manger, the precise opposite to "all the dictates of love and magnanimity" for which America should stand. The energy of the Irish, Germans, Poles, and Cossacks, of the Africans and the Polynesians, would, he believed, "construct a new race, a new religion, a new state, a new literature, which will be as vigorous as the new Europe which came out of the melting-pot of the Dark Ages." [2]

Emerson had nothing but scorn for the patriotism which was rooted in a sense of pecuniary gain, which ended in the maxims of trade, "so much for so much." No less did he abhor the equally materialistic fashion of estimating "nations by the census, or the geographical extent, by coin, or antiquity." [3] To measure miles and count hands was to his mind a brutish and hopeless formalism.

The Sage of Concord could speak of the "role of Providence" in America's past and future, knowing full well that every other country likewise believed that "the Divine Providence had a sneaking kindness for it." [4] He had no sympathy at all "with that boyish egotism, hoarse with cheering for one side, for one state," nor for the spread-eagle, who had best "fold his foolish wings and be less of a peacock." [5]

In a shrewd, if overdrawn, analysis of the functions of the patriotism he disparaged, Emerson proved himself to be a good psychologist. The dusty artisan, he wrote in his Journal in 1827, when he was but twenty-three years old, needs some consolation for the insignificant figure his sordid habits and feelings present in comparison with the great. Thus the humble man is "fain to remember how large and honourable is the confederacy of which he is a member, and, that however low his lot, his resources are yet reckoned an integral part of that awful front which the nation presents to the world. Hence the unaffected, boisterous enthusiasm with which any spirited allusion to the idea of country is always received by a mixed assembly." Emerson knew that it is not only "plebeian clay" that

[2] Ralph Waldo Emerson, *Journals* (Boston and New York, 1909–1914), VII, 115, 116.

[3] *Ibid.*, V, 369.   [4] *Ibid.*, X, 195.

[5] Emerson, *Complete Works*, XI, 413.

is thus touched—intellectuals too, need this vicarious glory. Nevertheless in his individualistic eyes the truly wise should perceive that the "advantage of the whole is best consulted in consulting the real advantage of the particular." [6]

This brings us to the essence of Emerson's critique of the emotional, chauvinistic type of national loyalty: all these things overshadow and drown the individual, the center of Emerson's universe of values. This is what he meant when he said that America, if her attainments are to equal her promise, must produce great individuals; when he wrote that "our nations have been mobs"; and, again, when he exclaimed "how much more are men than nations." This is what he meant when he so often declared that loyalty to America rests on America's devotion to humanity. The right patriotism, he said, consists "in the delight which springs from contributing our peculiar and legitimate advantages to the benefit of humanity. . . . I wish to see America a benefactor such as no country ever was. . . . I hope that America will come to have its pride in being a nation of servants, not of the served." [7] For "the office of America is to liberate, to abolish kingcraft, priestcraft, caste, monopoly, to pull down the gallows, to burn up the bloody statute-book, to take in the immigrant, to open the doors of the sea and the fields of the earth. . . . This liberation appears in the power of invention, the freedom of thinking, in readiness for reforms." [8] This, then, was the criterion by which Emerson judged America—her role in the universal struggle for the well-being and the growth of men and women individually and of humanity collectively. This was the foundation of his loyalty to his country.

The liberal, individualistic, and humane currents in American thought that Emerson stood for did not, of course, vanish with the rising emphasis on an integral, organic nationalism. All who insisted that the nation transcends men and women by substituting for their will and moral standards those of a living nation had to face the claims of innumerable individualists of many varieties. Much of the criticism that the new emphasis on an all-inclusive

[6] Emerson, *Journals*, II, 174.
[7] Emerson, *Complete Works*, XI, 387, 413, 422.
[8] Emerson, *Journals*, X, 195.

patriotism called forth rested on the traditional assumption that men possess natural rights to life, liberty, and the pursuit of happiness and that the nation is only a convenient instrument for realizing these rights. The time-honored identification of American patriotism with liberty still possessed vitality.

In protest against the doctrine that the nation is the highest end and achievement of civilization, the older cosmopolitan ideal reappeared in the form of the new internationalism. Likewise in the reassertions of the earlier conception of nationalism and patriotism the eighteenth-century emphasis on reason was once more invoked against mere feeling.

Perhaps the man in whom the older type of nationalism and patriotism and the newer currents of thought came closest was Walt Whitman. The "Good Gray Poet" in antebellum days had been representative, as Emerson was not, of a sort of spread-eagle patriotism which justified the Mexican War as an expansion of American liberty into a benighted country. The sacrifices and suffering of the Civil War on both sides had aroused in him a mystic compassion which often asserted itself in a symbolic conception of a new, reunited, organic nation. At the same time, even in the 40's and 50's, Whitman's individualism had checked his proneness to an all-inclusive patriotism and nationalism. The nationalism he sang in no sense kept him from singing even more lustily of the ability of human beings to live freely together without governmental restraint, in joyous, creative comradeship.

In the post-Civil War decades Whitman continued to think of the nation, not merely as a living organism, but as an instrument through which men can best realize and express their divine sense of fellowship, their immense capacity to cooperate for the common good. Few critics in the Gilded Age cut more deeply than he did in his indictment of "the national cancer" of materialism and greed, of public and private corruption, of poverty, inequality, and the growing power of great wealth. Nor did he abandon his faith in men's right and duty to revolt against a nation if it should betray its great function of enhancing the capacities of all men and women for free, creative, happy living:

> *Still though the one I sing:*
> *(One, yet of contradictions made)*
> *I dedicate to Nationality,*
> *I leave him in revolt,*
> *(O latent right of insurrection!*
> *O quenchless, indispensable fire!)* [9]

Nor did he identify the particular foreign policy of the government with the good of humanity, as he had done in 1846. Only insofar as America served mankind, he declared, did he reverence, love, and build for America.

The reassertions of the older, liberal, humanitarian, and individualistic type of patriotism can best be understood through representative illustrations. It was this traditional type of patriotism that led James Russell Lowell to write of George William Curtis, the crusader for honesty in public life:

> *I loved my Country so as only they*
> *Who love a mother fit to die for may;*
> *I loved her old renown, her stainless fame,—*
> *What better proof than that I loathed her shame?* [10]

Lowell developed the idea in 1886 by contrasting the martial type of patriotism that touches the heart and kindles the imagination and energies of men with that more sedate, less picturesque, and inspiring day-by-day patriotism that strives to enlighten public opinion by inculcating civic courage and independence of mind, by showing the fallacy of accepting clamor as argument and endlessly repeated slogans as syllogisms.

In their discussions of patriotism, leading Catholic thinkers deplored the tendency to regard the nation as the supreme end of life and the related emphases on a national honor and a national interest which easily ran into chauvinism. No voice in the Roman Church was more eloquent, more closely akin to the temper of the Emersonian insistence on the higher law of truth and morality than

[9] Walt Whitman, *Leaves of Grass* (New York, 1917), p. 14.
[10] James Russell Lowell, *Poems* (Boston and New York, 1890), IV, 144.

that of Bishop Spalding of Peoria. In his eyes, patriotism was a desire for a richer, wider life; love of country was "the love of truth, the love of justice, the love of righteousness." The national life was at fault, continued Bishop Spalding, if it "be not in harmony with the eternal principles on which all right human life rests; . . . and he alone is a patriot who is willing to suffer obloquy and the loss of money and friends, rather than betray the cause of truth, justice, and righteousness, for only by being faithful to this can he rightly serve his country." [11]

In a somewhat more concrete way the same pattern of thought was clear in the comments on patriotism from scores of other Americans. Thus Frederick W. Schultz, in his *Politics and Patriotism* (1895), declared that only free men, not slaves and serfs, can be patriots, and that therefore the growth of democracy is requisite for the advance of patriotism. It was this approach that explained the growing tendency to distinguish between "spurious" and "true" patriotism. The one, declared Louis F. Post in his *Ethics of Democracy* (1903), was mere instinct, uninformed emotion, hero response; the other was social intelligence. The one worshiped the flag as a sacred crystallization of the past; the other looked on the country's emblem as the symbol of the nation's highest aspirations. The one made a fetish of obedience to lawmakers and presidents on the ground of national policy; the other gave respect and obedience to those in office only when they meted out justice to all alike, at home and abroad.[12]

More concretely still, others applied this general idea of patriotism to the issues of the day. It was this outlook that in the 70's and 80's, for example, inspired civil service reformers to attack political corruption. In the name of patriotism Cardinal Gibbons demanded that the buyers and sellers of votes be declared infamous enemies of their country. Such a conception of patriotism as public conscience led to an insistence that men cultivate the same sort of honesty and integrity in dealing with the government—the nation's representative—that they were accustomed to observe in private transactions.

[11] John Lancaster Spalding, *Opportunity and Other Essays* (Chicago, 1901), p. 193.
[12] Louis F. Post, *Ethics of Democracy* (New York, 1903), p. 330.

Only then, declared one writer, would a citizen to whom one could trust his life shrink from cheating the government out of a postage stamp.

Even more pressing problems figured in the reassertions of earlier conceptions of patriotism as love of a land standing for human rights, justice, and abundance. Agrarian grievances, frequent widespread unemployment, the growing economic insecurity of small-business men, all these brought into high relief the relationship between national loyalty and economic well-being. On occasion, a champion of economic justice to the people spoke boldly. Thus a writer in *The Arena* declared that "men will love their country and look with hopeful assurance at the future, when their stomachs are filled and their backs clothed. . . . You make a patriot out of a man when you make him contented and happy." [13] Labor leaders in general did not talk so bluntly, but they did deplore the tendency of business and a large section of the public to regard unions and strikes as unpatriotic, and they insisted that the movement for better working conditions was only a continuation of the old struggle the forefathers had waged in the American Revolution when they proclaimed the rights of man and the right of self-determination of all people.

The most unequivocal and dramatic indictment of traditional patriotism was that of the small groups of anarchists and Marxist socialists who began to expound their doctrines in the last three decades of the nineteenth century. Differing indeed at a great many essential points, the diagnoses they made of nationalism and patriotism were strikingly similar.

The common element in these diagnoses was fairly simple. They traced the origin of the national state to the alliance which royal tyrants had made with the rising middle class in their efforts to overthrow feudalism. In the eyes of socialists and anarchists, the national state substituted the unity of a common language, a common blood, and a common past for the unity of the international working class. The emergence of the national state, dominated by the middle class, was an indispensable step in the evolution of a class-

13 *Arena,* XIX (June, 1898), 749.

less society, but it only slightly changed the subordinate status of the working class. For, the argument continued, the exploiting capitalists in the middle class now kept down the workers with an iron heel and the severity was tempered by the doctrine of nationalism and patriotism, a doctrine which proved highly suitable to their purposes. For patriotism and nationalism enabled them to divert attention from the struggles of the people within the nation to throw off the capitalist yoke and made it possible for them to rally the masses for wars in the interest of capitalism against brother workers in other lands.

On the basis of such a diagnosis of the ills of the time the socialists and anarchists logically sought to unite those of like economic interests the world over in a common cause, the overthrow of capitalism and its ally, the national state. "Patriotism," declared a typical socialist indictment, "by drawing together and mixing up rich and poor in one and the same country, stands in the way of that vision of the class war, just as by placing formidable armies at the service of the propertied classes it protects them against popular demands." [14] Thus the working masses in fact have no country. The patriotic analogy of the motherland is false and dangerous. No capitalist nation provides for the masses as any mother provides for her children: on the contrary, the nation is, if there must be such analogies, the cruel stepmother who strips all but a pittance from the pockets of all save the few, favored offspring of her own. The sooner the masses learn this, the sooner they will refuse to be blinded by flag waving and national slogans; the sooner they will understand that the only war they can properly support is social revolution. So the radical socialist argument ran.

No American figure in the left-wing movement spoke more frequently or more bitterly about patriotism than the anarchist leader, Emma Goldman. With burning zeal she made good use of the arguments not only of Bakunin and Hervé, but of the sainted Tolstoy as well. Patriotism, she declared, has been artificially created by the exploiting capitalists and their henchmen: it is the great super-

[14] *International Socialist Review,* XVII (April, 1917), 594.

stition, the most audacious lie of the modern age. But its days are numbered. The conceit, the arrogance, and the egotism that lie at its roots cannot insure its future. In the first place, the patriotic assumption that the world is divided into tiny specks each with its own iron gate is a denial, according to anarchist teaching, of the great fact of the international movement of workers whose only loyalty is to the revolution that is to destroy capitalism and the national state alike and to establish the freedom of all men and women from the chains of clericalism, militarism, nationalism, and wage slavery.

Emma Goldman went on. The time has passed, she said, when people can remember their childhood home as a place of freedom and joyous play, of heroic stories at their mothers' knees. It has become the grime of factory and mill, the battleground of workers and of the soldiers who serve the exploiter. The stories mothers now tell their children, the memories these children themselves will hold, are "of sorrow, tears, and grief." The awful waste involved in the patriotic myth—the waste of modern war in behalf of an imperialistic capitalism—can only speed the death of national loyalty and the triumph of freedom.[15]

Such a picture of patriotism did not, however, have much appeal for the American working people. It was easy to brand anarchism and socialism as alien importations, as un-American, as having no validity at all in the United States, which had presumably never known either social classes in the European sense or the class struggle as Marx and Engels expounded it. The fact that the indictment of socialism and anarchism as un-American enjoyed widespread popularity suggests how potent were the older concepts of national loyalty and patriotism.

Although socialism did indeed make marked headway between the Spanish-American War and the First World War, the 90's in truth witnessed the triumph of two ideas and policies which precluded, at least for the time, any victory of the class ideology of the extreme left. Insofar as the urban workers followed the

[15] Emma Goldman, *Patriotism: A Menace to Liberty* (New York, 1908), *passim*.

Populists, they accepted the idea that they were not a class, but merely a part of "the people." Insofar as they followed Samuel Gompers and the American Federation of Labor, the workers' movement that displayed the greatest strength, they rejected the doctrine of class conflict with its implications for patriotism. They accepted, rather, that of union control of jobs, hours, working conditions, and wages, a doctrine in no irreconcilable conflict with the conventional forms of national loyalty and patriotism.

The pattern thus laid down persisted in spite of the vigor displayed here and there by the International Workers of the World, who adopted the anarchist indictment of patriotism. In the social and political revolt of the first fifteen years of the new century, workers and the so-called middle class cemented the bonds between them in the crusade against the "wicked monopolists" for the restoration of the older America in which the little fellow had his fair chance to get ahead. The response to the call of patriotism by all but a minority of workers when the country declared war in 1917 was to prove again that the socialist and anarchist indictment of national loyalty had largely fallen on deaf ears.

In our own day, even the socialists and communists have come to speak in terms of the national traditions and purposes and to identify their programs with patriotism. They may yet revert to the old doctrines. In any case, in the history of American patriotism the earlier indictment of the left is significant as the most pronounced and relentless of all the criticisms that the concept of national loyalty has called forth.

In contrast to this very small but highly vocal minority of the extreme left, most of the advocates of specific radical programs for the solution of economic ailments identified their creed with the traditionally American conception of loyalty to a land that provides everyone with fair opportunities to win the good life. Thus William H. ("Coin") Harvey founded the Patriots of America for "restoring general prosperity and to again set the Republic firmly on its foundation, where it will be free from all vandal hands." [16] Henry George based his program on the philosophy of the Declara-

[16] William H. Harvey, *The Patriots of America* (Chicago, 1895), p. 46.

tion of Independence and identified it from start to finish with the American patriotic conception of a land which guarantees to man his inborn right to pursue happiness.

Edward Bellamy baptized his form of socialism "Nationalism" on the score that "what Socialism desires to reach in a universal way for the world, Nationalism desires to obtain within the limits of the nation. Inasmuch as there is a tendency in the human race to crystallize around national centers, Nationalism thinks it best to respect these boundaries." [17] America, being a self-contained nation, could embark on socialism far more easily than any European country, since here it was not necessary to ask leave, so to speak, of other lands. On another occasion, Bellamy declared that the term nationalism seemed appropriate because "its purpose was to realize the idea of the nation with a grandeur and completeness never before conceived, not as an association of men for certain merely political functions affecting their happiness only remotely and superficially, but as a family, a vital union, a common life, a mighty heaven-touching tree whose leaves are its people, fed from its veins, and feeding it in turn." [18]

The explanation of the term Nationalism, by the man who looked "backward," received further amplification. It was adopted, Bellamy confessed on one occasion, because it would thus be more difficult to stigmatize a socialistic movement so named. One of his followers remarked that "Nationalism stands for Patriotism, while European Socialism considers that sentiment a vice rather than a virtue. . . . We are proud of Uncle Sam, and what we intend to do is to enable him to grow on the very lines that were laid down by the Pilgrims when they landed on Plymouth Rock." [19] This was neither the first nor the last time that radicals identified their cause with patriotism.

The traditional association of patriotism with human well-being also figured in the movement to enhance the powers of the federal government as a public-service agency. John Bascom, Frank Good-

[17] Rabbi Solomon Schindler, "What Is Nationalism?" *New England Magazine*, n.s. VII (September, 1892), 54.
[18] *Edward Bellamy Speaks Again* (Kansas City, 1937), p. 28.
[19] Laurence Gronlund, "Nationalism," *Arena*, I (January, 1890), 158.

now, and Herbert Croly all favored increasing the powers of the national government that it might better promote social and economic justice, whether through control of predatory corporations or through the enactment of social legislation. In stoutly defending the duty of the government to end the ruthless exploitation of natural resources for private gain, President Van Hise of the University of Wisconsin declared that "he who thinks not of himself primarily, but of the race and its future, is the new patriot." [20]

Somewhat under the spell of the doctrine of evolution or perhaps of the pragmatic philosophy, President Alderman of the University of Virginia set forth in an address delivered in 1905 to the New York Chamber of Commerce a comparable conception of patriotism. At different times and under different conditions, the speaker declared, patriotism had expressed itself now in one form, now in another: in George Washington it was the struggle for manhood rights, a struggle still incomplete in Russia; in Emerson, it was arousing the intellect of the nation from its sluggish deference to an ill-suited and sterile Old World culture; in Lincoln and Lee, it was devotion to a particular theory of government; in the great leaders of post-Civil War industry, it was giving the nation a unity of steel and steam, and adapting to man's uses the resources of the land; and now patriotism had come to mean a reaction against the unsocial individualism of those industrial giants. It was now a movement for the economic rights of the common man, that he might share more equitably in the material wealth of the country and in its treasures of mind and spirit.[21]

The patriotism that spoke in terms of social responsibilities and humane values rather than in terms of national honor and national interest inspired the leaders of the anti-imperialist crusade at the turn of the century. In taking their stand against the conquest of the Filipinos and the retention of Spain's former colonies, the anti-imperialists believed they were merely abiding by the fundamental assertion in the Declaration of Independence of the right

[20] Charles R. Van Hise, *The Conservation of Natural Resources* (New York, 1910), p. 378.
[21] Edwin A. Alderman, "The Making of a National Spirit," *Harper's Weekly*, XLIX (December 9, 1905), 1776–1777.

of self-determination of peoples. In their minds the path of empire led away from the foundations of American patriotism. It led to false conceptions of national interest and national honor, to power politics, huge armaments, and inevitable war. It subverted the civil liberties. It brought heavy taxation. It meant increase of powers in the already dangerously overburdened central government. In denouncing efforts to identify imperialism with patriotism, William Everett in his Harvard Phi Beta Kappa oration in 1901 eloquently concluded: "Brethren, even as Athens began by patriotism and passed into tyranny, then into ruin, so shall every nation bow who interprets patriotism to mean that it is the only nation in the world, and that every other that stands in the way of what it chooses to call destiny, must be crushed." [22]

Within the peace movement itself, which likewise condemned imperialism, it was possible to draw on an old tradition in opposing the chauvinistic type of patriotism. American pacifism had always rested on the Christian concept of the sanctity of human life and on that higher law of God that forbade men, even at the behest of the state, to kill and to work injustice. No slogan enjoyed more favor among peace men than William Lloyd Garrison's "my country is the world." The economic burdens war brings to the common man; the profiteering of the well-to-do; the appeals of demagogues to patriotism and battle as a way out of their difficulties; the whitewashing of past wars in the name of patriotism —all these arguments filled the pages of peace literature long before the Civil War. Charles Sumner, moreover, had explored the notion of national honor and found that it was relative to time and circumstance, to what the foe in a given controversy deemed its honor. Gerrit Smith in his address before the American Peace Society in 1858 had gone even further in ridiculing the belief that a nation is a superbeing, above and different from the citizens composing it, endowed with a moral irresponsibility to which men must conform.

To such a body of thought friends of peace now appealed in

[22] William Everett, *An Oration, Delivered before the Phi Beta Kappa Society of Harvard College* (Richmond, Indiana, 1901), p. 23.

opposing the Spanish-American War and the imperialism that followed in its wake. The traditional doctrines were now implemented and called into service in criticizing what was deemed a hollow and explosively emotional patriotism. The true patriot was defined as one who is "above all things loyal to civilization, and includes under this head everything which brings human affairs under the control of reason, and fosters the larger hopes of the race for the good time coming when the war-drum shall beat no longer, and the battle-flags be furled. . . . There is no one," continued this exponent of the internationalist conception of patriotism, "so criminal, or so vicious, or so silly, or so empty-headed that he cannot be a patriot by longing and 'hollering' for war, and feeling 'insulted' by some foreigner, and wanting to have the insult washed out in somebody else's blood in a fight of which he will be a spectator merely." [23]

More pregnant for the future was the insistence that the growth of international trade, of a network of treaties and agreements, and of all sorts of unions for particular purposes had, in fact, created an international interest and an international mind. Thus national sovereignty, the basis of the my-country-right-or-wrong type of patriotism, was held to be no longer realistic. National well-being could not be pursued anywhere apart from the advancement of freedom and order in the whole world. This was the pacifist patriotism.

It was not only at peace meetings that this idea was expounded. On Washington's Birthday in 1914, only a few months before the flames of war broke out across the Atlantic, Chaplain Frank Oliver Hall forthrightly brought the doctrine before the New York chapter of the Sons of the American Revolution. Maintaining that men could no longer be true Americans unless they shared in that larger patriotism that expressed itself, not in loving the United States the less, but humanity the more, the speaker insisted that the great contribution America had made to history was

a demonstration that it is possible for all classes and conditions of men, all nationalities, races, and colors to live together in unity.

[23] *Nation*, LIV (February 4, 1892), 83.

America had shown the world the stupendous spectacle of thirteen independent nations, and then thirty and now forty-eight, different from each other in soil, climate, and history, coming together and organizing a federation, and forgetting their differences in a common loyalty. Men are beginning to see that what America has done the world can do. If a federation of fifty independent states, then why not a federation of the world? The United States of America has set people to dreaming of the United States of the Earth. That is our contribution and the glory will be America's. When the federation of the world is achieved . . . and the hatreds of the past shall have been superseded by the consciousness of human brotherhood, we need not fear that our love of the homeland will diminish.[24]

In depending, as they did, on education as the principal means for accelerating the victory of an internationalism of justice, friends of peace were compelled to direct their attention to the schools, the agency from which every group, including the integral nationalists, expected so much. It is true that there was little or no discussion of internationalism at the meetings of the National Education Association during the last decade of the nineteenth century. It is also true that teachers reported that the classrooms were commonly decorated with warlike pictures and that the main emphasis in the teaching of history was on a narrow type of patriotism. But winds from a different direction stirred the air. In 1885 the Quaker, Josiah Leeds, began a crusade to remove war propaganda and the chauvinistic type of patriotism from textbooks. Josephus Nelson Larned, public librarian and superintendent of schools in Buffalo, spoke out at the turn of the century against the prevalent stress in history teaching on "the bullying pride" of country, the concealment of national shortcomings, and the our-country-right-or-wrong slogan. With all its limitations, the new emphasis on objective history which had taken hold of college instruction in that subject, and the effort to apply this to teaching in the schools, gave substance to the growing optimism on the part of the critics of militaristic, integral nationalism.

The struggle between the two groups for the control of the mind

[24] Frank Oliver Hall, *The Expansion of Patriotism* (New York, 1914), p. 10.

of the child led in the first decade of the twentieth century both to a well-planned criticism of integral nationalism and to what its opponents thought of as a constructive alternative. This was closely related to the reaction in certain educational circles against the emphasis on routine and the mechanical inculcation of abstract generalities. Patriotism, according to this way of viewing things, could best be taught, not by ritual, not by flag salutes, not by insisting on lip service and the memorizing of slogans, but rather by day-by-day emphasis on actual service, by concrete object lessons of good citizenship.[25]

Thus a group of educators regarding themselves as an advance guard began to insist on a civic as opposed to a military patriotism. Civic patriotism took as its point of departure the small group—family, school, church, community—and pointed in concrete ways to the actual meaning of sacrifice for the common good. Only in this way, it was held, could the child learn the meaning of a constructive patriotism in terms of the nation as a whole. Emphasis on the achievements of the United States in promoting the well-being of all the people was to replace the time-sanctioned stressing of wars. Nor was the teacher to neglect pointing out the virtues of other lands. Advocates of the new point of view also urged the importance of making the child understand that the symbols of patriotism—the flag above all else—have importance only insofar as they represent the best the country has stood for, the ideals yet to be fully achieved.

In brief, then, Americans for whom love of and loyalty to country meant devotion to humanity and democracy, peace and freedom, deplored the prevalent idea that patriotism could be taught from a cut-and-dried manual. What the school should foster was not mere veneration and blind devotion to country, right or wrong, but an intelligent understanding of country, of its laws, institutions, its splendid domain and natural beauty, its spirit of freedom, its "triumphant march onward" in the sphere of democracy and humane values. Only through such an intelligent understanding, only if shortcomings and ways for overcoming them entered into the pic-

[25] A good example of this school of thought is William Burnham's "Every-Day Patriotism," *Outlook*, XC (November 7, 1908), 535 ff.

ture, could "progressive patriotism" manifest itself. All this, of course, represented not only the basic assumptions of the internationalists as such but also those of the various types of reformers who came to exert so much influence in the last decade of the nineteenth century and in the first dozen years or so of the twentieth.

All these ideas took classic form in the writings of John Dewey: it was he who gave systematic philosophical expression to the belief that the more exclusive types of nationalism and patriotism were no longer adequate instruments to test plans for the solution of pressing problems. He recognized the past services of even the narrower, more chauvinistic patriotism in forcing men out of limited sectionalisms into larger social units and in creating loyalty to a state which subordinated petty and selfish interests; but he pointed out that this type of nationalism and patriotism now stood in the way of continuing the same process by setting up a dislike of all who did not find themselves within the charmed national circle.

If in the past, Dewey continued, our geographical isolation had largely protected us from the "harsh, selfish, exclusive aspects of nationalism," this was no longer true. The task now was to develop the desirable aspects of nationalism, that is, those that served as the friend, not the foe, of the international society that had come into being. Only such constructive patriotism would enable people to prevent self-seeking politicians from cleverly playing on the emotion of national loyalty and the ignorance of other lands to advance their own interests.

Dewey believed that the integral emphasis in nationalism was as ill-suited an instrument for solving problems as was drawing a line to hem in loyalties at the national frontiers. What made the American nation unique and great, he held, was the richness, the variety of its peoples. "The same feeling that leads us to recognize each other's individuality," he declared, "to respect individuality between person and person, also leads us to respect those elements of diversification in cultural traits which differentiate our national life." [26] Thus he deplored the tendency, during the First World War, to insist on nation-wide conformity to conventional ideas of

[26] John Dewey, "The Principle of Nationality," *Menorah Journal*, III (October, 1917), 206.

national loyalty and patriotism. Desirable and necessary though unity in the crisis was, it could best be obtained, Dewey held, through intelligence and education, rather than through fear, compulsion, and violence. Such short cuts to the desired end could only, he urged, breed bitter hatreds.

In holding that the United States is a much more interesting and promising country because of local diversity, because Southerners, New Englanders, Midwesterners, and Far Westerners all differ, Dewey, the instrumentalist, was joining hands with a distinguished philosopher of a very different school. Josiah Royce, an absolute idealist, had first given serious consideration to the relations between provincial and national loyalty. In 1908 he had urged the need of preserving and developing provincial loyalty, as a useful, if not indeed a necessary, factor in national loyalty. Provincial loyalties, urged the Harvard philosopher, need not be of a jealous nature; they need not be narrow; they need in no sense detract from national loyalty. If vigorous and sustained, they would help give newcomers in any community—and American communities were in large part made up of newcomers—the feeling that there was something to attach themselves to, that by finding the roots of the community they might become genuinely a part of it.

Such provincial loyalty, Royce insisted, was the first and natural step toward national loyalty of a meaningful sort. The standardization and conformity so uppermost in modern civilization, especially in America, in Royce's eyes needed the counteractant of provincial differences and provincial loyalties. The place to foster the ideals of service and loyalty to the nation was in the province, with its own traditions, its own ways of thinking and speaking, its own way of setting up social wisdom to guide into channels of safety the emotional mob psychology of the day.[27]

A variant of this approach was made by Mary P. Follett in her book, *The New State* (1918). Patriotism, if it were not to be a blind, herd instinct, must be creatively developed, and this, Miss Follett held, could best be done in small groups in every neighbor-

[27] Josiah Royce, *Race Questions, Provincialism, and Other American Problems* (New York, 1908), pp. 61 *ff.*

hood. As these groups learned to cooperate and join with others for larger community ends, they were taking the first steps toward a truly creative loyalty to the nation and—at length—to the world-state.

The emphasis which Royce, Dewey, Follett and others were putting on loyalty to the community and the province was reinforced by the local-color school of literature and by the researches and studies of historians who discovered and developed the histories of the various sections. Geographers and sociologists helped to broaden the old type of political-economic sectionalism into a comprehensive regionalism. This was based not only on economic and political differences, but on geographical, climatic, ethnic, and sociological peculiarities. In the spirit of Miss Follett, the new regionalists urged the importance of a creative, regional planning in relation to the needs, potentialities, and well-being not only of the people of the region, but of the whole nation as well. This type of regionalism did not become a well-formulated social philosophy until the 1920's and the 1930's, but the foundations for it were laid earlier.

Although the approach of Royce and the exponents of community and regional activity was in no sense a thrust at national loyalty—quite the contrary—it was a significant protest against that conformity, mob spirit, and loss of local leadership and initiative which the organic, integral type of patriotism seemed to breed, especially in a culture that tended to become ever more dominated by technology.

In certain expositions of loyalty to the nation which may properly be regarded as critiques of the organic, all-inclusive type of patriotism, there were apparent qualities of thought that reflected in an even more striking way frontier developments. A case in point is the turn that Josiah Royce's colleague at Harvard, William James, gave to the discussion of the warlike impulse so closely associated with national loyalty. In his epoch-making *Principles of Psychology* (1890) he had attached much weight to what he regarded as inborn instincts, such as warlike aggressiveness. Now our ancestors, James believed, had, as it were, bred pugnacity into our very bones and marrow; nor would thousands of years of peace breed it out.

Yet the instinct theory was not the last word for James. He likewise attached much importance to the possible control of instincts through intelligent habit formation. He moreover made a great point of the similarly instrumental or functional role of what he called "energy-releasing ideas." In the front rank of these, he held, stands patriotism with its various components, such as "fatherland," "flag," "Union," "Monroe Doctrine," and "national honor." When effective in an individual's life, such ideas can transfigure it by unlocking innumerable and unsuspected powers.

Thus it was, James continued in his memorable essay, "A Moral Equivalent for War," that no one thinks "patriotism . . . discreditable; nor does anyone deny that war is the romance of history." [28] In point of fact, the conventional type of patriotism that emphasizes the martial virtues, whatever its limitations, is the enduring cement that holds society together. It is indispensable so long as there is no higher form of social intelligence. In consequence, the martial virtues so intimately associated with patriotism would somehow insist on being preserved.

In James' mind it was not necessary for them to be perpetuated through war. All the basic impulses of patriotism—the pugnacious instinct "bred in the bone," the energy-releasing ideas such as that of country, the martial virtues so necessary for the coherence of society, can find suitable expression, he thought, in socially useful activities. Such activities might be arduous ventures like road building, the irrigation of the desert, and the reclamation of swamps. In cooperative attacks on these and other obstacles that stand in the way of realizing a better society, youth may find a suitable outlet for their aggressive instincts without forfeiting loyalty and without endangering the cohesiveness of society.

For the time—and it was a time when the idea of laissez faire still enjoyed much lip service in our essentially unplanned culture —James' constructive proposals fell largely on deaf ears. But the probing into the very heart of the problem of patriotism did not end. William Graham Sumner, the Yale economist and sociologist

[28] William James, *Memories and Studies* (New York, 1911), p. 275.

whose defense of laissez faire made him a celebrated figure, had long taught that much which man deemed above time and place in the sphere of values actually could be better understood in terms of folkways and mores—unconscious social habits that had emerged in some remote era in response to needs which might or might not still survive as actual needs. The implications for patriotism of such a sociology were sensed and developed by the penetrating Norwegian-American scholar, Thorstein Veblen, who as a student at Yale had become familiar with Sumner's teachings. Veblen, however, gave a very different turn to Sumner's conception of mores and folkways.

Veblen defined patriotism as "a sense of partisan solidarity in respect of prestige." [29] The patriotic spirit for Veblen was a spirit of emulation, but a spirit of emulation shot through with a sense of solidarity. Patriotism ennobles the individual's urge to be of and in a group; it provides him with ideals that mask his desire for privilege and prerogative by enabling him subtly to enjoy and to pursue privilege and prerogative under the sanction of love of, and devotion to, country.

In patriotism Veblen saw even more significant functions. As property rights develop, community interests are emasculated, he argued, and one after the other disappear. Collective prestige, which patriotism unconsciously means for almost all men, remains the sole interest holding the community together. In glorifying and in making sacrifices for the nation, the common man, Veblen remarked, is guided by no consciously sordid zeal. In point of fact, the modern economy with its great inequality of wealth and its vast aggregations of corporate capital, needs an over-all sanction and ideal to enlist the common people in its competitions with foreign industry and trade.

Patriotism, Veblen argued, provides business with just that sanction and ideal. The common man himself does not profit from imperialist wars, waged for the advantage of capital under the banner of patriotism; but he does not know this. On the contrary, he has

29 Thorstein Veblen, *On the Nature of Peace* (New York, 1917), p. 31.

come, as a result of the way in which patriotism had embedded itself in the folkways and mores, to identify almost all that is desirable with patriotism.

In its fully developed form, Veblen's critique of patriotism went even further. With penetrating shrewdness he compared the nation's allegedly inalienable right of self-direction and self-help with the so-called similar right of the individual to direct his activities and aid himself—a right that Sumner made the core of his social philosophy. To Veblen in each case such a so-called right was in the nature of a "divine right," incapable of bearing scrutiny. "There is the further parallel," he continued, that "the ordinary exercise of these rights confers no material benefit on the underlying community. In practical effect, the exercise of such divine rights, whether by sovereign monarch or by the officials of a sovereign nation, works damage and discomfort to one and another, within the national frontiers or beyond them, with nothing better to show for it than some relatively slight gain in prestige or in wealth for some relatively small group of privileged persons or vested interests." [30]

Yet Thorstein Veblen saw a future check to all this. As industry came to be internationalized in cartels, overrunning all national boundaries, the old concept of "national integrity" would have no meaning for it. National pretensions, prestige, patriotism itself, would cease to be serviceable in the new order. No doubt Veblen underestimated the pull and lasting qualities of the emotion of patriotism—his analyses oversimplified a highly complex phenomenon. No doubt he had little immediate influence on the thought of others. Yet no one can read his discussion without recognizing that among all the psychological and sociological analyses of patriotism, his is outstanding by reason of its acute approach.

[30] Thorstein Veblen, "Live and Let Live." *Dial.* CXVI (January 11, 1919), 19.

IX: LOYALTY IN WORLD CRISIS

*Our Government's greatest danger lurks in those pagan patriots who,
without malice, without evil designs of any kind, but heedlessly,
support any cause, however menacing it may be to American ideals,
if its promoters decorate it richly enough with the American flag.*

LOUIS F. POST, 1923

*Lives of nations are determined, not by the count of years, but by
the life-time of the human spirit. The life-time of man is three-
score years and ten: a little more, a little less. The life of a nation
is the fullness of the measure of its will to life. A nation, like a
person, has a body—a body that must be fed and clothed and
housed, invigorated and rested, in a manner that measures up to the
standards of our time. A nation, like a person, has a mind—a mind
that must be kept informed and alert, that must know itself, that
understands the hopes and the needs of its neighbors—all the other
nations that live within the narrowing circle of the world. A nation,
like a person, has something deeper, something more permanent,
something larger than the sum of all its parts. It is that something
which matters most to the future, which calls forth the most sacred
guarding of its present.*

FRANKLIN D. ROOSEVELT, 1941

THE FIRST WORLD WAR heightened certain aspects of American
patriotic thought and feeling. Among these was hatred of an ex-
ternal foe, the association of military power with loyalty and devotion to country, and that intensely emotional insistence on unity
which had been so central a feature of the integral type of nationalism. The war gave mass expression to all these aspects of patriotism.
Hitherto they had been most frequently articulated by intellectuals,
professional patriotic organizations, and public men. Now they became thoroughly organized and widely and efficiently publicized,

Two factors explain these developments, at least in large part. The broadening and intensification of fear and hatred of an enemy, the fervent insistence on unity and conformity—if need be, by compulsion—resulted in the first instance from the essentially new nature of war. Former struggles by and large involved the civilian population only in minor ways. Now war required mass morale, support, and participation. Hence patriotism could hardly be left to casual education, to chance. It must be highly organized, skillfully directed. It must be, if necessary, commanded and enforced outright. In the second place the availability of new media for influencing mass opinion—the technique of the "drive," the use of the movies and of advertising in particular—added a fresh element to the whole picture.

Almost from the start of the war in Europe a group of Americans, small at first, agitated for great increases in the armed strength of the nation. Some said that only thorough preparedness for war could enforce American neutral rights and thus safeguard peace for America. Others urged that the United States must sooner or later become involved in the war, that both our interests and our honor demanded it. And some declared that in full preparation for war American society would find the unifying principle, the patriotic discipline, the need of which was so apparent. Whatever the argument, the sponsors of preparedness always identified it with loyalty to the nation. The two chief champions of the movement in its early stages—General Leonard Wood and Theodore Roosevelt—denounced Wilson as blind, misguided, cowardly, and, by implication at least, unpatriotic, for his indifference to the cries for a big navy and a big army. The Democrats in turn suspected that Roosevelt was mainly seeking a popular issue for the presidential campaign of 1916.

The preparedness movement, as the crusade was called, aroused great fervor. General Wood converted hundreds of men of substance and influence into impassioned missionaries through the civilian training camps which he had begun at Plattsburg in the summer of 1913. The older patriotic societies, such as the D.A.R., gave the campaign their blessing and their support. New groups, notably the Navy League, the American Defense Society, and the National Security League, flooded the country with high-pressure speakers, sensational books and pamphlets, and spirited articles in magazines and newspapers. Emotional movies laid bare the defenseless state of the nation and pictured graphically the catastrophe that would follow invasion by a foreign foe. As if to startle complacent Americans still more an army officer claimed, in a widely publicized volume, that in previous wars Americans had fought inefficiently and often wretchedly for mere lack of adequate training and preparation: our past wars thus appeared very different from the glorious episodes patriots had long pictured them.

No technique used in the preparedness movement—not even the highly effective lobbies in Congress—proved more impressive than the mammoth parades. The one in New York on May 13, 1916, was, as the New York *Times* described it, the "greatest civilian marching demonstration in the history of the world." [1] Sixty-three divisions of men and women, two hundred bands, and fifty drum corps marched past cheering throngs on the sidewalks and notable personages in hundreds of grandstands. The procession took over eleven hours to pass a given point. Hundreds of thousands of flags decorated public and private buildings. The Union League Club was magnificently illuminated by an electric sign reading "Absolute and Unqualified Loyalty to Our Country."

The demonstration did much to impress influential and articulate groups throughout the country. It was soon followed by similar parades in all the great metropolitan centers of the nation. Never before had the military aspect of patriotism been organized on such a high-pitched emotional level. Never before had it enjoyed such wide support.

The preparedness movement won the day, thanks to skillful leadership and ample financial backing, thanks to the intoxicating glamor of the parades and to the broad character of its argumentative appeals, thanks above all to our vexing relations with Mexico and our far more troubled relations with European belligerents. The warning of the pacifists that the crusade was the first step to mili-

[1] New York *Times*, May 14, 1916.

tarism and war failed to exert any great influence in government circles. The efforts of Senator LaFollette to associate the movement with the desire of munitions makers and Wall Street financiers to feather their nests went for the most part unheeded. So too did the socialist indictment, which identified national pride and military power with the nefarious designs of an imperialistic capitalism. Nor was favor shown Carlton Parker's attempt to explain the opposition of such dissidents as the I.W.W.'s to the whole matter. This farseeing labor-relations specialist contrasted the "cynical disloyalty and contempt for the flag" of the Wobblies, "for whom the United States stirs no memories of satisfaction and happiness," with the vehement enthusiasm for preparedness displayed by the fifty thousand volunteers for the Officer Training Camps, whose patriotism reflected "a rich background of social satisfactions, which in the mind of the young officer had sprung from his country, America." [2]

After the *Lusitania* crisis President Wilson, hitherto largely indifferent to preparedness, was convinced that it was necessary to preserve peace, or, should war come, to insure victory. The pacifists who approved the sentiments of the popular song, "I didn't raise my boy to be a soldier," were, he declared, trying to put pigtails on Uncle Sam! Early in 1916 the president toured the country, seeking public support for the military and naval program he had recommended to Congress. The victory was impressive. It was a victory which created closer and more comprehensive association than ever before between military power and virtues and love of country. Pride in the heroic achievements of American "doughboys," once war was declared and fought out on the battleground of France, confirmed that association.

The closer tie-up of patriotism with military preparedness—and finally with war against an impressive foe—was not the only shift in emphasis in patriotic thought and feeling. Long distressed at what appeared to them the disunity of the country, many Americans saw a powerful cohesive force in the general consciousness of an alien

[2] Carlton Parker, "The I.W.W.," *Atlantic Monthly*, CXX (November, 1917), 655.

foe. In the brief and easily won Spanish-American War the enemy, in more realistic moments looked on as a weakling, only inadequately fulfilled the function of an alien foe to whip up fear and durable hatred. But the Germans were another matter. The effort to arouse patriotism and to stimulate unity in the nation by focusing hatred on everything Teutonic was both systematic and effective.

In the name of patriotism and national loyalty German books were burned by order of educational authorities; German music was proscribed by the influential members of local communities; and instruction in German in schools and colleges was in great measure forbidden by those who directed their fortunes. Even in the most bitter days of Anglophobia the British had never been so widely and so vehemently detested and excoriated as the new foe. Never had the embrace between patriotism and hatred of a foe been so fervent and so intimate.

Hatred of the enemy across the sea was extended to German-Americans at home—again in the name of loyalty to the nation. It was no doubt true that many German-Americans continued to sympathize with the fatherland and to look on the war as a calamity for which British propagandists and sinister Wall Street interests were to blame. But the loyalty of a substantial number of the men and women of German background did not greatly mitigate the hysteria that was directed indiscriminately against German-Americans by self-constituted groups such as the Councils of Defense and even by government-sponsored agencies. It did little good when patriotic German-Americans urged their fellows to buy bonds and to show their loyalty to America in every possible way, including "fighting in the front ranks for freedom." [3] Equally ineffective were admonitions to Americans to recall the devotion and loyalty of German-Americans throughout the nation's past. Far from bringing about the unity of spirit which the denunciators and persecutors of German-Americans professed to desire, the crusade drove a deeper wedge between the "hyphenated Americans" and other groups making up the nation. Nor, as we have seen, did the Ameri-

[3] Julius A. Coller, *Loyalty of German-Americans to the United States* (Washington, 1918), p. 7.

canization movement, which the war greatly intensified, succeed in realizing the transformation of immigrants into thoroughly assimilated Americans.

The German-Americans and related immigrant groups were not alone in being suspected of disloyalty: the confusion of loyalty and morale reached considerably further. Pacifists and socialists, many of whom regarded the war as a mistake or as an incident in capitalistic imperialism, found it increasingly dangerous to express their views. In some instances they were brought to trial for treason under the Sedition Act and sentenced to long terms of imprisonment for alleged interference with the prosecution of the war. In other instances citizens took it upon themselves to mete out violence to those whose loyalty was under suspicion. The I.W.W.'s, who made no secret of their conviction that the war was one for the preservation and expansion of capitalism, met with rough handling in many parts of the country. Even mildly liberal and devoted Americans who merely insisted that the Germans were not all beasts and that German culture had much to commend it were condemned as disloyal or at least utterly lacking in patriotism. Thus, for example, when professors at the University of Nebraska were publicly tried for alleged disloyalty, only the flimsiest evidence was forthcoming. Yet some were dismissed, and the careers of others ruined.

Since the American people had been divided about the wisdom of entering the war and since unnumbered men and women continued to entertain grave doubts about the decision, it is significant that all the prosecutions under the Sedition Act and all the unofficial or quasi official witch-hunting revealed few cases of flagrant or even clear-cut disloyalty. Yet the knowledge that many Americans had felt little enthusiasm for the war explains in part the impassioned and even hysterical efforts to enforce unity. War enthusiasts demanded of their fellow citizens proof of their patriotism and loyalty to America, proof in the form of such visible things as the knitting of sweaters and the folding of bandages, the buying of war bonds, the denunciation of the Germans and of all who did not give unstinted support to the war.

These efforts to mobilize patriotism were immensely facilitated by the discovery of new methods for influencing public opinion through various types of propaganda and pressure. But all this hardly explains the intemperate character of so much patriotic thought and feeling. Much of the intemperance probably resulted from the reluctance of the government in the campaign for the conservation of food and fuel to adopt such controls as rationing. The reliance rather on voluntary cooperation seemed to the patriotic supporters of the war to necessitate steam-roller methods for the desired ends.

Yet it would be a mistake to assume that patriotism during the war was confined to vitriolic hatred and frenzied hysteria, that it was merely the frantic insistence that Germans be damned out of hand, that German-Americans be dealt with summarily, that liberals, pacifists, and socialists be persecuted and thrust into prison for alleged disloyalty. It would be a mistake to see in it merely a compulsory insistence on buying war bonds, accepting curtailments of food, and cheerfully eating substitutes on the famous meatless days. It would be a mistake to suppose that patriotism was mere swagger that concealed the selfish activities of war profiteers piling up their millions in the name of rendering service to the nation in its emergency. Nor was the patriotism of Negroes, Jews, and trade unionists fully expressed in the somewhat pathetic pledges of loyalty by their leaders that appeared in the press. Patriotism was something more than all of this.

In a memorable editorial the *Nation* reminded its readers of what it termed "the minor patriotisms." Over and against all the hysteria, over and against the much publicized contributions of the wealthy dollar-a-year men and the comfortable subscribers to the largest issues of war bonds, stood the contribution of that mass of undistinguished men and women, who without pressure and at great personal sacrifice, willingly made their contributions to their country in its time of trial. "There will be no decorations or memorials for those who have given the nation this service, yet the War would have spelled defeat had they hesitated or refused," the *Nation* wrote. "It were better to recognize the unpretentious loyalty of the men who individually can do but little, to whom even the smallest extra outlay means a very real sacrifice, yet who day by day are giving of their labor and their savings and parting with those that are dear to them because of their deep belief that injustice may be thus redressed and right prevail." [4]

What was felt in the hearts of the lesser folk of whom *The Nation* spoke was, of course, best exemplified on a literary level by the war president, Woodrow Wilson. Indeed, Wilson's addresses brought together almost all the idealistic, liberal, and humane aspects in the American tradition of love for, and devotion to, country. In his historical account of the Civil War and Reconstruction, *Division and Reunion* (1893), he maintained that the United States had never in actuality been a nation until the great struggle between North and South imparted "to the national idea diffused vitality and authentic power." [5] But the young Southerner was too much under the shadow of Reconstruction and the doctrines of state rights and individual liberty to subscribe to the tenets of integral nationalism. He was profoundly influenced by the Christian conception that ideals and spiritual purposes, not material interests and strength, constitute true national greatness. This idea was central to his whole conception of nationalism and patriotism. It was supplemented by faith in moral progress and in cooperation. Wilson was also much influenced by Bagehot's notion that the modern nation is essentially a debating society in which argument and constructive criticism replace the appeals to force represented by such outmoded states as militaristic Prussia.

These general ideas were first systematically advanced by Wilson in an address made in 1899 before the New England Association of Colleges and Preparatory Schools. The Princeton political scientist who was later to be president began by defining patriotism as a principle rather than a sentiment—a principle of devotion to those highest ethical ideals which America was destined to realize and to extend. "I have heard some very selfish purposes served by the expression of the sentiment of patriotism," he remarked with

---

[4] *Nation*, CVII (September 7, 1918), 244–245.
[5] Woodrow Wilson, *Division and Reunion* (New York, 1893), pp. 208 ff., 242, 261.

realistic insight. True service to country, he said, rests first and last on an understanding of what the nation really stands for, what its true meaning actually is. The most notable characteristic of America is, in Wilson's view, its "debating and intellectual polity." Our nation, be it never forgotten, originated in the sharpest sort of criticisms of existing public policy. How deplorable, then, Wilson continued, is that type of patriotism which teaches school children unthinkingly to genuflect to a flag when they are quite ignorant of its true meaning! The teacher must see to it that her pupils "know that this is a flag of liberty of opinion, as well as of political liberty in questions of organization." [6]

There being no known prescription by which love of the individual or love of country can be compelled, patriotism must therefore rest, Wilson concluded, on an understanding of the essentials in the American tradition—self-government, liberty, and equality. But let no one think, he hastened to add, that the flag of the United States is the only flag that stands for these values. Thus, Wilson's was the liberal, humane, and cosmopolitan type of national and patriotic thought for which Jefferson, Emerson, Whitman, and Lincoln had likewise stood.

In theory, at least, Wilson maintained the essential outlines of his earlier conception of patriotism during his presidency. "No man can be a true patriot," he declared in 1914 at the unveiling of the statue in memory of Commodore John Barry, "who does not feel himself shot through and through with a deep ardor for what his country stands for, what its existence means, what its purpose is declared to be in its history and its policy." [7] The individualism he held so dear was reflected in a Fourth of July address at Independence Hall in 1914, when he said that "the most patriotic man . . . is sometimes the man who goes in the direction that he thinks right even when he sees half the world against him." [8] His respect for minorities, above all for the cosmopolitan make-up of the

6 *School Review*, VII (December, 1899), 603.
7 Ray Stannard Baker and William E. Dodd, eds., *The Public Papers of Woodrow Wilson: The New Democracy* (New York, 1925), I, 106–107.
8 *Ibid.*, p. 140.

American people, found expression in his Memorial Day address in 1916. He had no criticism for men who loved the places of their birth so long as that feeling did not drown out their loyalty to the land of their new and voluntary allegiance. The United States was to assimilate its newcomers, not by compulsion, but by education, by intelligence, and by a spiritual process which emphasized, not that which divided Americans, but that which united them.

Once President Wilson committed himself to preparedness it became necessary to harmonize his conception of a liberal, humane, and individualistic debating-society patriotism with the problem of power. Without in any sense losing the ethical note from his patriotic thought, Wilson now emphasized the subordination of the individual that national service implied. A little military training, he urged, would breed in young men "the spirit of obedience, the thought of the Nation, the consciousness of having some kind of personal connection with the great body politic they profess to serve." [9] Without defining national honor precisely, the President again and again asked how he was to maintain it if the country denied him adequate military power. Only power, he concluded, would enable the United States to preserve peace with honor and, if that effort failed, to sustain righteousness, justice, and the golden rule by drawing the sword against the enemy of these virtues.

It was above all Wilson's identification of patriotism with righteousness that provided the keynote to his wartime philosophy. America, he declared, "was given birth to" by a patriotism spiritual and unselfish in type. Her destiny in the world "was to show men the paths of liberty and mutual serviceability, to lift the common man," and to enable him to secure the best possible development.[10] The eloquence of the President's idealism captured the consciences and imaginations of countless Americans who responded to his interpretation of American patriotism.

In reluctantly accepting the issue of war, Wilson came to see the necessity on the international stage of supporting justice with force: he came, in brief, to accept the position of Theodore Roosevelt, his most bitter critic. But at home, at least in most matters

[9] *The Public Papers of Woodrow Wilson*, II, 34.
[10] *Ibid.*, I, 437–438.

involving the rights of private property, the president continued
to rely on ethical appeals to justice and disinterested love of country. Thus he assumed that "patriotism leaves profits out of the
question." In addressing miners and manufacturers in the midsummer of 1917, he insisted that "patriotism and profits ought never
in the present circumstances to be mentioned together. . . .
When soldiers are giving their lives will not he [the patriot] give
his money? No true patriot will permit himself to take toll of their
heroism in money or seek to grow rich by the shedding of their
blood." [11] The President went on to declare that shipowners and
railroad men were doing all they could through high charges to
make the war a failure, though they did not realize or intend that.
Yet despite all these appeals, profits, fortunes even, were made.
Wilson's noble words were not in actuality of much help in di-
vorcing profits from patriotism.

Though in the heat of battle Wilson modified his earlier conceptions of patriotism, he did not qualify at all his conviction of
the patriotic duty of Americans to champion throughout the world
the principles of order, decency, peace, and freedom. He condemned
without mercy those of his opponents on the issue of the League
of Nations who identified Americanism with "isolation and defiant
segregation." In his mind they were only perverting patriotism by
insisting that the dignity and interest of the nation consisted in
standing apart, watching for opportunities to advance selfish interests, involving ourselves in no responsibility "for the maintenance of the right in the world or for the continued vindication of
any of the things for which we entered the war to fight." [12] The
fathers had thought of America as the light of the world, destined
to lead mankind "in the assertion of the rights of peoples and the
rights of free nations; as destined to set a responsible example to
all the world of what free Government is and can do for the maintenance of right standards, both national and international." [13]

Wilson could with good reason regard the type of Americanism

---

[11] Baker and Dodd, eds., *The Public Papers of Woodrow Wilson: War and
Peace* (New York, 1927), I, 75.
[12] *Ibid.*, II, 503–504.
[13] *Ibid.*

which seemed to triumph in the election of 1920 as "spurious and invented for party purposes only." [14] Nevertheless his downfall symbolized the temporary triumph of a kind of Americanism largely alien to his mind. The tragedy was only the more pronounced because he lent himself to—or at least failed to check—the reactionary tendencies that characterized the last two years of his presidency: the deportation, without due regard to the best traditions of American legal procedure, of aliens deemed subversive; the penalties meted out to dissidents and sustained after the shooting stopped; the triumph, in short, of the hysterical type of patriotism so much at odds with his conception of patriotism as intelligence, criticism, freedom, and humanitarianism.

The triumph which the more conservative interests and ideas won during the war itself and which always, of course, were identified with patriotism, found full and feverish expression after the armistice. When unstrung nerves encountered little to check them, this intense national self-consciousness and social-economic conservatism, publicized by its supporters as Americanism, expressed itself in international relations by a repudiation of the whole—or almost the whole—of that world-oriented type of patriotism Wilson had fought for so valiantly and so stubbornly. In the name of the fathers of the republic, the League of Nations—in fact any responsibility for world peace and order—met with denunciation. Pacifists and internationalists protested and became the special *bête noire* of the champions of "Americanism." These damned their opponents by identifying them with the Reds. They also emphasized the importance of national military strength. "America first, last, and all the time" became a cliché in discussions of international cooperation, high tariffs, and the collection of war debts.

Nor was this all that made up the content of "Americanism." The United States was regarded as having been always right in the past and bound to be always right in the future. American government and American institutions surpassed all others in excellence. America was conceived, not as a process, a development, but as a finished and perfect product, not to be changed, not to be criti-

[14] *The Public Papers of Woodrow Wilson*, II, 509.

cized. Our late ally, Great Britain, provoked bitter condemnation
from Irish-Americans, German-Americans, and others who declared
that the Wilson regime had stupidly pulled chestnuts out of the
fire for perfidious Albion. In all but closing the door against the
great stream of immigration the government still further exemplified the program of Americanism, as it did in discriminating
against Southern and Eastern European immigrants in favor of
the so-called Nordics. All this was justified in the name of patriotism.[15]

In domestic matters no less than in foreign affairs a conservative
social and economic philosophy, again identified by its champions
as Americanism, met with relatively ineffective protests, especially
during the early years of the post-war decade. Dislike of the New
Freedom program of the first Wilson administration, which subjected business to certain controls in the name of public interest,
and the fear of the so-called Bolshevik menace to the family, to
religion, to individual freedom, and to private property lay back
of the doctrine known as one-hundred-percent Americanism. In
some instances, no doubt, the Bolshevik "menace" was used as a
canard for publicizing business dislike of organized labor and for
dealing blows against anarchists, socialists, and even old-fashioned
American liberals of the Populist-Progressive tradition. However
disguised such an Americanism might be under glittering generalities about freedom, democracy, and justice, it actually identified
loyalty to the nation with support of the dominant economic system.

The program of the one-hundred-percent-American "patriots"
was not lacking in concreteness and practical application. In the
name of loyalty to the United States, legislature after legislature
condemned as treasonable any expression of belief in the right of
revolution. The fact that the country had originated in revolution
and that almost all the notable figures of the nineteenth century had
openly expressed their belief in the right of revolution was con-
veniently overlooked. In the name of devotion to American institu-

[15] See, for examples, George B. Lockwood, *Americanism* (Washington, 1921)
and *National Republic Magazine* (1925–1926).

tions conservative patriots launched a crusade against such social legislation as the child-labor amendment. In the name of Americanism, furthermore, the open shop was proclaimed as sacrosanct and the activities of labor unions curtailed. The worship of an unchanging and unchangeable Constitution became the bulwark of those who insisted on the preservation of the social and economic *status quo*. The fact that the Constitution contained within itself provision for amendment was readily brushed aside.

Two organizations contributed substantially to spreading these ideas and to putting them into practice. The one was the American Legion. In addition to looking out for the interests of the veterans and to maintaining a fight for a bonus and a liberal pension policy, the Legion worked through both its central organization and its local branches for the maintenance of military and naval strength, including conscription, for isolation or a very cautious type of international cooperation in foreign affairs and for a generally "antiradical" and antiprogressive program in domestic affairs. The other organization was the Ku Klux Klan, a secret society given to the use of violence and notable for its antiradicalism and for its bitter prejudices against Catholics, Negroes, Jews, and "foreigners" generally.[16] Appealing to the insecure lower middle class, the Klan became a potent political influence in more than one state. Its importance did not, to be sure, prove lasting. Yet for a time it frightened old-fashioned American liberals by demonstrating the ability of skillful organizers to capitalize on the honest if bigoted fears and prejudices of citizens who identified these fears and prejudices with patriotism. Huey Long subsequently inherited from the Ku Klux Klan some part of the "Americanism" program on which he rode to power in Louisiana.

Many, though by no means all, of the conceptions of patriotism and Americanism for which the American Legion and the Klan stood, found friendly support in such businessmen's service organizations as Rotary, Kiwanis, and the Lions, in Boy Scout leadership, and in the older type of patriotic societies as well as in those

---

[16] Hiram W. Evans, "The Klan: Defender of Americanism," *Forum*, V (December, 1925), 805–814.

that had taken shape during the war itself. There can be little doubt that some of the so-called professional patriotic organizations enjoyed appreciable financial support from the well-to-do and from large corporations whose interests were deemed to be threatened by the internationalism, pacifism, and liberalism which, lumped indiscriminately together, were stigmatized as unpatriotic, subversive, and un-American. One patriotic organization, the National Security League, appeared to be operating for a brief time, at least, on an annual budget of $235,000 a year.[17]

With such considerable support for the pattern of ideas and feelings termed "Americanism" it was inevitable that educational agencies should become the special object of solicitude on the part of the one-hundred-percenters. The Lusk Laws in New York, which evoked much criticism from both educators and the liberal public before they were repealed in 1923, initiated a program copied in other states. These laws supervised textbooks and the appointment and tenure of teachers in the interest of Americanism—defined in broad, general terms of liberty and democracy but actually stipulating loyalty to the American social and economic *status quo*; they required flag salutes and pledges of allegiance from pupils and loyalty oaths from teachers; and their enforcement made possible the dismissal not only of teachers of socialist and labor sympathies but even of those committed to old-fashioned American liberal faith.

Prodded on by the Hearst press, by the Knights of Columbus, and by such demagogues as Mayor Thompson of Chicago, school boards threw out texts in American history on the ground that by pro-British treatment of the Revolution and by failure to inculcate an ardent patriotism they were poisoning the youthful American mind. A careful investigation by Professor Bessie L. Pierce of four hundred social science textbooks proved that none in fact presented a version of the American Revolution which could be regarded as pro-British by the canons of historical scholarship and that virtually all were written within a framework of pride in the United States, respect for private property, obedience to law, and belief in

[17] Norman Hapgood, *Professional Patriots* (New York, 1927), p. 23.

democracy.[18] At the same time a federal investigation revealed that a few textbook writers severely critical of government ownership, which they labeled as un-American, had taken retainers from public-utility corporations. Such evidence confirmed the belief of many Americans that the crusade of the one-hundred-percenters was needless and harmful interference in the educational process.[19]

By the end of the 1920's the high-water mark in the campaign had been passed. Yet in 1940 an indictment by the National Association of Manufacturers of the Rugg textbooks was to prove that the attack on school texts on the score of un-Americanism and disloyalty to the nation died hard, if indeed it died at all.

The heightened emotionalism of so much of the patriotic thought and feeling of the post-war decade did not, of course, go unchallenged. Throughout the history of American patriotism two opposing major themes recurred at intervals. And so now the more reflective, critical, and humane pattern of patriotic thought was reasserted. Thus Jane Addams and Horace Kallen emphasized cultural pluralism as the essence of Americanism. This, rather than a unified integration, they insisted, explained whatever was truly unique in America: many minds, one heart; many roads, one goal. In like vein Edwin E. Slosson, the popularizer of modern chemistry, wrote that "America is one of the fine arts, the finest of all the fine arts, the art of getting along peaceably with all sorts and conditions of men." [20]

Others deplored the influence of one-hundred-percentism in keeping America from that international cooperation for world peace, freedom, and order which so many regarded as the core of American destiny. "Patriotism, as practised in the United States," wrote Earnest Elmo Calkins in the *Atlantic Monthly*, "seems to be egocentric, radiating from a point occupied by the patriot and diminishing in intensity as it gets further from home." [21] If pa-

[18] Bessie L. Pierce, *Civic Attitudes in American School Textbooks* (Chicago, 1930), pp. 253–254.
[19] Howard K. Beale, *Are American Teachers Free?* (New York, 1936), pp. 555 ff.
[20] *Independent*, CI (March 20, 1920), 431.
[21] *Atlantic Monthly*, CXLVIII (December, 1931), 689.

triotism could overleap so many barriers separating town, state, region, and country at large, continued this writer, should it stop at the national frontiers? Why should it not embrace the entire world, now so closely interrelated in all its parts? Thus was asserted once more the internationalists' demand for a reinterpretation of patriotism.

To this noted educators and historians such as George A. Coe and J. Montgomery Gambrill added the familiar criticism that one-hundred-percentism was only another name for partisanship and the closed mind. Gambrill called attention to the dangers involved in such a slogan as "America first" when it was not intelligently interpreted to school children. "Are we aiming," he asked, "to instil into these young people certain dogmas and creeds [extreme militarism, or extreme pacifism, or what-not], or are we anxious to develop as far as may be, a type of citizen trained to keep his mind open until he has some facts and some evidence, who is actuated by a spirit of fairness, who has the courage to look even at the unpleasant facts in his community and his country, who is acquainted with real human beings and not sentimental Sunday School heroes, who has some equipment for dealing with the world as it is?" [22]

The criticism of one-hundred-percent patriotism sprang not only, as in this instance, from the humane and liberal American tradition of faith in testing general concepts by facts and results and focusing on them the light of reason. It also rested on the equally traditional Christian conception of a higher law than that of man. The vigorous and broad-based contribution of the churches to the peace movement in the post-war decade, accompanied as it was by a criticism of one-hundred-percent Americanism, issued in the last analysis from the faith that when the altar and the flag are in conflict, the altar takes precedence. It would, in fact, be hard to overemphasize this element in the criticisms of the chauvinistic patriotism of the post-war years.

[22] *Report on the Conference on the Teaching of History with a View to International Understanding* (Philadelphia, 1926), p. 19. See also J. Montgomery Gambrill, "Nationalism and Civic Education," *Teachers College Record*, XXIII (March, 1922), 109–120.

There was also a new accent in the innumerable articles and speeches which took to task the professional patriots and their allies. This was part and parcel of the disillusionment that affected many intellectuals and a considerable part of the sophisticated or would-be sophisticated post-war generation. The type of patriotism for which the Legion, the K.K.K., the Boy Scouts, the National Security League, the D.A.R., and the Rotarians stood met with jesting quips in the *American Mercury* and with cutting rebukes in the *Nation*, the *New Republic*, and the *Freeman*. The great showman, George M. Cohan, spoke in this same vein when, on being asked to explain the secret of notable stage successes, he replied, "many a bum show is saved by the American flag." [23] Such frankness on the part of America's song-and-dance hero invited second thought about patriotism. It also became more fashionable than ever before, probably, to belittle American civilization, and to identify it with the crass materialism, the get-aheadism, the Philistinism, and the syrupy moralizing of the Babbitts and the Main Street characters of Sinclair Lewis.

The disillusioned mood of the 1920's found expression in the much-read "debunking" biographies of national heroes. Iconoclastic writers won applause for striking down from their pedestals the cold, noble images of the fathers of the Republic. Even though in some accounts there was excessive derogation, such biographies, showing that the fathers were after all only human, had their use as a corrective to the earlier canonical accounts of the patriots. A similarly severe critical note stole into some of the histories of the country.

The criticism which one-hundred-percent Americanism evoked displayed some relatively new points. For the first time scholars seriously concerned themselves with objective studies of patriotism. Empirical sociological investigations seemed to support the theory of pluralistic sovereignty expounded by the brilliant visiting British scholar, Harold J. Laski. According to this theory the nation or state is only one of the various groupings of mankind which have ever been in the process of combination and recombination. Hence,

[23] *Freeman*, VII (July 4, 1923), 391.

Laski argued, the nation "no longer enfolds and absorbs the allegiance of the individual; his loyalties are as diverse as his experiences of life." [24] The investigations of Earle Hunter analyzed patriotic expressions called forth in the press during four crisis situations and provided much evidence in support of his contention that actually there is no abstract loyalty to an abstract nation, but merely specific loyalties to the specific functions of a state: for example, to the protection of life and property by the police, both at home and in those foreign countries where Americans find themselves, and to the maintenance of services designed to promote the profits, comfort, and well-being of citizens. Patriotism, this investigator concluded, is chiefly the projection of the aims, desires, and views of the several specific groups in order to give or to secure to them social control and the sanctions of universality.[25] Thus fact-finding investigations provided documentation for the interpretations Veblen and others had earlier made of the nature and functions of patriotism.

A leading social psychologist, Floyd Allport, applied to the whole problem, with telling effect, the theories and findings of behaviorism. Allport showed specifically how children are "conditioned" to think and believe that the nation is an "over-person" capable of willing and feeling, worthy of being honored, loved, and protected. For purposes of convenience the nation came to be spoken of as a unit; from so speaking of it, the step to believing this to be the fact, to forgetting that the nation after all is but a figure of speech, is short and easy. The nation, in Allport's analysis, is but a situation in which individuals, and only individuals, perform specific political acts. Thus the nation "stands merely for the point of view from which we see the citizens all behaving in a similar and patriotic manner." [26]

Allport went on to elaborate his thesis by arguing that, through the mechanism of the conditioned reflex, the emotions of love, fear,

[24] Harold J. Laski, A Grammar of Politics (London, 1925), p. 666.
[25] Earle Hunter, A Sociological Analysis of Certain Types of Patriotism (New York, 1932), passim.
[26] Floyd Allport, "The Psychology of Nationalism," Harper's Monthly Magazine, CLV (August, 1927), 291.

and anger and the sentiments of loyalty, obedience, and pride are merely *"forms of human reaction"* to situations or stimuli, including the national symbols. The last step in the process is the rationalization of the reactions into a belief that the "nation" is the superperson of the organic theory, something independent of, and greater than, the individuals in their group relationships. This psychologist admitted that it would be justifiable to believe in the nation if the national ideal were one of promoting human welfare. He struck, however, a severe blow at one-hundred-percent patriotism in his conclusion that "this supposed reality is a National Being whom we can neither see nor prove; but yet a Being for whom we must fight, killing those whom we do not hate and wasting our substance upon an empty dream." [27]

This theory of the nation and of patriotism drew immediate fire. Its critics held that it did not adequately take into account pertinent realities. However much the nation might be an abstraction or a rationalization of responses and symbols built up through the conditioned reflex, it nevertheless, they argued, is an actuality in the sense of being an historical continuity of traditions and outlooks shared by members of a given community. A Catholic writer in the *Commonweal* no doubt spoke for many intellectuals and for many simple folk not given to writing or even to formulating in words their beliefs. To his mind behavioristic and psychoanalytical interpretations of nationalism and patriotism were merely efforts to get around the job of explaining a phenomenon "whose strength and especially whose spiritual content bothers and baffles . . . by using scientific terms which clumsily describe those outer aspects and effects of it clearly visible to everyone." [28] However much the naturalistic approach might protest against the use of such a vague term as "spiritual," the plain fact is, according to this writer, that this term and the feelings associated with it are far too deeply imbedded in the culture to yield readily to scientific criticism or to empirical investigation.

Techniques for measuring attitudes in the post-war era throw

[27] Allport, *loc. cit.* See also his *Institutional Behavior* (Chapel Hill, 1933).
[28] *Commonweal*, XVIII (September 22, 1933), 477–478.

little light on the degree to which one or another of the competing conceptions of national loyalty and patriotic sentiment influenced the public. Such evidence as there is suggests that the great majority of Americans held implicitly or consciously to one of three conceptions of Americanism: the "my-country-right-or-wrong" attitude; the association of patriotism with the fathers and with such abstractions as liberty and equality; and the constructive adaptation of these and other inherited principles to modern conditions. On the other hand, a relatively small group seems to have thought of patriotism in terms of wisecracking exposés or the radicals' identification of it with rationalizations of class interests.[29]

The years of depression and of the New Deal did much to emphasize that conception of patriotism which has been defined as the constructive adaptation of inherited principles to new situations. The fact that the national government, in a profound emergency which exacted a bitter toll of suffering, took responsibility for the well-being of the disadvantaged millions, inspired confidence and faith in the power and readiness of the nation to meet human needs. What local communities, what private philanthropy, what the states failed to achieve, the national government undertook and in an impressive degree carried through. The Republicans, traditionally the party of federal power, now clamored for state rights in response to the big-business interests that largely directed its fortunes. The power of the national government nevertheless swept forward to meet rising emergencies and in doing so gave new life to the economics of national loyalty. So marked was all this that even the Socialists and Communists, sensitive to the power of patriotism, identified their aspirations with American traditions. To cite a single example, Socialists referred to their national assembly as "the Continental Congress."

Among the minor but not insignificant aspects of the impact of the New Deal on patriotism were the efforts of the Federal Arts Projects to bring to the people recreation and esthetic satisfactions —the theater, music, painting, and the dance. The program pro-

[29] *Forum*, LXXV (June, 1927), 801–802, and LXXXII (September, 1929), lii–liv.

moted a greater familiarity with traditionally American folk arts and with the beauty and rich variety of the American landscape. The state guidebooks and the growing importance of the national parks and monuments in the common life of the nation helped to strengthen pride in country and love of it.

The new emphasis on the positive aspects of patriotism was re-enforced by the rising threat of European totalitarianism to American security and to American ideals. In the midst of world crisis the meaning of American democracy was thoughtfully reconsidered. Writers pointed to the inadequacies in both the one-hundred-percent type of patriotism and in the "debunking" and allegedly destructive emphasis on American shortcomings. The tendency to "sell America short," or, in other words, "to undersell America to the American people" was deplored. So was the tendency to be-little American heroes and the American past. All this was con-trasted with the positive fashion in which the totalitarian leader-ship abroad had capitalized on love of country in meeting inter-national problems and in enhancing national strength.

The new approach was a frank search for a middle ground which might avoid the narrowness and bigotry of one-hundred-percentism and the negation of mere criticism. This search inspired the discus-sions of patriotism by men like Lewis Mumford, Struthers Burt, and Howard Mumford Jones. The mood of these writers was well expressed in the remark of Professor Jones of Harvard: "Why has American democracy mislaid its mythology and lost its glamor . . . ? How shall we restore patriotism without chauvinism, economic self-interest, or racial snobbery? . . . If we really want to believe that political democracy is worth fighting for, we need to be told over and over again what pain and suffering it has cost." [30]

Ever sensitive to new currents in popular thought, educators began publicly to confess their dereliction in having overemphasized both the value of pacifism and the shortcomings of the American nation. With the amazingly rapid domination of a large part of Europe and Eastern Asia by Fascism, Nazism, and "Japanism," and

[30] Howard Mumford Jones, "Patriotism—but How?", *Atlantic Monthly*, CLXII (November, 1938), 586, 592.

with the new movement for American preparedness, it was clear that another chapter in the history of patriotism in the United States was beginning. That chapter, in the light of a future historical perspective, will have to be written in years to come. It may be helpful now, however, to suggest some of the problems and topics which will then have to be treated.

When the chapter is written, it will be clear that there was little basis for the diagnosis of American patriotism which Nazi and Fascist leaders made in the years and months before Pearl Harbor. Insensitive to the new mood of appreciative democracy and patriotism and ignorant of the deep roots of loyalty to the nation, these leaders pointed with brash glee to the divisions, the doubts, the confusions in American thought and feeling. In the cleavages they saw evidence of basic weakness, of disintegration, of the dwindling to the vanishing point of national spirit and patriotism. Loyalty to the common good and readiness to sacrifice class and individual interest to it, they declared, had been so weakened that Americans could put up no sustained, effective resistance in modern total war. Even some thoughtful Americans shared these gloomy views.

Once the Axis blow fell unexpectedly and disastrously at Pearl Harbor the doubt, confusion, and division in the American mind seemed almost instantly to disappear. The reality of a treacherous and dangerous foe called forth a unity of feeling, purpose, and endeavor. For the time, at least, those whose loyalty to America had been weakened or dissolved by devotion to totalitarianism in one form or another—and there were such among immigrants and natives, among the common people and leading men of business —these held their tongues. Those whose loyalty to America had never been in doubt, but who had honestly opposed military conscription, lend-lease, and all other preparedness measures of the administration which in their eyes made ultimate war likely or even inevitable rallied to the flag, suspended their opposition to war, or quietly stood upon the ground of conscientious objection. Election decisions were accepted with some grumbling but with no basic opposition; industrial mobilization for total war made amazing headway; war loans were subscribed on an impressive scale; the conscription law was generally obeyed. It was clear that loyalty to the nation was by no means in the feeble state of health that the Japanese, German, and Italian leaders had maintained and that some Americans had feared.

It is true that the pre-Pearl Harbor debate over the wisdom and inevitability of the war reappeared in one form or another. An unknown number of men and women raised doubts about the war in private conversations. It is, however, possible to speak with precision regarding opposition to the war only when that opposition was clear-cut and overt. In spite of the decision of the federal government to make concessions in the treatment of conscientious objectors which in 1917 a more hysterical Washington had denied, a great many more Americans were imprisoned for conscience than in the First World War. In addition, between 12,000 and 15,000 young Americans chose on grounds of conscience to enter the Civilian Public Service camps in preference to serving with the armed forces. These conscientious objectors maintained that their position represented the highest type of patriotism.

In some instances immigrant or minority groups cherished divided loyalties and no longer concealed the fact. Reports of fifth-column activities and trials for treason took a prominent place on the front pages of the daily press and the trials dragged on month after month. The Negro, anxious to show his loyalty to the American promise of equality, to all that America might become, resented the discriminations he frequently met with both in the armed forces and in war plants. By and large, however, minority groups, including the Japanese-Americans who were subjected to special restrictions, seem to have cherished little disloyalty to America.

Thus the differences and tensions in American life were not resolved by the unity which the first stages of the war gave to the American people and by the evidences of loyalty among minority groups. Political bickerings and antagonisms reappeared and, as the war pursued its course, became sharp and bitter. Labor leaders declared that business was putting profits above disinterested service to the country. That there was some truth in the indictment seemed apparent when early in 1944 a federal court found evidence that one firm had, in the interest of profits, sold the government inferior war material and when one factory owner, Vivien Kellems, advised Americans to refuse to pay their income taxes. Despite denunciation of the black market as unpatriotic, the fight against it did not entirely succeed. Many decried the appeals of radio advertisers to buy a specified brand of razor blade in order to "help conserve the nation's steel supply" or to purchase other products from allegedly patriotic motives. On the other hand business denounced labor as unpatriotic for insisting that wages keep pace with living costs or even advance more rapidly than such costs, for absenteeism, and for refusing to give up, without strings, the right to strike. In spite of the fact that only a minute proportion of man hours in war production plants was lost as a result of strikes, spokesmen for management conveyed the impression that labor was in this respect sadly lacking in patriotism.

All these differences and tensions did not, of course, show that Americans by and large were lacking in loyalty to the country. In the light of the long history of American patriotism it is clear that in identifying their own interests and loyalties with the good of the country, even when many fellow Americans saw only selfishness in their actions, both leaders and rank and file were following a well-worn path. The American distinction between loyalty to government or officials and loyalty to the general good, to the nation, still flourished in a world in which totalitarianism, with its complete denial of the validity of such a distinction, at last met effective resistance.

What the future of American patriotism would be in the postwar world, no one could comfortably predict. The past history of American patriotism suggests that as long as conflicting interests within the United States struggle for existence and for power, so long will conflicting conceptions of patriotism continue to flourish. The older, humanitarian, individualistic, and liberty-loving patriotism is tenacious and it seems unlikely that it will in the near future be supplanted by the more integral, exclusive, and chauvinistic type.

Yet the latter pattern is still sufficiently imbedded in American thought and still sufficiently supported by concrete interests, to challenge the older views. Thus there is a real question whether these older attitudes, more in keeping with our leading national traditions, can maintain their hold on Americans. Will this individualistic type of loyalty, based on recognition of the service of the nation to the needs of individuals, and on belief in the right of all individuals in the nation to those services, continue to be a dominant factor in American thought? What comfort and assurance will there be for those who hold that the nation can survive in an interdependent world only through the development of a wider patriotism, a loyalty to mankind in any and every nation?

BIBLIOGRAPHICAL NOTE

WHILE NO comprehensive history of American patriotism has hitherto been written, scholars have laid the foundations for the present study through their explorations of the development of nationalism and patriotism in the modern western world. These studies are briefly evaluated in Merle Curti's "Wanted: A History of American Patriotism" in *Proceedings of the Middle States Association of History and Social Science Teachers*, Vol. XXXVI (1938). The work of Carlton J. H. Hayes, *Essays on Nationalism* (New York, 1926) and *The Historical Evolution of Modern Nationalism* (New York, 1931), together with the monographs of his students, put all who are interested in this field into deep debt. So does Hans Kohn's *The Idea of Nationalism* (New York, 1944), the sixth chapter of which deals explicitly with the emergence of American nationalism. Relevant to the subject are such suggestive and well-documented studies as Frederick Jackson Turner, *The United States, 1830–1850: The Nation and the Sections* (New York, 1932), Charles A. Beard, *The Idea of National Interest* (New York, 1934), Albert K. Weinberg, *Manifest Destiny* (Baltimore, 1935), Paul H. Buck, *The Road to Reunion, 1865–1900* (Boston, 1937), Howard Odum and Frank Moore, *American Regionalism* (New York, 1938), and Ralph H. Gabriel, *The Course of American Democratic Thought* (New York, 1940). The role of national feeling in American culture is one of the leading themes in Merle Curti's *The Growth of American Thought* (New York, 1943).

Those wishing to explore the more philosophical aspects of American patriotism will find several books and essays of considerable interest and importance. Among these may be mentioned Thorstein Veblen's *An Inquiry into the Nature of Peace* (New York, 1919), Chapter Two, Floyd Allport's *Institutional Behavior* (Chapel Hill, 1933), Roberti Michels, "Über den Amerikanischen Nationalitätsbegriff," in *Weltwirtschafliche Archiv*, XXVIII

(1928), and Earle Hunter's *The Sociological Analysis of Certain Types of Patriotism* (New York, 1932). Josiah Royce's *The Philosophy of Loyalty* (New York, 1908), Julius Drachsler's *Democracy and Assimilation* (New York, 1920), Horace Kallen's *Culture and Democracy in the United States* (New York, 1924), and Herbert A. Bloch's *Concept of our Changing Loyalties* (New York, 1934) are also important. Bishop John Lancaster Spalding's essay, "The Patriot," in *Opportunity and Other Essays* (Chicago, 1901) presents the Catholic position, more fully developed in John J. Wright's *National Patriotism and Papal Teaching* (Boston, 1942). Mention should also be made of Shailer Mathews's *Patriotism and Religion* (New York, 1918) and of James R. Angell's *The Higher Patriotism* (Stanford, 1938).

Pertinent monographic articles and larger studies on various aspects of Americanism, American nationalism, and American patriotism have in general been cited in the footnotes of the text itself. Special attention should be called to Harry R. Warfel's *Noah Webster, Schoolmaster to America* (New York, 1936), E. F. Humphrey's *Nationalism and Religion in America* (New York, 1924), Ray A. Billington's *The Protestant Crusade, 1800–1860* (New York, 1938), Wood Gray's *The Hidden Civil War* (New York, 1942), Dixon Wecter's *The Hero in America* (New York, 1941) and *When Johnny Comes Marching Home* (Boston, 1944). Arthur M. Schlesinger's delightful essay, "Patriotism Names the Baby," in *New England Quarterly*, Vol. XIV (December, 1940), a by-product of research in another field, is an important contribution to our understanding of patriotism during the American Revolution. Special attention should be called to Benjamin T. Spencer's "A National Literature, 1836–1855" in *American Literature*, Vol. VII (May, 1936), and to the charming interpretation by Percy Boynton, *Changing Ideas on American Patriotism* (Chicago, 1936). The best brief interpretation of the history of American nationalism is the little-known essay of Charles A. Beard, "Nationalism in American History," in Waldo G. Leland, ed., *Nationalism: Papers Presented at the Fourth Chicago Meeting of the American Association for the Advancement of Science* (Bloomington, Indiana,

1934). The forthcoming study of Wallace E. Davies, "A History of American Patriotic Societies" (Harvard doctoral dissertation) will replace older studies of the several organizations designed to promote patriotic sentiment.

But this present book, indebted though it is to secondary literature, is based principally on an investigation of primary materials. Some of these may properly be regarded as classics in the expression of American nationalism and patriotism. Examples are *The Federalist*, Hamilton's *Report on Manufactures*, Washington's *Farewell Address*, Monroe's famous message to Congress, William Ellery Channing's *Remarks on National Literature*, Emerson's *The American Scholar*, Webster's *Reply to Hayne*, Samuel F. B. Morse's *Imminent Dangers to the Free Institutions of the United States*, Whitman's *Leaves of Grass*, Lincoln's *Gettysburg Address*, Turner's *The Significance of the Frontier in American History*, and Theodore Roosevelt's *American Ideals* and *The New Nationalism*. Less well known, but of much importance, are the writings of Tench Coxe, Caleb Strong, Noah Webster, George Perkins Marsh, Thomas Starr King, Francis Lieber, John Hurd, Elisha Mulford, John W. Burgess, William T. Harris, Josiah Strong, Alfred Thayer Mahan, and Robert Ellis Thompson. The writings of Washington, Hamilton, Jay, Samuel Adams, John Adams, Thomas Paine, Jefferson, John Quincy Adams, Henry Clay, Daniel Webster, Charles Sumner, William E. Seward, John C. Calhoun, Robert Winthrop, Edward Everett, Abraham Lincoln, Carl Schurz, Edward Everett Hale, Chauncy M. Depew, Homer Lea, Theodore Roosevelt, Woodrow Wilson, and Franklin D. Roosevelt are indispensable. This is likewise true of the *Journals of the Continental Congress*; *Letters of Members of the Continental Congress*; *Records of the Constitutional Convention*; the *Annals of Congress*; the *Congressional Globe*; the *Congressional Record*; and the *Messages of the Presidents*. Such government reports as those of the Immigration Commission and the Lusk Committee and the most relevant decisions of the Supreme Court, particularly the opinions of Chief Justice Marshall, are likewise of basic importance.

Considerable use has been made of the thought of both major

and minor figures in American literature. The writings of Joel Barlow and of the other Hartford Wits, of Philip Freneau, Washington Irving, James Fenimore Cooper, Nathaniel Hawthorne, Henry Wadsworth Longfellow, James K. Paulding, William Gilmore Simms, Ralph Waldo Emerson, Theodore Parker, James Russell Lowell, Walt Whitman, Mark Twain, and Stephen Crane deserve special attention. Two secondary studies, Rebecca W. Smith, *The Civil War and Its Aftermath in American Fiction* (University of Chicago dissertation, 1937) and Dorothy Leeds Werner, *The Idea of Union in American Verse, 1776–1786* (Chicago, 1932), are useful guides. The principal collections of American stage plays likewise provide significant material. Some two thousand "dime novels" were examined at the Huntington Library to discover their implications for the history of American patriotism, and the results were reported in my article, "The Dime Novel and the American Tradition" in *Yale Review* for the summer of 1937.

The bearing of the nonliterary arts upon American patriotism have not been overlooked. The standard histories of American painting and sculpture and the lives and autobiographies of artists have proved useful, as have the several histories of American patriotic music. James Stone's "War Music and War Psychology in the Civil War" in *Journal of Abnormal and Social Psychology*, Vol. XXXVI (October, 1941), is a significant contribution.

American periodicals have been one of the main sources of this study. An effort has been made to sample periodicals adequately by taking into account the several sections of the country, the principal chronological periods, and the constituencies to which the magazines appealed. Those which have proved most fruitful are: *American Museum; Port Folio; Niles' Weekly Register; Hunt's Merchants' Magazine; American Whig Review; Democratic Review; Biblical Repository; Southern Literary Messenger; De Bow's Review; North American Review; Brownson's Quarterly Review; Western Literary Journal and Monthly Review; Knickerbocker Magazine; Godey's Lady's Book; Methodist Quarterly; Congregationalist; New Englander; Atlantic Monthly; Scribner's Magazine;*

Century Magazine; Harper's Monthly Magazine; Dial; Arena; Mc-Clure's; Independent; Outlook; Literary Digest; Nation; New Republic; New Masses; Internationalist Socialist Review; Overland Monthly; Youth's Companion; Catholic World; Commonweal; Saturday Evening Post; American Federationist; Nation's Business; National Republic; Woman's Home Companion; Ladies' Home Journal; Common Ground; American Mercury; Popular Science; Crisis; and *Journal of American Folklore. Vital Speeches of the Day* has been indispensable for the contemporary period.

No effort has been made to do more than sample the newspaper press. The pattern of Fourth of July celebrations over a long span of time has been studied in the local press of Northampton (Massachusetts) New York City, Charleston, Augusta, New Orleans, Beloit (Wisconsin), and San Francisco. Much work in the newspaper press, and especially in the foreign language press, remains to be done. In determining the drift of public opinion the various polls provide, during the past decade, a valuable supplement to the newspaper press.

Of special interest, in connection with the Fourth of July and other patriotic holidays, are W. DeLoss Love, *The Fast and Thanksgiving Days of New England* (Boston, 1895), "The Day We Celebrate: from the Journal of a Country Parson, 1836–1860," *Atlantic Monthly*, XCIV (July, 1904), and Cedric Larson, "Patriotism in Carmine: One Hundred and Sixty-Two Years of Fourth of July Orations," *Quarterly Journal of Speech*, XXVI, (February, 1940). Among the essays on patriotic symbolism not cited in the footnotes of the text, Ralph Barton Perry's "Uncle Sam and the Statue of Liberty," *Century Magazine*, Vol. CVII (February, 1924) is particularly valuable.

There is a useful body of writings intended specifically to inculcate patriotism. Representative of this material is Ignatius Thomson, *The Patriot's Monitor* (Randolph, Vermont, 1810), William McCary, *Songs, Odes, and Other Poems on National Subjects* (Philadelphia, 1842), D. Macaulay, *The Patriot's Catechism* (Washington, 1843), Addison T. Richards, *American Scenery Illustrated* (New York, 1854), William H. Ryder, *Our Country;*

or, The American Parlor Keepsake (Boston, 1854), John Henry Hopkins, *The American Citizen* (New York, 1857), James E. Murdoch, *Patriotism in Poetry and Prose* (Philadelphia, 1864), Frederick Saunders, *Our National Jubilee* (New York, 1877), Selim H. Peabody, *American Patriotism: Speeches, Letters, and Other Papers which Illustrate the Foundation, the Development, and the Preservation of the United States of America* (New York, 1880), George T. Balch, *Methods of Teaching Patriotism in the Public Schools* (New York, 1880), and Charles R. Skinner, *Manual of Patriotism for Use in the Public Schools of New York* (Albany, 1904). Special attention has been given to schoolbooks, especially in the pre-Civil War period. Among the authors whose textbooks have been examined are John McCulloch, C. A. Goodrich, Samuel Goodrich, Noah Webster, Jedidiah Morse, John Pierpont, Emma Willard, William Grimshaw, and Samuel Hall. In the post-Civil War period textbooks have been merely sampled; one of my former students, Ruth V. Miller, is exploring this field. Chief reliance has been placed on the excellent studies of Bessie L. Pierce, *Civic Attitudes in American School Textbooks* (Chicago, 1930) and *Public Opinion and the Teaching of History in the United States* (New York, 1938). Howard K. Beale's *Are American Teachers Free?* (New York, 1936) and *A History of Freedom of Teaching* (New York, 1941) are important studies which contribute to the understanding of the whole problem of patriotism and education.

Considerable light on American patriotism is shed by the voluminous travel literature familiar to all students of social and intellectual history. Representative of this material are Adlard Welby, Esq., *A Visit to North America and the English Settlements in Illinois* (London, 1821), Henry Durhing, *Remarks on the United States* (London, 1833), Harriet Martineau, *Society in America* (London, 1837), Alexis de Tocqueville, *Democracy in America* (New York, 1840), and James Bryce, *The American Commonwealth* (New York, 1888). Likewise useful is an extensive body of reminiscences and diaries, including such items as Charles Fraser, *Reminiscences of Charleston* (Charleston, 1854), *The Diary of Philip Hone, 1828–1851* (New York, 1889), Charles H. Haswell,

Reminiscences of an Octogenarian of the City of New York (New York, 1896), T. H. Nichols, *Forty Years of American Life* (London, 1874), and George Cary Eggleston, *Recollections of a Varied Life* (New York, 1910). Systematic exploration of materials of this type has been confined to the study of the reminiscences, letters, and diaries of pioneers published by the historical societies of Michigan, Wisconsin, Texas, Nebraska, and Oregon.

In general, manuscript material has not been extensively used in this investigation. A thorough exploration at the Huntington Library of the Francis Lieber papers has proved useful. The Brock Collection at the same library includes the records of the Mount Vernon Memorial Association, one of the early patriotic societies. The Rhees Collection, the James Fields Collection, and the Fiske Collection, also at the Huntington, throw considerable light on the patriotic motives and activities of an influential group of scientists and writers. Especially useful is the David Cronin Collection of War Relics and Reminiscences at the New York Historical Society.

Those interested in pursuing further the contributions of minority groups to patriotism will find revelatory the autobiographies of Negro leaders, the Negro press, and the publications of the Association for the Study of Negro Life. The records of the conventions of free colored people in the Northern states in the pre-Civil War period are significant documents. The letters, reminiscences, and autobiographies of immigrants also provide pertinent material. The publications of several state historical societies and of the organizations concerned with the historical experiences of the several national groups can be used to good advantage. Among the many interesting immigrant recollections and letters a few may be mentioned as representative: *The Reminiscences of Carl Schurz* (New York, 1907–1908), the *Memoirs of Gustav Koerner* (Cedar Rapids, 1909), Abraham Rihbany, *A Far Journey* (New York, 1914), M. E. Ravage, *An American in the Making* (New York, 1917), Horatio Bridges, *On Becoming an American* (Boston, 1919), Michael Pupin, *From Immigrant to Inventor* (New York, 1924), William I. Thomas and Florian Znaniecki, *The Polish Peasant in*

Europe and America (Chicago, 1918), David S. Lawlor, *The Life and Struggle of an Irish Boy in America* (Newton, Massachusetts, 1936), and Osland Birger, *A Long Pull from Stavanger* (Northfield, Minnesota, 1945). Especially useful is Robert Stauffer's *The American Spirit in the Writings of Americans of Foreign Birth* (Boston, 1922). Related material is easily accessible in Marcus L. Hansen, *The Atlantic Migration, 1607–1860* (Cambridge, 1940), William Adams, *Ireland and Irish Immigration to the New World from 1815 to the Famine* (New Haven, 1932), Carl Wittke, *We Who Built America* (New York, 1939), and Philip Davis, *Immigration and Americanization* (Boston, 1920).

The main source for this study has been a body of material hitherto little exploited: the occasional sermon, the Fourth of July oration, and the academic address. The rich Eames Collection at the Huntington Library has provided the basis for the research, but materials in this field in many other libraries have also been examined. After random sampling, an effort was made to obtain a representative selection by taking into account place of publication, the social and economic status of the author, and the audience to whom the appeal was chiefly made. Evans's *American Bibliography*, Sabin's *Bibliotheca Americana*, Roorbach's *Bibliotheca Americana*, Poole's *Index to Periodical Literature* (and its successor, the *Reader's Guide to Periodical Literature*), and the numerous guides to imprints in the several states by D. C. McMurtrie and his associates have proved useful in the sampling process. The sermons collected in *The National Preacher*, the orations published in Charleston by the Revolution Society and by the Fourth of July Association, and the addresses given at patriotic festivals in various cities under the auspices of the New England Societies are especially valuable. Of the approximately three thousand titles in this general category that were read or inspected, it has been impossible to cite in the footnotes more than a few. Titles cited in the footnotes do, however, give the reader some conception of the themes emphasized and of the nature of the orations and addresses.

INDEX

INDEX

Adams, Abigail (Mrs. John Adams), 102
Adams, Brooks, 64
Adams, Henry, 64, 150
Adams, Herbert Baxter, 182
Adams, John, quoted, 8; view of relationship of America to Britain, 10; use of term "country," 23; views on immigration, 69; preparation of seal of the United States, 130; designation of thanksgiving days, 135; views on celebration of Independence Day, 137
Adams, Samuel, 8, 16
Addams, Jane, 238
Adirondacks: landscape painting, 35
Alderman, Edwin A., 212
Alien Act (1798), 75
Allport, Floyd, 241
America: early optimism in, 6; development of human rights in, 8; early use of name, 21-22; advantages, described by Washington, 24; popular faith in future, 60; asylum for the oppressed, 68
American Crisis, The (Paine), 26
American Defense Society, 225
American Federation of Labor, 210
American Flag Association, 191
Americanization: first formal movement, 74; basis in organic nationalism, 182-85; First World War, 186
American Legion, 236, 240
American Mercury, 240
American Peace Society, 213
American Protective Association, 184
American Revolution: non-British element in colonial population prior to, 7; and formation of loyalty, 16-29; views of soldiers in, 21; compared with French Revolution, 53; Puritan belief in divine guidance during, 53; role of Negro soldier in, 88;

failure to provide solidarity, 92; textbook presentation of, 237
Anarchism, 209, 235
Anglo-American patriotism, 12
Anglo-American superiority as argument for expansion, 45
"Anglo-Saxon": views on superiority of, 76; dominant role of, in concept of organic nationalism, 182
Arena, The, 207
Arizona, 44
Atlantic Monthly, 71, 238
Avery, Mrs. R. J., 35
Axis view of American patriotism, 245

Backwoods, unifying elements in, 9
Bagehot, Walter, 230
Baines, Thomas F. O'Malley, 83
Baldwin, Simeon, 95
Bancroft, George, quoted, 42; sees hand of God in history, 54; "race" concept in his writings, 76; urges abandonment of regionalism, 159
Barlow, Joel, 34
Barnes, Mary Sheldon, 190
Bartram, William, 4
Bascom, John, 211
Beard, Charles A., 27
Belknap, Jeremy, 34
Bellamy, Edward, 211
Benjamin, Park, 116
Beverly, Robert, 6
Bible, as a patriotic symbol, 78
Bierstadt, Albert, 36
Bingham, Caleb, 124
Bishop, Abraham, 98
Bland, Richard, 10
Bolshevik "menace," 235
Boucher, Jonathan, 16
Boutwell, George S., 113
Boy Scouts, 236, 240
Bradford, William, 4, 135
Bradley, Joseph, 116